CIARAN CARSON: CRITICAL ESSAYS

Ciaran Carson
Critical Essays

Elmer Kennedy-Andrews

EDITOR

FOUR COURTS PRESS

Set in 10.5 on 14pt Garamond for
FOUR COURTS PRESS
7 Malpas Street, Dublin 8, Ireland
e-mail: info@fourcourtspress.ie
http://www.fourcourtspress.ie
and in North America for
FOUR COURTS PRESS
c/o ISBS, 920 N.E. 58th Avenue, Suite 300, Portland, OR 97213

ISBN 978-1-84682-156-1 hbk
978-1-84682-162-2 pbk

Printed in England
by MPG Books, Bodmin, Cornwall.

Contents

Abbreviations

TiC	*The insular Celts* (Belfast, 1973)
Tne	*The new estate* (Belfast, 1976)
Tle	*The lost explorer* (Belfast, 1978)
Itm	*Irish traditional music: Appletree pocket guide* (Belfast, 1986)
Tneop	*The new estate and other poems* (Loughcrew, 1988)
Ifn	*The Irish for no* (Loughcrew, 1987; Newcastle upon Tyne, 1990)
Bc	*Belfast confetti* (Loughcrew 1989; Newcastle upon Tyne, 1990)
Fl	*First language* (Loughcrew, 1993)
Oec	*Opera et cetera* (Loughcrew, 1996)
Lnf	*Last night's fun: a book about music, food and time* (London, 1996)
Tsf	*The star factory* (London, 1997)
Ttn	*The twelfth of never* (Loughcrew, 1998)
Tap	*The alexandrine plan* (Loughcrew, 1998)
bHMSB	*The ballad of HMS Belfast* (Loughcrew, 1999)
Ffa	*Fishing for amber* (London, 1999)
St	*Shamrock tea* (London, 2001)
Ti	*The inferno of Dante Alighieri: a new translation* (London and New York, 2002)
Tmc	*The midnight court: a new translation of 'Cúirt an Mheán Oíche' by Brian Merriman* (Loughcrew, 2005)
TT	*The Táin* (London, 2007)
Fawk	*For all we know* (Loughcrew, 2008)

Preface

Ciaran Carson: critical essays makes a timely appearance not only in being the first book-length study of this highly original and prolific writer's work to be published so far, but also in saluting him in this the year of his sixtieth birthday. The book represents a critical stock-taking of Carson's work as both poet and prose writer, from his earliest publications in the early 1970s up to his latest work, the prose-poem *For all we know* (2008), and two as yet unpublished novels, $X + Y = K$, and *The pen friend* (the latter to be published by Blackstaff Press in Autumn 2009). Throughout his career, Carson has been interested in both poetry and prose writing, oscillating between the two genres, at times – even as far back as *Belfast confetti* (1989) – experimenting with the possibilities of fusing the conventionally discrete categories of 'prose' and 'poetry', 'narrative' and 'lyric', 'fact' and 'fiction'. Indeed, Carson's penchant for boundary-crossing and hybridization of all kinds is a recurrent theme of the essays in this book.

Seven of the essays were originally given as conference papers at the University of Ulster's sixth international Ulster Symposium (2002) which was devoted to Carson's work. Other essays were subsequently commissioned to enlarge and update the coverage of a career which, after something of a lull between the late 70s and the late 80s, has since been marked by a quite remarkable resurgence of energy and productivity. Stan Smith's essay, 'Cruising to the podes: Ciaran Carson's virtual realities', which was one of the original symposium papers, appears as a chapter in his book, *Irish poetry and the construction of modern identity* (2005), and is reprinted here by kind permission of the author.

The opening 'conversation' between Ciaran Carson and myself, conducted by email over a period of several months between December 2007 and April 2008, was intended to elicit Carson's own account of his background and early life, his education and career, his views on life in Belfast, on art and politics, on his own writing and writing in general. It was also intended to introduce some of the critical issues which his work raises, and which are taken up in more detail in the following essays.

Peter Denman's essay is a close, detailed examination of Carson's verse forms to show how they both draw on and extend traditional English structures. David Wheatley extends the formalist analysis of Carson's work to more recent poems. Focusing on the breakdown and collapse of the lyric in *Breaking news,* Wheatley concludes that if the aim of the book is less lyric transcendence than an expression of the violent breakdown of history, the poems, slender though they may be, yet 'hold their own against the immense bloodshed, waste and violence they describe'.

Two essays concentrate on Carson as an urban poet. The major point of reference for John Goodby's essay on space, narrative and surveillance in Carson's early poetry is Michel de Certeau's chapter 'Walking in the city', in his highly influential book *The practice of everyday life* (1974). Goodby discusses Carson's postmodern urban poetics as an attempt to redefine tradition in terms of 'acceptance of un-location and dissenting from essentialism'. Eamonn Hughes's essay focuses on Carson's complex negotiations between traditional forms and practices on one hand, and the forces of urban modernity on the other. Carson's Belfast, Hughes, argues, is an amalgalm of traditional and modern, oral and print, Irish and English in what is an always absent totality: the logic of binary oppositions gives way to postmodern contingency, in which each element is always traced through with its opposite, and the traditional and the urban become mutually defining.

Concentrating on a particular aspect of contemporary culture, Michael McAteer examines Carson's treatment of the nature and function of the commodity, and its relation to language. Highlighting Carson's concern with the power that objects and instruments – including language – exercise over their creators, McAteer proceeds to a consideration of *Breaking news*, in which he discovers the kind of poem in which word and object coalesce.

Stan Smith's theme is Carson's deconstruction of the grand narratives of Irishness and the conventional language in which an Irish 'identity' has usually been rehearsed, and his imagining of a new and contemporary Ireland, open to the cross-currents of a wider European and international semiotics. Smith proposes the term 'ambilocation' to describe Carson's subject position – 'being always in neither place, or of being between places, or of being always in one place which may be Belfast, but also at the same time in many other places, dis-located, relocated, mis-placed, displaced, everywhere and nowhere'.

Tim Hancock considers the way in which Carson finds an authentic voice in the complicated interplay of the 'sophisticated' and the 'primitive', thus delineating another kind of liminality or hybridity in the poet's writing, one which relates to the postmodern erasure of the line between 'high' and 'low' culture.

A number of the essays are concerned with placing Carson in context of various poetic traditions – English Romantic, European Symbolist, Modernist, Irish language, contemporary American, and so on. Patricia Horton, using Borges' notion of tradition as fluid and unpredictable, investigates Carson's preoccupation with perception, vision and visionary states *à la* Keats, De Quincey, Rimbaud, Baudelaire and Borges himself. Horton's conclusion is that while remaining deeply suspicious of visions, Carson retains a longing for the ideal that leads him to challenge conventional forms of thought and representation, even in the knowledge that our time-bound human condition and the distorting mirror of language make it impossible for us ever to access the realm of the transcendent and the eternal.

Frank Sewell considers the ways in which the Irish language, Irish music and oral storytelling traditions, and Carson's own bilingualism have affected the poet's thinking, vision and poetry, while Ciaran O'Neill turns attention to Carson's American influences – C.K. Williams's long-lined poem, William Carlos Williams's short-lined poem, Frost's metaphysicality.

Three essays focus on Carson's prose writing, with particular reference to his handling of narrative. Jerzy Jarniewicz, focusing on *Fishing for amber*, shows how Carson's suggestion of a neat, ordered and conclusive alphabetical sequencing of material is overpowered by an unruly narrative energy which defies organization and wholeness, and leads the reader deeper and deeper into labyrinthine depths. My own essay, referencing *The star factory, Shamrock tea, The inferno* and *For all we know*, takes up the metaphor of the labyrinth and, using John Zilcosky's theoretical framework of Romantic, Modernist and Postmodernist models of lostness, compares and contrasts Carson's and Heaney's representations of the art of getting lost. In the final essay, Alan Gillis examines two novels, the unpublished *X + Y = K* and the soon-to-be-published *The pen friend*, and discovers in their conflation of Symbolism and Spiritualism, and their atmosphere of political paranoia and a culture of seemingly omniscient surveillance a concept of art as 'a Twilight Zone' infused with 'Special Powers', imaginative as well as political. Within environments of oppression and negation, Gillis argues, Carson's art moves like 'acoustic perfume' which 'might be meaningless, or that might somehow contain the totality of every meaningful thing'.

The premise underlying this book is pure Carson. His obsessive concern with maps and mapping is not only the subject of these essays, but also provides a convenient model of critique – the idea of a critical map which, instead of imposing a single reading from above, has multiple entry-points and contributors, is negotiable, revisionary, open – open to different critical approaches, method-ologies, performances and conclusions. It is in this spirit of prompt and query that this book has been compiled. From a range of standpoints, the essays collected here reflect on the ways in which Carson's writing makes us think about writing, about what it can and cannot do; the ways in which it opens up new imaginative pathways, makes new connections; how it raises doubts and ideas, poses new questions, forces us to look for new answers, suggests new epistemologies.

Grateful acknowledgment is made to the following for permission to quote copyright material: Blackstaff Press, Gallery Press and Granta Books.

ELMER KENNEDY-ANDREWS
Coleraine, April 2008

For all I know: Ciaran Carson in conversation with Elmer Kennedy-Andrews

EK-A (Elmer Kennedy-Andrews): You were born in 1948, on the Falls Road, Belfast. Your father, who makes recurrent significant appearances in your work, was a postman. You went to St Gall's Public Elementary School on the Falls ... What are your lasting impressions of your Belfast childhood? Did you have much experience of 'the other side'? Did you feel any of the tension that Montague and Heaney felt of being 'balanced as a fulcrum between two buckets'?

CC (Ciaran Carson): Two memories of 'the other side' stand out. One is going with my mother to the Berlin Street pawnshop on the Shankill Road, and being kitted out with what I suppose were Protestant shoes. 'Clarke's shoes, Mrs Carson, a very good wee shoe'. The other is being stopped by a gang of small boys (who were nevertheless bigger than me), one of whom was armed with two little handmade charity-type flags, one a tricolour and the other a Union Jack. This was in Cupar Street, which ran between the Falls and the Shankill. I evaded the question and ran away. At the time, I assumed they were from 'the other side', but in retrospect, perhaps they were from my own. In any event there was much more intercourse between the Falls and Shankill in those days – the 1950s – than there is now. Falls Road people shopped on the Shankill and vice versa, thinking that there were better bargains to be had on 'the other side'. As for the fulcrum between two buckets, the buckets, for me, were not so much religious as linguistic, as I teetered between Irish and English. My father and mother had learned Irish and spoke it exclusively at home. The other world was English, both alien and familiar.

EK-A: Were there aspects of your childhood experience that you can see now contributed importantly to the kind of moral/social/political/aesthetic vision expressed in your writing?

CC: There is a sense in which my name is emblematic of whatever I am, an oxymoron of a kind. My first name is Irish, meaning 'little dark-headed one'. The second is also that of the Unionist leader and prosecutor of Oscar Wilde: the Lord Carson whose image, in the form of the statue at Stormont, was familiar to me from an early age. My father, in some perverse act of homage, would bring us there every Easter to roll our eggs. I began to realize that his single-minded attachment to a Gaelic Catholic Ireland was complicated by some irony, an irony also evident in his translating classic English tales into Irish – those of Conan Doyle, G.K. Chesterton and Robert Louis Stevenson spring to mind – and recounting them to us children as bedtime stories, in addition to the more conventional fare of Fenian sagas, Irish folk tale, and anecdotes (sometimes embellished, as I now realize) of his own childhood. In any event I was always aware that there was a world of story coterminous with the 'real' world: an alternative universe with its own codes of practice and negotiation. Some kind of Celtic Twilight Zone, perhaps. I should say at this juncture that my representation of my father in books like *The star factory* and *Fishing for amber* is sometimes more fictional than biographical; though when he read the books he did not demur from this representation, and seemed happy enough, or more than happy, with the character thus portrayed. Perhaps I learned that blurring of fact and fiction from him, or from the peculiar domestic and linguistic circumstances he had engendered.

EK-A: Your first language was Irish. Irish was spoken exclusively in your home when you were a child. Why were you drawn to English as the medium in which to write?

CC: In my teens I began to rebel a little against my Irish upbringing and what I perceived as its moribund nineteenth-century nationalistic implications. In any case the vast proportion of my reading was done in the English language, and the first language in which I wrote was English (hence the ambiguity of the title of one of my books, *First language*). One of the reasons for writing – one of the most important – is to try to follow the examples of great writers, to see how their linguistic perception of the world might shape yours. I still remember the great joy I got from our Senior Certificate English Literature textbook, *A galaxy of poems old and new*. It was here that I first encountered the poetry of Gerard Manley Hopkins, Robert Frost, Dylan Thomas, Edward Thomas and T.S. Eliot, for example. Spurred by nostalgia, I bought a copy on the internet some months ago and I still get a palpable frisson when I open it: apart from anything else, it's a beautifully designed book, with little woodcuts ('Decorations by Edward Nolan') interspersed between the poems. I was talking to Frank Ormsby recently and it appears he had an identical experience: the shock of the new, the feeling that you had been empowered and enabled by the language. I was encouraged in my appreciation of the poetry by our English teacher, Brother Hickey, but I didn't write anything of substance until I went to university in 1967. There, encouraged by my reading of *The portrait of the artist as a young man*, I embarked on my own very bad version of *The portrait of the artist as a young man*. I still shudder with embarrassment when I think of it. The poetry came a little later, I think, and was not so bad. At least Frank Ormsby, then the editor of *The Honest Ulsterman*, thought fit to print the first poems I sent him, which was very encouraging.

By then I had overcome my discomfort with my upbringing in Irish: now I saw it as a uniquely empowering heritage, and I began to write poems inflected or infected by the metres and assonances of Early Irish verse, many of which found their way into my pamphlet, *The insular Celts*, which, again, Frank encouraged me to put together. It also included translations or versions of Irish poems. I fell deeply in love with the music of Early Irish. Again, the spur was an anthology, Gerard Murphy's *Early Irish lyrics*. More latterly, I've translated Brian Merriman's eighteenth-century *The midnight court*, and the Old Irish epic *The Táin*. Both those projects were an education for me. I'm in awe of the energy and sophistication of the language as represented – in very different ways – by those two great pieces of literature.

EK-A: For 23 years, between 1975 and 1998, you were Traditional Arts Officer in the Northern Ireland Arts Council. Could you tell us about your work there? What, in your view, is the importance of Traditional Arts in the life of the community? What importance have Traditional Arts had in your development as a poet?

CC: Regarding the Arts Council, I was someone who enabled what was already there. Indeed, I learned from whatever was already there. One of the great joys of the job was bringing together musicians and singers who would not otherwise have met, but who had heard of each other by reputation. I immersed myself totally in the music for many years. I began to realize that the circumstances in which it is played are just as important as what is played. Some of my own work has been called 'genre-defying': maybe I learned that from the music, since every tune recalls other circumstances in which it has been played; and the conversation and anecdotes sparked off by the tunes are essential to a good session. It's a mix of tunes, songs, stories, drinking, eating, whatever happens to be going on, including smoking, in the days when you could smoke in bars. The tunes themselves are ostensibly simple, but capable of infinite variation. The music is always renewable in the light of the now. There's no one way of doing things, but there is a known framework in which to do them, and a deep acknowledgement of the history and practice of the tunes and the songs. I'd like to think of my own work as having that attachment to the vast reservoir of what has been done in the language.

EK-A: Looking back at the development of your career as a writer, who would you say have been the formative influences (apart from Frost)? Would you say you've been shaped more by other Irish writers or by writers outside Ireland?

CC: In no particular chronological order: John Ashbery, Italo Calvino, Jorge Luis Borges, W.G. Sebald, Alan Gillis, Anthony Powell, John Keats, Marcel Proust, Georges Simenon, Walter Benjamin, Arthur Conan Doyle, Robert Louis Stevenson, the earlier George V. Higgins. This is just a random sample. As you can see, most of these are prose writers. So be it. There's lots more. Last year I was knocked out by *The Door*, a novel by the Hungarian writer Magda Szabo. A really great book, and, from what I could see without knowing Hungarian, a great translation. Lately I've been reading Paul Celan in the parallel text translations by Pierre Joris (Green Integer Books). I don't pretend to know what the poems mean, but I'm astonished by their immense linguistic depths, their venturing into a world which seems to use language to go beyond language, or beyond our normal understanding of it.

EK-A: And, on the question of influence, how would you describe your religious background and the influence it has had on your development as a poet?

CC: I am a typical lapsed Catholic. Like many of my kind, I feel privileged to have had a Catholic upbringing. The sounds of the Latin Mass, the smell of candle wax and incense, the chill of the holy water font, still linger in my consciousness, as does the idea that there is a language beyond language, or things inexpressible in ordinary language.

Besides that aesthetic, I'm drawn more to mysticism than dogmatism. 'The cloud of unknowing'. In my case the logical outcome of Catholicism seems to have been agnosticism, or atheism. Or at least not knowing, as indicated by the title of the book of poems I finished in the summer of 2007, *For all we know*.

EK-A: An agnostic or atheistic mystic sounds like an interesting combination. Could you elaborate?

CC: I don't think you need to believe in a personal God to be in awe of the vast and beautiful complexity of the universe insofar as we know it.

EK-A: You also speak of 'a language beyond language': is there, as far as you are concerned, a metaphysical or transcendent dimension of meaning in your writing

– an order of reality independent of human construction? Or is such an idea merely re-cycling a religious essentialism from which you've lapsed?

CC: It seems self-evident that words cannot do justice to the aforesaid complexity, that there are more things in heaven and earth than are dreamt of in any philosophy. Celan's poetry tries to grapple with that enduring problem.

EK-A: Michael Longley has said that he thinks the only real poetry is religious poetry, by which he seems to mean poetry capable of absorbing and dealing with and transforming the most terrible experiences … poetry with a redemptive potential. Is your idea of 'real poetry' anything like that?

CC: We all need to make stories of our experience. We need to try to make sense of things. Again, I come back to Paul Celan, who wrote in the wake of the Holocaust, despite Theodor Adorno's admonition that to write poetry after such an event would be barbaric. I don't know whether Celan's sometimes intractably difficult poetry is redemptive: but it certainly makes the reader ponder the apparatus of language and its responsibility to communicate, if not necessarily redeem, the human condition.

EK-A: Heaney, Mahon, Paulin all left the North. You stayed. Has staying been important to you and your writing, especially during the Troubles?

CC: As you know, a lot of the poems I wrote in the 1980s and 90s were some kind of reflection of the Troubles. Hardly a commentary; I thought of the poems as snapshots of what was going on, the sometimes surreal circumstances of the violence. I never thought of leaving, so it was inevitable that was going on around me should get into the writing. I didn't choose to write about it, it chose me. I used to be very absorbed in the fabric of Belfast, but it's changed so much in recent years that I hardly know where I am any longer. Nevertheless its fractured history keeps impinging on what I write. *For all we know*, for example, began as some kind of fictional love story, an attempt to put the war behind me, but before long elements of various conflicts, including our local row, found their way into the poems. It seems inescapable. There's always a war somewhere.

EK-A: Do you think there's such a thing as 'Northern poetry'? Do you think the resurgence of Northern writing at the same time as the re-irruption of the Troubles in the late 1960s was any more than a coincidence?

CC: It seems self-evident that any writer is the product of his or her society and the political circumstances attached to it. Having said that, we don't know what would have happened had Northern Ireland been a 'normal' society, whatever that might mean. I believe Thomas Kinsella once called the Northern 'revival' a 'journalistic entity' or words to that effect. In any event, the writer is bound to write about what is there, whatever it might be. I can't speculate on what we might have written had we been born into an alternative universe. Having said that, maybe writing is itself an alternative universe.

EK-A: What do you make of the theory that violence spurs and validates creativity? Does this idea have any particular relevance to the specific nature and quality of your own writing?

CC: As I've said, I write about what's there. If there's violence about or abroad, so be it. And of course I'm always interested in other models of writing, in other modes of discourse. Japanese *haiku*, Early Irish syllabic verse, the prose of Italo Calvino and Stanislav Lem, the poetry of Baudelaire, whatever. I write as much from the anxiety of those influences as I do about the 'real' world. I'm interested in the ways that the language offers itself to continual negotiation, how its syntax and deep grammar can lead me somewhere I've never been. I want whatever world I live in to be defamiliarized so that it can make sense to me, so that I can see it anew.

EK-A: You've travelled all over the world giving readings of your poetry. How has the experience of travel affected you as a poet? Have you been aware of people in different countries reading or responding to your poetry in different ways? Has awareness of the accelerating globalization of culture affected your aesthetic in any significant ways?

CC: Some of my experience of elsewhere – Berlin, Paris, Dresden – is reflected in the poems I've just referred to. When you're abroad, removed from your habitual environment, you could be anyone, and I'm fascinated by how we represent ourselves to different people, be they people we know or complete strangers. Or how we communicate in an unfamiliar language. As regards the actual readings, especially at festivals of poetry, they have brought me into contact with many other poets, writing in other languages, and that has been an education. One discovery has been that true poets all seem to share the same philosophy, that they are subservient to the language rather than in command of it. And I'm constantly surprised by how accurately people from other countries perceive my own work:

sometimes better than I do myself. There seems to be some kind of global poetic common denominator involved.

EK-A: Critics have remarked on the way your poetry plays the oral against the literary. Could you say something about this aspect of your poetry?

CC: It began as an attempt to get into the poetry something of what I'd experienced in traditional music sessions, a kind of sophisticated gabble. I don't know if it's so true about what I'm doing now. But I do want to play around with as many registers as I can, whether ostensibly spoken or written. I was pleased to discover that the *Táin*, when I came to translate it, was a compendium of various styles and registers, from blunt and laconic to baroque prose to verse and the peculiar genre known as *rosc*, which is a deliberately gnomic utterance. And of course ordinary speech can often be as gnomic as any poem. I like that mix of clarity and obscurity. Again, as regards the literary, I'm attracted to the speculative fictions of writers like Borges and Calvino, and I'm sure my prose has been affected by them; and latterly, some of that otherworldliness, the sense of alternative universes, has crept into my poetry.

EK-A: Childhood, memory, father, family, location, place – usually Belfast: these are important themes in your work. Are you in any way a 'rooted' poet? Or do you think of yourself more in terms of being 'neither here nor there', 'in-between'?

CC: In-between, I think. I'd like to fall into the cracks in the pavement. Having said that, Belfast is important to me, or was. Maybe its provisional nature, its ongoing dispute as to what it was, what it is and what it might become, has provided a ground – a shifting ground, like the sleech on which the city is built – for the exploration of other modes of being, other possibilities. In the same way, I consider myself Irish, if Irish means to welcome other influences and other cultures, and recognising one's obligation to them. I am indebted to the English language, for one thing. And I've suggested elsewhere that Irish traditional music, historically, has always assimilated other kinds of music – Scottish, English, and European, among others. They are made Irish by an Irish style of playing. So style is the thing, whether in writing or music.

EK-A: For Montague and Heaney the rural native place, which is sacral as well as ancestral, has a grounding force for both self and community. Those poets have their dolmen or their *omphalos*. You, however, situate yourself on the urban ground of plurality and difference. Presumably, you're very conscious of opening new ground? Of putting Belfast on the poetic map? Doing for Belfast what Joyce did for Dubliners?

CC: Joyce has always interested me, as much for his rendering of the music of the city – sounds of traffic, printing shops, cutlery in restaurants, songs, fragments of speech – as for any overarching narrative, more *Ulysses*, perhaps, than *Dubliners*. I love his delight in the particular, and I'm sure it lies behind many of my own attempts to render the actuality of things. When I began writing about Belfast in the 1980s I don't think I did so with any conscious urge to put it, as you say, on the 'poetic map', or as a reply to the landscapes of Heaney and Montague. I just saw myself as describing what was there. The multifarious sounds and sights of the city impressed themselves on me as a kind of instant onomatopoeia. Not so much about Belfast, as *of* Belfast.

EK-A: When Derek Mahon writes about Belfast in, say, 'Spring in Belfast' or 'Ecclesiastes', it is a forbidding, unchanging, unyielding city. Your Belfast can be a site of alienation, confusion and violence too, but it also appears to be a place of new opportunities, where the stories of place, identity and nation become mobile, encyclopaedic, multivoiced, a place where a new post-national conscience is being forged. You seem to have a capacity to evoke disparate and contradictory views simultaneously. Would you recognize this reading of Belfast in your work? Do you see yourself giving the reader a very different image of Belfast from the picture Mahon or Paulin gives us?

CC: Again, I don't think I was conscious of measuring my poems about Belfast against those of Mahon or Paulin. I'm sure they had a good deal of influence on me. I was very attracted to the spareness of the Mahon of *Lives*, for example, which seemed to me not too far off the bleak clarity of some Early Irish verse. Paulin, too, with his spiky consonantal shifts. Perhaps it is true that their Belfast is a less welcoming place than mine (for all its terrors). But then I've always lived here. I have to deal with the situation on the ground. I have to see some redeeming qualities – those of provisionality and the change, for instance. Then again, one could put it in blunt terms by saying they are Protestant and I am Catholic. I think Edna Longley says something like that in one of her essays, that as a Catholic I see the possibility of redemption in the city. But you'd have to check that out, as I wouldn't like to misquote Edna. Who would?

EK-A: There's a notable shift in your poetry from the long Whitmanesque line of your early work to the short-lined verse in *Breaking news*. What took you from the long line to the short line?

CC: Maybe I just felt I'd gone as far as I could along that line. As it happens, I was re-reading Carlos Williams at the time. I'd always been attracted to the freshness of his writing. And as it happened, the first poems that emerged in the short line were conceived when a helicopter used to come and perch above my house night after night. I could hear some kind of minimalist staccato beat going on throughout that unceasing din. But I think maybe the lines were a kind of attempt to register some kind of fractured reported speech. Snippets of dialogue or reportage spoken by someone else, just as the longer poems in 'The war correspondent' were partly gleaned or stolen from William Howard Russell's newspaper reports of the Crimean War.

EK-A: I suppose the term 'translation' in the Irish context has acquired a special significance since Friel's play *Translations* inaugurated the Field Day enterprise in 1980. You've undertaken a great variety of translations: nineteenth-century French poetry, Dante's *Inferno*, *The Tain*; there's the series of Latin-tag poems in *Opera et cetera*; other forms of encryption have also attracted you – the radio operators' code, for example, in 'Letters from the alphabet'. Could you comment on the importance to you of some of these forms of linguistic and cultural exchange? For example, why Mallarmé, Rimbaud and Baudelaire? Why Dante?

CC: The *Inferno* was a commission. Otherwise, I would never have thought about doing it. But when I ventured into it, it seemed inevitable. Likewise Merriman's *The midnight court*, and *The Táin*. I felt blessed that this triumvirate should come to me, rather than me to them. I felt confirmed that I was a part of a much larger pattern. The French poems were a hangover from my study of A Level French. I loved the sounds and the rhythms, the decadence, the implication that an aesthetic impulse could change the world, or at least change our ways of seeing it. And of course as someone who is at least partly bilingual, I've always been fascinated by the way other languages, other codes, affect our knowledge, or lack of knowledge, of what we think is familiar and given. Translation is a serious business for me. It's also serious play. I like play.

EK-A: With reference to the *Inferno* specifically: could you say what significance Dante has for you?

CC: Dante seems a very modern writer in his ability to delineate or summon up a character in a few lines. And his concerns about the intersection of language, politics and poetry also appeal to me. I love the way he shifts his registers, from vituperative vernacular to high philosophy, just as he moves through a gamut of feelings, from anger to pity to tenderness to awe. It's a very attractive and vigorous music, and one of the challenges of the translation was to try to get that music, which I felt was missing in a great many of the English translations I read. But I think I've said as much, and more, in the Introduction to my translation.

EK-A: Your most recent work, *For all we know,* is a kind of novel-poem (an 'in-between' literary genre) though of course your poetry has always displayed a novelistic discursivity – even the collection *Belfast confetti.* The curious English idiom, 'for all we know', which you use as title highlights your theme – knowledge, its nature and limits – a theme which runs through all your work. Could you comment on how you see *For all we know* continuing, or marking a departure from, previous work, in terms of both content and form?

CC: Certainly, *For all we know* is the most unified book of poetry I've written to date. It became clear to me after some five or six poems that it would have to be a sequence of sorts, and as I wrote more, it became clear that it would be a book, a kind of hall of mirrors with poems reflecting and commenting on others. It's also the quickest book of poems I've ever done. Much of it was written in the summer months of 2007. At one stage I was writing a couple of poems a night, night after night. The book seemed to generate its own energy, and I am still wondering how it was done, still grateful for it. The initial thought was to try and write a conventional love poem. As it turned out, my suspicions that I was temperamentally incapable of doing anything in that genre were confirmed. The poems arrived in another voice, that of a persona, or rather two personas, man and woman, engaged in a dialogue which casts some doubt on whatever it is they are doing together. And it seemed to me that I was dealing with a new kind of language, a way of saying things I hadn't considered until then. I didn't know at the beginning of any of the poems (70 poems, written in 14-syllable lines) what I was going to say until I said it, so every line was a venture into unknown territory. The book was a kind of magical mystery tour, and it was a great experience to explore that hitherto unknown world, discovering new tropes and turns of phrase on the way. It seemed to me that I was being informed by some kind of *aisling* woman, a creature from another universe which resembled ours and was contiguous to it, but was not our world. So many of the poems are voiced by the woman, with the man responding in a sometimes perplexed manner to her stories or her accounts of their past. Writing in the voice of a woman was something I'd never considered before. Not that I *considered* it in this instance; it just happened that way. I should say that the book very possibly emerged from a novel I'd written some years back, *The pen friend*, which failed to find a publisher until recently – it'll be published by Blackstaff Press in Autumn 2009. That, too, concerns a love affair, and is as full of epistemological uncertainties as *For all we know*. I wrote the poems, I think, as another way of dealing with the same material, but then the poems began doing something else again, which is as it should be. The author should always be surprised.

EK-A: There is much 'learning' and 'erudition' in your work, but you've warned your readers about taking it too seriously. Is knowledge always primarily rhetorical? As far as your poetry is concerned, is there any difference between 'book learning' and 'pub-slabber'?

CC: My 'erudition' is very much in inverted commas. If asked to speak for twenty minutes on the subjects touched on in my books – especially the prose books – I would be very hard put. Much of the ostensible knowledge is the result of magpie forays into libraries, and, more latterly, the internet. It's stolen, cogged. I sometimes insert into a book whole paragraphs taken verbatim from some erudite source; but I have the illusion that I am writing these words myself, or that they become different because I am writing them, or that they become different because they're now in a different context, a different milieu. Like Borges' Pierre Menard, who rewrites Don Quixote word for word, except now it is completely different because the times that are in it are different. *The pen friend* was written almost entirely in fountain pen, or by fountain pen, or rather a whole set of different vintage fountain pens which I bought on eBay 'for purposes of research'. I told myself that each pen, with its different quirks and characteristics, had its own story to tell, and I pretended to myself that it was the pen writing, and not me. It's a kind of magic, or conjuring trick. A way of letting the story tell itself.

As for 'pub-slabber', I know I've used that term myself in the past, but it's a rather flippant way of referring to the sometimes profound knowledge, wisdom even, that I've encountered in my dealings with traditional musicians – people like Bobby Casey, Joe Burke, Junior Crehan, Mick Hoy – all great musicians, all great tellers of yarns and anecdotes, masters of the one-line put-down. They are immensely sophisticated, and not entirely without 'book-learning' either. What does interest me is that with them oral, musical and literary culture are all part of the same spectrum. It's all art, and it's all life.

EK-A: You have long demonstrated an interest in narrative – a desire to organize perceptions in larger patterns as opposed to seeing the world in terms of discrete units. Yet no sooner do you set up a narrative run than you're looking for ways to escape or subvert it. The narrative is swiftly turned into a labyrinth, a hall of mirrors, a Russian doll, which mocks and frustrates the desire for knowledge, enlightenment, wholeness. Similarly, what one might think were the more straightforwardly teleological systems of alphabets, catalogues and A–Z directories are complicated by an imaginative and linguistic exuberance which makes a mockery of taxonomic systems and the idea of simple, single, directional meaning. You lay down forms and structures, but you know that 'the world is everything that is the case' – that reality overflows any particular version of it. You want focus and precision, a concentration on the *haeccitas* of the vividly rendered fragment, but you also want a long rambly poem. Could you comment on this play-off between the particularizing and totalizing impulses in your work?

CC: When I first embarked on a long line, in *The Irish for no*, it seemed to me that each of the long lines could be seen as a haiku of sorts. So that discrepancy or marriage between the general and particular became an organizing principle. I think every writer strives to 'put things into words', if not 'words into things'. But every writer knows that things are not words, so the search is endless. All we can hope for is better failures, to paraphrase Beckett.

EK-A: The blurb on the dust-jacket of *The star factory* refers to the 'place of imagination' where history is turned into stories. Heaney believes in art's redemptive or curative force – the 'redress of poetry'. Muldoon jokes about art having any such elevated function. What is your idea of what you want your art to achieve in moral, social or political terms? What is the importance of stories?

CC: Stories are very important. They might be everything regarding writing. And it seems to me that the moral of every story is to put the reader into another place, to make them consider other possibilities, to imagine what it might be like to be someone else, or see the world through another's eyes. To make them think again. To make them examine their preconceptions. To disturb them, sometimes without their knowing. To leave them wondering. To see their world anew.

EK-A: *Shamrock tea* holds out the possibility of magical transformation, yet at the same time seems to enforce a sense of endless cyclical recurrence. What for you is the ratio of hope and hopelessness in this book?

CC: That's an interesting question. Let me try to begin to answer it by suggesting that Flann O'Brien's *The third policeman* might have been at the back of my mind when I wrote *Shamrock tea*. At the end of O'Brien's novel we find that the protagonist is, unbeknownst to himself, trapped in a circular hell. But its geography is fascinating and attractive in its detail: as hells go, it's not such a bad place to be in. *The third policeman* is also a parody – of philosophical and scientific method, of Irish rural genre novels, of crime thrillers and science fiction, among others. It's a play with genre. Our own lives are conceived in terms of genre. Our social being is governed by received ideas and rules: weddings, births, funerals, the worlds of work, politics and play, are all attended by familiar narrative procedures. Our urge to make stories of whatever happens or has happened, or why we are here, is inescapable. Hence the need for sacred books. The narrative of *Shamrock tea* might be fantastical, but no more so than the Bible, the Koran, or the Tibetan Book of the Dead. Which reminds me that maybe *Shamrock tea* is a parody of the Narnia books – the Christian apologetics – of C.S. Lewis. In any event it seems we must experience the world through narrative. Memory is narrative. Even the future, in so far as we can speculate about it, is a narrative of possible outcomes. That being so, what is the relevance of hope, or hopelessness? For better or worse, we are trapped within our own perceptions of the world, within our narratives.

EK-A: The labyrinth is a central and recurrent symbol in your work. You use it to describe the city, memory, history, text. Could you explain your attraction to this symbol? Is there ever a way out of the labyrinth? And if so, to where or to what?

CC: I never deliberately started out to get into the labyrinth as a recurrent symbol. But it so happens that I have a recurrent anxiety dream in which I am trapped between the Falls Road and the Shankill, or trapped on the wrong side, which to me is the Shankill: a labyrinth of side streets, cul-de-sacs, fences, rivers, factory complexes, dams. It seems inescapably ingrained in my experience, in my psyche. I had one of these dreams just last night, and woke up feeling strangely comforted by it, engrossed by its wonderfully complicated familiarity. For all its familiar dread there is something beautiful about its clarity and recurrence. Perhaps the way out of the labyrinth is to get deeper into it, more fully to explore its ramifications.

EK-A: You introduced the word 'fugue' in *Shamrock tea,* and it's clearly a term with considerable resonance for you. Could you comment on the relevance of 'fugue' to your writing practice?

CC: Latterly I became more interested in the concept of fugue (in musical terms) from reading the writings of Glenn Gould. He's a great writer, by the way, full of mischief and paradox. I used one of his sentences as an epigraph for *For all we know*: 'Fugue must perform its frequently stealthy work with continuously shifting melodic fragments that remain, in the 'tune' sense, perpetually unfinished.' But fugue is also a medical condition, a kind of trance where the victim walks out the door and, forgetting who he is, takes up another existence and another name in another place. He wakes with no knowledge of how he had become that person. So 'fugue', both in musical and psychological terms, has all sorts of implications as to who we are and what we are doing in this world. It's from Latin, *fugere*, to flee. Are we all fugitives? 'Fled is that music: – Do I wake or sleep?'

EK-A: How does a poem begin for you? With a rhythm, an image, an idea, a line or two … ? Are you a constant reviser of poems like Derek Mahon?

CC: Very much with a line or a phrase out of nowhere: a snippet of pub conversation, a sign on the street, a line by another writer. Words before I even have an idea as to what they might mean. Once the poem is in book form, I never revise. One has to make an end somewhere. There's no such thing as perfectibility. Well, maybe there is, but it's an ever-receding target.

EK-A: There are a number of references in your work, especially in *For all we know*, to the new technological culture which has clearly revolutionized the agenda for critical and cultural analysis in recent years. Indeed, your whole writing practice has much in common with the new digital aesthetics, and one doesn't have to look too far to see the relevance of the new media language of 'hypertext', 'virtuality', 'simulation', and so on to your work. What for you is the importance of this connection between poetry and technology, especially in the contemporary Northern context?

CC: I don't think about it that much. One uses whatever materials or technologies that are at hand. Having said that, I use the internet a lot for quite a lot of my writing. Sometimes I Google a phrase I intend to use, putting it into inverted commas, just to see if it has been used before. And very often – surprisingly often – words that I thought original have indeed been used before, sometimes in contexts that wouldn't have occurred to me. As you know, a lot of my prose is research driven. I used to haunt libraries, and still do, but to a lesser extent; now I tend to go wandering in hyperspace. Looking for whatever might crop up between the lines, whether it's information or disinformation; and of course it's always difficult to know on the internet what is true, or false, or a garbled amalgam. *For all we know* attempts to deal with some of those issues between truth and lies, including the lies we tell ourselves.

EK-A: *For all we know,* being a love poem, was a break-through for you. Your oeuvre is certainly marked by variety and a willingness to try new things (though I don't think pastoral has ever had much appeal to you). Is there anything you haven't had a go at that you'd still like to have a go at?

CC: If I knew what I was going to do next, there'd be no fun in it. For all I know, the next project might be a pastoral. I spend my life looking and waiting to see what happens next.

EK-A: Finally, how would you assess the state of poetry in the North of Ireland today?

CC: I've mentioned Alan Gillis above: he has immense linguistic resources, and a great sense of serious play. He's now based in Edinburgh. But it seems to me there's a lot going on here too: Leontia Flynn, Sinead Morrissey, Maureen Boyle, to name a few. And I'd like to think that the Seamus Heaney Centre of Poetry, of which I am the director, does something to create an atmosphere in which poets might learn and flourish.

Language and the prosodic line in Carson's poetry

PETER DENMAN

Ciaran Carson's poetry exhibits many departures from the normative structures of verse in English, but the degree of these departures is nearly always marked by a discernible reference to what is accepted as the conventional norm. To take the most prominent feature: his long lines are individual and distinctive, but they can be discussed and analysed by reference to their difference, first of all, from lines that are not considered long, and secondly by referring them to long-lined poetry produced by other poets. The accompanying features of lineation and rhyme in his poetry are distinctive in a similar and related way, because they also resist the accepted conventions. This is a characteristic that finds its culmination and clearest expression in his translations, where entire poems, even books, are produced in what might be termed 'separated language'. The distinctiveness of the translation operates against and around an original text that is always there in the background, and in many cases is printed on the facing page. The original text is a structural matrix. Carson's versions are generated not by a need to make the already well-known poems of Baudelaire, or Dante, or Ní Dhomhnaill available to an Irish readership, but to enlarge the poetic and linguistic space that the poems occupy. A number of Carson's book and poem titles, such as *First language*, 'Second language', 'The Irish for no', focus immediately on the linguistic and intertextual game of translation. 'The Irish for no' derives its momentum from the space that is opened up between the two languages, Irish and English.

> we were debating,
> Bacchus and the pards and me, how to render *The Ulster Bank – the Bank*
> *That Likes to Say Yes* into Irish, and whether eglantine was native to Ireland.
> *I cannot see what flowers are at my feet*, when *yes* is the verb repeated, ...

But there is another space being opened up in this poem, pointing at the distance between contemporary poetic idiom in Ireland, on the one hand, and what arguably stands as one of the normative and defining poems in the English tradition, Keats' 'To a nightingale', on the other. It is primarily on this latter aspect, the relation to and departure from normative form in Carson's poetry, that this essay will concentrate.

Carson's first collection, *The new estate* (1976), is very much in the standard idiom of Irish poetry in the 1960s and 1970s. A number of observational poems fix the significance of objects seen: stamps, an engraving in an encyclopaedia, a dead sheep. There are some versions from early Irish, for so long favoured test-pieces for Irish poets in English. There are poems recording moments allowed to speak for themselves with the minimum of narratorial comment. Formally the poems are of lyric length and are mostly unrhymed, except for the translations where rhyme is judged to be appropriate. Many of the poems are organized in regular stanza blocks, which range in length from couplets to eleven-line segments. The line length rarely exceeds ten syllables.

The poems in *The new estate* are very competent poems, but unremarkable; they appear distinctive only when set against the formal extensiveness of Carson's later poems. And those later poems were considerably later. There was a gap of over ten years before the next book, *The Irish for no* (1987), in which radically different approach and diction were employed. The poems in this collection established what came to be regarded as the characteristic Carson language, which might be briefly described as an idiomatic discursiveness set out in long lines playing against a stretched prosodic formalism in rhyme and rhythm. This remains the case, even though his more recent volumes, *The inferno of Dante Alighiere* (2002) and *Breaking news* (2003), exhibit preferences for conventional and very short lines respectively.

Although the publication of *The Irish for no* in 1987 brought with it what can now be seen as the foundation of a radically new diction, it was followed soon afterwards by a sort of throwback. Carson's first volume was issued in a revised form as *The new estate and other poems*: a few poems from the first edition were omitted, and quite a few new pieces added. Most of the newly added poems had been included in a pamphlet, *The lost explorer* (1978), published just two years after the original *New estate*. Even in these there is already a progression from the generally tight and contained poems that marked Carson's debut volume. Pieces such as 'The great Fitzpatrick' and 'The incredible shrinking man' are beginning to open out. Although the poems may be shaped in carefully blocked-out stanzas, they can be left inconclusive and open-ended as if hinting at larger forms. 'Twine' is a good example of this:

My father's postman sack
Hung on a nail behind the kitchen door,
Its yellow straps undone. I stuck my head inside
The canvas flap and breathed the gloom.

The smell of raffia and faded ink
Was like the smell of nothing. The twine lay in
My mother's bottom drawer, the undelivered
Letters were returned to sender.

I thought of being shut up under stairs.
Outside it was snowing, and my father's hands
Were blue with cold. Soon he would return,
His hands would warm me.

Christmas came. He worked all day.
His dinner would be kept hot in the oven.
There was the twine to tie the turkey's legs.
There was the tawse behind the kitchen door.

In this poem there are four uncompromising quatrains. The lines hover around the median ten-syllable length. Although many of the lines are run on, each stanza ending is firmly closed syntactically. The poem starts with a quatrain of almost unrelieved rhythmic regularity, a succession of iambics varied only by the inversion at the start of the second line. What metrical variation there is in the stanza is brought about by the different line lengths, with three, five, six and four beats respectively. The rising duple pattern (or iambic metre) continues to underpin the rhythm of the second and third stanzas, but with marked variations. At the end of the poem there is return to a strict regularity to mark the closure, which is here provided not by terminal rhyme but by a forcefully repeated line structure. The final stanza is the only one without run-on lines; its lines move towards being self-contained units. The last two lines are duplicates, structurally and metrically. Both can be scanned as classic iambic pentameters, each incorporating a reversed first foot. They both introduce slightly dialect words: 'tawse' is an Ulster English word for a strap; and standard English would generally say 'string' rather than 'twine'. Both words occur in the same position in their respective lines, but they bring very different imaginative weights to the poem.

'Twine' has already been mentioned prominently earlier on, in the title and in the second stanza; it is part of a steady and closed process of imagery within the poem. It has a clear and stated function – to tie the turkey's legs. Figuratively it suggests the ties and conjunctions of family relationships. The tawse springs out from behind the kitchen door, unexpected, strange, and sinister. The tawse is left hanging there. Where the twine is what we might call a closed image, the tawse is an open one. The twine remains in the poem with the bottom drawer, the raffia and the title; it operates within the space circumscribed by the text. The tawse swings back to the previous stanza to rewrite the image of the father's hands blue with cold that would warm the speaker; implicit with a potential threat as yet unfilled, it stretches out to a time beyond that enclosed by the poem.

Most of the rest of the examples discussed here are taken from those gathered in *The ballad of HMS Belfast* (1999), a compendium volume that stands as a sort of *Selected Poems*. The only poem from *The new estate* to make it into the book is 'Dunne', from the revised 1988 edition; it is as if the earlier material and methods are being discarded. The Dunne in question is Ben Dunne, which enables us to date the poem to sometime after October 1978 when the kidnap it describes took place. The poem makes a clear formal distribution of its material over five eight-line stanzas. The stanzas are end-stopped. Each line is constructed with reference to the five rising beats of the iambic pentameter line, although the variations may drop or add syllables and some of the lines are reduced to four beats.

> From Camlough, Silverbridge and Crossmaglen
> The military were closing in. He was
> It seemed, the paste on the wallpaper, or
> The wall, spunked out between the leaves, etched
> At last into the memories of what might have been.

This gazetteer of names is one of the early instances of a trope that is to become frequent in Carson's work, that of the list. The rhythm in 'Dunne' varies, as in the switch from the predominant rising iambic pattern to a falling trochaic one at the end of the first stanza:

> *I reached an avenue of darkened yews.*
> *Somewhere footsteps on the gravel.*

Elsewhere a line of anapests can be detected, as in the second line of the last stanza. These observations are not of huge significance in themselves, and are made primarily to show that Carson's early poems work within a standard framework of English verse and are susceptible to analysis through broadly traditional scansion.

The subsequent poems seem to depart markedly from this. There is a tendency when discussing innovative poems to identify them negatively, by saying what they are not. It may indeed be the case that resistance to a known form is often an important part of their making. Take, for instance, the ghost of the sonnet form that underpins the unrhymed *Belfast confetti* poems:

> Suddenly as the riot squad moved in, it was raining exclamation marks,
> Nuts bolts, nails, car-keys. A fount of broken type. And the explosion
> Itself – an asterisk on the map. This hyphenated line, a burst of rapid
>   fire …
> I was trying to complete a sentence in my head, but it kept stuttering,
> All the alleyways and side-streets blocked with stops and colons.
>
> I know this labyrinth so well – Balaclava, Raglan, Inkerman, Odessa
>   Street –
> Why can't I escape? Every move is punctuated. Crimea Street. Dead end
>   again.
> A Saracen, Kremlin–2 mesh. Makrolon face-shields. Walkie-talkies. What is
> My name? Where am I coming from? Where am I going? A fusillade of
>   question-marks.

The five/four division of these nine-line poems mimics the eight/six division of the sonnet form, and the reduction in the number of lines is compensated for by making each line longer. In fact each poem ends up rather longer in total than the normative English sonnet, having about 170 syllables rather than the 140 one gets in fourteen ten-syllable lines. But when Carson does come to write conventional sonnets he favours 'the alexandrine plan', using alexandrine twelve-syllable lines which give a total of just about 170 syllables (14 x 12 = 168, if the form is rigorously observed).[1]

---

1 *The Alexandrine plan* contains Carson's translations of sonnets by Baudelaire, Rimbaud and Mallarmé.

A formal instance of duplication has already been pointed out in the parallelism of the closing two lines of 'Twine'. Phrases of duplication are employed so frequently in Carson's poetry as to make duplication a basic figure. Often it is a simple verbal construction. All the following examples are from the poem 'Judgement': 'Nods and winks'; 'Spectacles put on and off'; 'The Tullyallen and the Ummeracam were dry'; 'Priests had a great way with ropes and knots'; 'Something to do with chasubles and albs'; 'The tracks began to shimmer and hum'. Sometimes this feature is extended to become a list (what classical rhetoric would term a catalogue) as in 'Belfast Confetti': 'Nuts, bolts, nails, car-keys'; 'Balaclava, Raglan, Inkerman, Odessa Street'; 'A Saracen. Kremlin–2 Mesh. Makrolon face-shields. Walkie-talkies'. This device of almost tautological inclusiveness would amount to over-determination if used in a prose fiction description, but in poetry it has a long lineage as a rhetorical figure that serves primarily for ornamentation. In the opening canto of *The faerie queene*, for instance, when Spenser wants to convey an image of a forest he offers an extended descriptive catalogue of different trees – cedar, laurel, yew, birch, oak, pine, etc. – which would never be found growing together in nature. This is an imaginative precision that supersedes reality

The duplications become multiplications when more than two elements are involved, and they may be structural rather than ornamental, as in the following passage from 'Loaf':

> I chewed it over, this whiff I got just now, but trying to pin down
> That aroma – yeast, salt, flour, water – is like writing on the waxed sleeve
> That it's wrapped in: the nib keeps skidding off. Or the ink won't take. Blue-black
> *Quink* is what I used then. I liked the in-between-ness of it, neither
> One thing nor the other. A *Conway Stewart* fountain-pen, bluish-green
> Mock tortoiseshell ... the lever sticking sometimes in the quick of my thumb,
> I'd fill her up: a contented slurp like the bread you use to sup up Soup.
> McWatters' pan loaf, some said, was like blotting-paper: I thought of
> Leonardo's diary, or a mirror code ending with, *Eat this.*
> Well, some people *like* blotting-paper. I used to eat chalk myself. Raw
> Flour, oatmeal. Paper. A vitamin deficiency? The corners of
> My books weren't dog-eared, they were chewed. But neatly chewed, like the thumb-index
> Of a dictionary. I ate my way from *A* to *Z*, the list of weights
> And measures. So now I'm in McWatters' flour-loft. Grains, pecks and bushels:

An undefined 'it' is immediately glossed as a 'whiff', then an 'aroma'. Next comes a list of constituents. In the poem they are presented as the constituents of the indefinable aroma, but of course they are in fact the ingredients of the loaf. It is difficult to attach any smell, even an indefinable one, to the water used in a bakery, or to salt. The lack of definition is compared to an act of writing (or rather of not-writing), and this is figured in two alternative images: 'the nib keeps skidding off. Or the ink won't take.' The duplication in this lack of definition is continued across the hyphenated terms: the ink is described as 'Blue-black' and 'I liked the in-between-ness of it, neither / One thing nor the other'. The pen itself is bluish-green. At the end of the section are more lists and duplications: 'Chalk ... Raw Flour, oatmeal'; not 'dog-eared' but 'chewed. But neatly chewed'; 'weights and measures', 'Grains, pecks and bushels'.

The loaf is compared to blotting paper, and it is apparent that the simile is the characteristic trope for the passage. The prepositional 'like' for comparative purposes occurs four times: 'like writing on the waxed sleeve', 'like the bread you use to sup up / Soup', 'like blotting paper', 'like the thumb-index /Of a dictionary'. This use of simile is a particular form of duplication, as it inevitably joins two images or concepts, with one being compared to the other. 'Like' is then modulated into a verb. It has already occurred in this form in the fourth line. Two lines after the reflection that 'McWatters' pan loaf ... was like blotting-paper' some said, we get the statement that 'some people *like* blotting-paper', where a reader (aided by the italics) has to make an effort to put a distance between the two usages of 'like'.

In Carson's poetry the suggested meaning lies not outside and around a single image, as in Pound's formulation for Imagist poetry, but is located somewhere between two or more images that become the co-ordinates of a conceptual space.

> It's all the go, here, changing something into something else, like rhyming
> Kampouchea with Cambodia ...
>
> ('Queen's gambit')

These are phrases which may function phonetically, creating their own local sound patterns within a phrase: The phrase may be a well worn one, its meaning slightly stretched in the context of the line, or it may link two phonetically similar lexical items in an unexpected way, as rhyme does conventionally according to Roman Jakobson.[2] But also they mark out an imagined space within which the action or objects of the poem may reside. This is a particular characteristic of Carson's writing, occurring so frequently as to be almost a signature.

2 Roman Jakobson, *Language in literature*, ed. K. Pomorska and S. Rudy (Cambridge, MA, 1987), 62–94.

Another feature associated with Carson's poetry is the long line. The long line has some notable precedents in English and American verse: Chapman's translation of Homer, Christopher Smart, William Blake, Walt Whitman, Ogden Nash, Allen Ginsberg, Carl Sandburg, C.K. Williams, Charles Olson. Is it possible to establish just what are the aspects of Carson's use of the long line that make it individual? The normative length of the poetic line in English is between eight and twelve syllables, with a strong propensity for ten. This sets a lower limit, and a line can be described as long when it is typically longer than this. It is more difficult to fix an upper limit, but generally something around thirty-five or forty syllables seems to be the upper extent. Go much beyond that and one is getting into the territory of the prose poem, which is a different form. In the particular case of Carson's poetry one can be more precise and say that the normative length for his own long-line poems is a line of sixteen to eighteen syllables. The lines can be considerably longer than this, up to twenty-five syllables or more on occasions, without breaking the pattern. Again, his long lines cannot vary towards the other extreme, because if they drop much below sixteen syllables they then become normal lines, or even short lines. So, one can have long 'long lines' but not short 'long lines'. Can we be more descriptive of Carson's long line, beyond counting the syllables and saying that it is long, or very long, and identify what distinguishes Carson's use of long line from the other practitioners of the form?

We might begin with some generalizations about the long line in poetry. It functions in various ways. Sometimes it stands as a unit: an item – albeit an elaborate one – in a sort of catalogue, as in this well-known passage from Whitman describing a sea-fight ('Song of myself xxxvi'):

> Two great hulls motionless on the breast of the darkness;
> Our vessel riddled and slowly sinking – preparations to pass to the one
>   we had conquered;
> The captain on the quarter deck coldly giving his orders through a
>   countenance as white as a sheet;
> Near by, the corpse of the child that serv'd in the cabin;
> The dead face of an old salt with long white hair and carefully curl'd
>   whiskers;
> The flames, spite of all that could be done, flickering aloft and below;
> The husky voices of the two or three officers yet fit for duty;
> Formless stacks of bodies, and bodies by themselves – dabs of flesh upon
>   the masts and spars …

The lines can be self-contained statements. We could find examples of that in Whitman also, but here is a part of Smart's *Jubilate agno*, where each line is a sort of incantatory antiphonal response in praise of his cat Jeoffry:

> For he keeps the Lord's watch in the night against the adversary.
> For he counteracts the powers of darkness by his electrical skin and glaring eyes.
> For he counteracts the Devil, who is death, by brisking about the life.
> For in his morning orisons he loves the sun and the sun loves him.

The long line can be a qualification of a previously announced concept, as in Allen Ginsberg's *Howl.* For instance:

> who loned it through the streets of Idaho seeking visionary indian angels who were visionary indian angels,
> who thought they were only mad when Baltimore gleamed in supernatural ecstasy,
> who jumped in limousines with the Chinaman of Oklahoma on the impulse of winter midnight streetlight smalltown rain,
> who lounged hungry and lonesome …

Prosodically, the line becomes the primary rhythmic unit; that is to say, the line itself, not a constituent of it such as a pattern of beats or stresses, is the repeated element that generates the rhythm of the poem. In fact, one could go further and say that it appears that internally the long line unit must be metrically irregular once it gets extended beyond about fourteen syllables. It is quite easy to find poems with long lines that do display a metrical pattern and that do rhyme, but these lines tend to break down into smaller units precisely because they have such a metrical pattern within them. For instance, Robert Service's 'The shooting of Dan McGrew' typically has a sixteen- or seventeen-syllable line (about the same length as Carson's). It is immediately apparent that the strong beat pattern allows the line in Robert Service's poem to subdivide into predominantly two-beat and three-beat units, with the line always ending on three beats:

> A bunch of the boys / were whooping it up / in the Malamute Saloon
> The kid that hand / les the music-box / was hitting a rag-time tune;
> Back of the bar/ in a solo-game / sat Dangerous Dan McGrew
> And watching his luck / was his light-o'-love, / the lady that's known as Lou.

At times these divisions are further pointed up by internal rhymes:

> There's men that somehow/ just grip your eyes/ and hold them hard like
> a spell;
> And such was he/ and looked to me/ like a man who had lived in hell;
> With a face most hair/ and the dreary stare / of a dog whose day is done
> As he watered the green stuff/ in his glass,/ and the drops fell one by one.

The continuity of each line is subverted by the prosody that brings shorter rhythmic units into play. A similar effect can be observed in fourteener lines, where the fourteen syllables almost inevitably fall into an eight/six ballad pattern. 'The lake isle of Innisfree', (roughly contemporary with 'The shooting of Dan McGrew', but more respectable), has thirteen- or fourteen-syllable lines, where the caesura in mid-line is very evident.

> I will arise and go now, and go to Innisfree,
> And a small cabin build there, of clay and wattles made,
> Nine bean rows will I have there, a hive for the honey bee,
> And live alone in the bee-loud glade.

In a long-line poem in free verse the prosodic pattern is built up primarily by the repetition of line units, not of syllabic patterns within the line. As a result the poem becomes almost a chant, especially when the line is a breath-unit. The long line does not rely on end rhyme, except as in Ogden Nash for comic effect, where the technique of the long line is used to defer the expected rhyme which, when it comes, is usually a 'surprise rhyme' and additionally comic in its deformation of language. Nevertheless, as the line – even when long – remains the basic unit of the poem, the line break has to be marked. In metrical verse this is generally marked by the completion of a recurrent metrical pattern, and often additionally by end-rhyme. With the long line, given that end-rhyme is often dispensed with and that there is no regular metre, other expedients are found. For instance, the line ending is nearly always marked by the completion of a grammatical unit. The line is grammatically complete, and enjambment is unusual.[3]

One of the functions of end-rhyme in a poetic line is to signal the completion of the line. This can be signalled prominently, as in Pope's end-stopped lines, or almost subliminally as in the run-on couplets of Browning's 'My last duchess'. In

---

3 William Blake does employ run-on long lines.

long, metrically irregular lines of serious poetry (as distinct from the light verse of Ogden Nash) end-rhyme is not used. However, there very frequently is a repeated element serving to mark the division between one line and the next. In long-line poems this repeated element tends to be relocated from the line-ending to the start of the line; the rhythmical emphasis in the long line is initial rather than terminal. As the function of the repeated element is to mark a division between lines, it can do this as well at the start of the succeeding line as it can at the end of a preceding one. The extracts from the Smart and Ginsberg poems quoted above demonstrate this feature.

So, while recognizing that the long line is a deviant form identified by difference in that it steps outside the bounds of conventional length, one can establish a rough idea of the general characteristics of the typical long line: something in excess of fourteen syllables long, without a regular recurrent metre or beat pattern, usually end-stopped, unrhymed at the end, but often with an initial emphasis generated by repetition at the start of the line. Further, because the line is end-stopped it usually makes a unit of sense in itself and it may constitute a breath unit, or a typographical unit. To these features one can add that a long-line poem is generally set out in extended verse paragraphs; it is not stanzaic.

Although this has been a brief and hurried generalization about the long line form in English, it will serve as a sort of matrix against which to measure what is distinctive in Carson's use of the line.

First of all, Carson never really abandons the stanza form. It may not be there in as hard-edged a structure as it is in 'Twine' or 'Dunne', but his poems are blocked out stanzas of two lines, or of three lines as in 'The ark of the covenant' in *First language*, or five lines as in 'The brain of Edward Carson', or in quasi-sonnet form as in *Belfast confetti*. Nor does Carson abandon end-rhyme. He favours rhyming lines in couplets, or sometimes in groups of three. The rhyming lines are nearly always contiguous, and we do not get much use of the envelope or interlaced patterns of ABAB rhyming schemes etc. A simple explanation for this is that such interlaced patterns extend the gap between the rhyming sounds, and as the length of Carson's lines already opens up a distance between the line endings and their rhyme words, further extension of the distance is challenging. As to the type of rhymes, he seems to run through the gamut: triple rhyme, slant rhyme, consonantal rhyme, off rhyme, pararhyme, homoteleuton (essentially the same word repeated). The rhymes and repetitions of Carson's work would be worth a study in themselves. Perhaps the most remarkable aspect is the way in which he has been able to submerge his rhymes. The rhyming effects often rely on linking words in unusual or surprising ways, yet they generally do not attract undue attention to themselves.

The poem 'Eesti' demonstrates this compromise between the free verse form of the long line and the formalism of the stanza. It is written in long-line couplets. Each couplet constitutes a stanza.

> I wandered homesick-lonely through that Saturday of silent Tallinn
> When a carillon impinged a thousand raining quavers on my ear, tumbling
>
> Dimly from immeasurable heights into imaginary brazen gong-space,
>   trembling
> Dimpled in their puddle, rain-drop halo-pools, concentrically assembling.

Of the eleven stanzas, six are run on, setting up an immediate tension between the closural containment of the stanza and the continuity of the poem's discourse. The end-rhymes linking the two lines in the couplets are various. There are full rhymes, slant rhymes, multi-syllabic rhymes, rhymes on unstressed syllables – the only full rhyme is the 'trembling'/ 'assembling' of stanza two. Again, the concept of rhyme is at once summoned and resisted. While the first pre-rhyme word 'Tallinn' – picking up the place name of the title – has one of the vaguest of all the rhymes, 'Tumbling', that word 'tumbling' does anticipate the rhyme sounds of the next couplet much more strongly. There is a strong pattern of internal rhyme imposed on the opening stanzas. If 'Tallinn' is without a strong end-rhyme correspondence, there is a definite rhyme in the very first stressed syllables of the next line: 'Carillon'. The strongly end-rhymed second stanza also rhymes its line openings, 'Dimly' and 'Dimpled', and these are associated with the cluster of initial 'im-' sounds in lines nearby: 'impinged', 'imaginary', 'immeasurable'.

The internal rhyming becomes more complex further on. In the second line of the fourth couplet, there is the characteristic duplication effect of 'shrines' and 'niches' which are lit by 'tapers and the sheen of ikons'. These two semantic pairings are further linked phonetically by rhyme; 'shrines and niches' share the consonantal sounds 'Sh' and 'n'; the sounds are picked up even more forcibly in the word 'sheen', which is a sort of phonetic anagram or reversal of 'niches'.

> I thumbed the warm brass worn thumb-scoop of the latch. Tock.
>   I entered into bronze-
> Dark, shrines and niches lit by beeswax tapers and the sheen of ikons.

This device is carried through the poem in another doubling of 'poised and pointed'; further down 'patina and faces' is found in almost anagrammatic conjunction with 'painted faces'. Later on, towards the poem's end, 'clinking' and 'chinking' is a duplication linked both semantically and phonetically.

> Silk tasselled missals. Rosaries. Statues stricken dumb

> Beneath their rustling purple shrouds, as candles wavered in the holy smoke.
> The mosaic chapel echoed with a clinking, chinking censer-music.

> This red-letter day would not be written, had I not wandered through
>   the land of Eesti.
> I asked my father how he thought it went. He said to me in Irish, *Listen: Éist.*

In the penultimate stanza there is an approximate end rhyme between 'smoke' and 'music', but 'smoke' also anticipates the first stressed word in the next line, 'mosaic' – a phonetic rearrangement of 'smoke' and a pararhyme for 'music'. This process culminates (as it should) in the final stanza. The end-rhyme used for the couplet is consonantal and anagrammatic. The Irish 'Éist' is an anagram of most of 'Eesti'. But 'Éist', as well as being the translation, is also contained anagrammatically in the heart of 'Listen', making '*Listen: Éist*' a very strong semantic and formal pairing or duplication. There is something going on here formally, and more than what we have identified so far. Line lengths have varied in the poem up to this, but here they become metrically regular. Both lines can be scanned as displaying ten beats or stressed syllables, and ten unstressed syllable. Or, break the lines at their mid-line divisions, marked by the comma and full stop respectively, and the stanza becomes a perfectly acceptable quatrain in an iambic pentameter rhythm. And for a rhyme to mark the ending of what would be the first and third line, we have 'written' and 'it went', where the six letters of the second element are contained anagramatically in the first. The doubling of letters and sounds leads to this sort of linguistic hybridization. As in the early poem 'Twine' considered above, the conclusion of the poem moves towards a closural finality in the form. Where 'Twine' opened beyond itself with the menace of the tawse, this poem doubles back upon itself.

Carson's poems consistently refer to the stanzaic structure, but do not submit to it. The ghost stanzas in his poems may be two lines long as in 'Eesti', 'Second language', and many others, or they may contain a greater number of lines: five in 'The brain of Edward Carson', six in 'Serial', nine in 'Snow'. The tendency of the stanzas to run on means that there is a tension between the formal containment associated with the stanza and the verse paragraph more usually associated with the long line. In fact Carson's stanzas, while quite apparent visually as organizing the lines on the page, have a diminished structural function. The rhythms of the poem as a whole resist the stanza structure rather than submit to it. The run-on quality means that the long line does not function as a self-contained unit (except in the translation from Rimbaud, 'Drunk boat'). Lines and stanzas flow into one another syntactically, and use of enjambment extends down to the level of words. Few poets use the hyphen more frequently than Carson. His hyphenation is not so much to provide compound words as to break down the difference that defines the individual lexical items.

In furtherance of this, he searches for interruptions and interpolations within the line unit. Sentence endings, parentheses, ellipses, punctuate the line so that its autonomy is resisted. Here, for instance, is a line from 'Loaf':

Soup. McWatters' pan loaf, some said, was like blotting-paper: I thought of

There are four sentences or part-sentences distributed across this line. 'Soup' is the completion of a sentence from the previous run on line. 'I thought of' is the commencement of another sentence. Between them is a complete statement, 'McWatter's pan loaf was like blotting paper', and interpolated into that is another statement that qualifies and erodes its authority: 'some said', – not the author/poet (who 'thinks' later on in the line) saying it. While simile is a basic poetic figure, the simile in this poetic line has only the ghost of its poetic function. The gist of the statement is to diminish the loaf, shading it into blotting-paper, in the perception attributed to the vaguely demotic 'some'. The simile does not really heighten our awareness of the image of the loaf, as a straightforward poetic simile would; it tells us about a possible perception of it. But images do work across the line. Soup and loaf come from the same semantic range of food; loaf and blotting paper are linked by the figure of the simile. There are two verbs conveying perception, 'said' and 'thought of', accompanied by different but equivalent agents: 'some' and 'I'. The co-presence of 'some' with 'I' diminishes the authority of the lyric first-person 'I'. It might be possible to offer a scansion of this line. The first-level phrasal rhythm of it is

Soup.//McWatters' pan loaf,/some said,/was like blotting-paper.//I thought of

At its centre is a strong rising beat pattern:

> McWatters' pan loaf, / some said,

This changes to a falling beat in the second part. This is superficially similar to what was noticed above in 'Dunne' – a switch from an iambic line to a trochaic line. But in that case each line retained its basic rhythmic pattern; here the radical change in rhythm takes place within the line, and the significant aspect is not the move from a rising to a falling rhythm but the opening up of the prosodic structure to accommodate such changes. It can incorporate practically anything – from the regularity of the closing couplet of 'Eesti' to the transitions within the line we have just been looking at.

This very partial look at Carson's prosody and versification has attempted to identify some of the features of his poetry, and to relate them to our understanding of verse forms generally. In so far as innovation is characterized by departure from the norm, the extent of that departure always carries along with it a shading of the normative measure to which it can be related. The process of verse translation, which by definition refers to a base version, is cognate with this.

While it might be argued that versions from early Irish constituted the test pieces for twentieth-century Irish poets, then equally versions of Dante represent *the* test piece for poets in English. There have been notable translations by Pinsky, C.K. Williams and others; as a form it is there in the background of Heaney's 'Station Island', Eliot's 'Little Gidding', Walcott's *Omeros*. Carson's translation of *The divine comedy* displays a return to a strictly conventional formalism, in which he has risen to the challenge of the *terza rima* form much more rigorously than most recent translators. Formal considerations are often the crux of versions of Dante in English. *Terza rima* requires three words for each rhyme, as opposed to the more usual two. This upping of fifty per cent is relatively easy in Italian which, as a romance language, has lots of similar word endings; it poses more of a challenge in English which, while it has a large lexicon, has a more restricted stock of rhyme words. Different translators have dealt with it in different ways: some, like Robert Pinsky, adopt a flexible definition of rhyme to include consonantal and slant rhyme. Others, (like Heaney in his versions of Dante), opt to rhyme only two of the three lines in each tercet. Another expedient is to leave the lines unrhymed, on the grounds that the blank verse iambic pentameter line is an English measure of equivalent weight to the Italian *terza rima*. C.K. Williams opts for a sixain of short lines with partial rhymes.

Considering this, and against the background of his own flexible verse forms, it is perhaps remarkable that Carson emerges as a scrupulous and almost traditional formalist in his version of Dante. The rhyme scheme is strictly observed; the lines are scannable in generally iambic patterns; the syllable count for each line is either ten or eleven, a nice compromise between the dominant ten-syllable line of English prosody and the eleven-syllable line of the Italian original. Carson's fit into the *terza rima* form is remarkable, and this essay will conclude by hazarding a half-explanation for the ease with which he uses it – an explanation based on prosodic features we have noticed. The particular characteristic of *terza rima* is the projection forward implicit in its rhyme arrangement; the middle line of each tercet provides the pre-rhyme sound for the two outer lines in the next tercet. In Carson's poems it was noticeable that there is a predominance of enjambment, where lines or stanzas run on to the next unit. This feature has its prosodic equivalence in the anticipatory nature of the *terza rima* rhyme scheme, where each stanza looks forward to and generates features of the next line grouping. The end sound of the middle line anticipates its recurrence in the succeeding stanza. The run-on quality here is phonetic rather than syntactic.

> And as I walked inspecting down the line,
> I saw one with a yellow leather purse
> emblazoned with a rampant azure lion.
>
> Then, my look continuing its course,
> I saw another with a pouch of scarlet
> on which was displayed a milk-white goose.
>
> And one who had a little argent wallet
> featuring a pregnant azure sow
> cried out: ' What business have you in this pit?

It is apparent that Carson's handling of form and language derives its strengths from an awareness of 'strong' patterns. In his book on traditional music, he observes that 'one of the beauties of traditional playing is the way a good musician can produce a pulse against the ostensible rhythm of the tune. The result is a kind of *double entendre* – like hearing two beats at once and it is appropriate that many tune titles are on the verge of *double entendre*, or maybe oxymoron' (*Lnf*, II). This brief description moves from music, though rhythm, to language and semantics.

It suggests, if only by analogy, something of what is to be observed in Carson's poetry. His verse forms work back against standard measures, extending and complicating them. At the same time, his language suggests additional ways of meaning in its accretions and duplications.

'Pushed next to nothing': Ciaran Carson's *Breaking news*

DAVID WHEATLEY

Ciaran Carson's *Breaking news* teems with ghosts: the blackbird of its opening poem is ghosted by a ninth-century predecessor, 'The blackbird of Belfast Lough'; many poems are thin to ghostly in their proportions: 'Spin cycle 2' is a mere four words long, if we count compound words as one; descriptions of parked cars, soldiers and horses are slowed down to almost freeze-frame speed before the spectre of destruction is unleashed on them; remote imperial campaigns are revisited and insinuate themselves into the ghostly baggage of present civil unrest; the words of William Howard Russell, William Carlos Williams and Isaac Babel and the images of Goya, Géricault and Hopper ghost through Carson's language and imagery, pentimento-like; and, inching forward in the slenderest of lines, the poems inhabit intervals such as that described in 'Wake' between a bomb and its aftermath, exploring their ghostly spaces like a blackbird whistling in 'a chink /of light //between /that world /and this.' (*Bn,* 53) Chief among Carson's presiding artistic ghosts is William Howard Russell, to whose memory *Breaking news* is dedicated. Russell (1820–1907) was a Dublin-born reporter for *The Times* who pioneered the role of the modern war correspondent during the Crimean War. Sixty years before the First World War poets bypassed official accounts of conflict to address the public directly from the battlefield, Russell wrote candidly to a mass audience of the horrors of war. Launched as a countermeasure against Russian ambitions in the Middle East and Asia, the Crimean War he describes was an incompetent and blood-soaked affair, whether in the loss of more than 16,000 troops to dysentery and other diseases, or the infamous Charge of the Light Brigade, in which British cavalry were ordered into the line of enemy fire ('Surely that handful of men were not going to charge an army in position? Alas! It was but too true'.[1]) Tennyson's poem on the subject adds a further dimension to the modernity of the Crimean War: a wax cylinder recording of him survives from 1854, sounding as though addressing us through a hailstorm as he salutes the cavalrymen mown down in the 'valley of death'. Technology played an important

---

[1] Nicholas Bentley (ed.), *Russell's despatches from the Crimea, 1854–1856* (London, 1970), 126.

part in the war too: the Crimean War was the first conflict to see the use of ambulances, trenches and telegraphy. Photography also came of age in the war: Roger Fenton was made the first official war photographer at the insistence of Prince Albert, in the propaganda campaign against Russell's reporting for *The Times*, and produced haunting images such as 'Aftermath of Battle' of the ammunition-strewn battlefield in the wake of the Charge of the Light Brigade.[2]

His adoption of the Crimean War coincides with innovations in Carson's poetry too. *Breaking news* is an anomalous volume in the Carson *oeuvre*, announcing a break with the rhyming long-lined style of his previous several books. 'The poem is the cry of its occasion', according to Wallace Stevens,[3] and in few of its occasions is the poem more inimitably itself than in its lineation. When a reviewer rearranged some of her lines as a prose paragraph (though with line-breaks indicated), Ciaran Carson's Canadian namesake Anne wrote to *Thumbscrew*: 'To print verse as prose is an act of contempt that verges on falsification'.[4] Modern poetry sounds a gamut of line-lengths from the massive diapasons of Ginsberg's *Howl* to the miniatures of Lorine Niedecker, but seldom has a writer forsaken one extreme for another as dramatically as Carson in *Breaking news*. It usefully illustrates the timbre of (Ciaran) Carson's short-lined style to compare a poem as printed with an alternatively laid-out version. An arrangement of 'Breath' in something like alexandrines, with the supplementary impertinence of punctuation, might look something like this:

> Watching helicopter: gone. There's a clear blue space
> above my head. I feel rinsed clean. You know that
> quiet: when the washing-machine stops shuddering.

As printed this becomes:

> watching
> helicopter
>
> gone

---

2 Cf. Susan Sontag, *Regarding the pain of others* (New York, 2002), for more on representations of war in Fenton's work. 3 Wallace Stevens, 'An ordinary evening in New Haven', *Collected poems* (London, 1955), 473. 4 Anne Carson, Letters, *Thumbscrew* 14 (Autumn 1999), 58.

there's a
clear blue

space

above
my head

I feel

rinsed

clean

you know
that quiet

when the
washing-machine

stops
shuddering (*Bn*, 23)

In my synthetic version, omission of the article and use of a colon offer a small advance on simply declaring 'A watching helicopter disappears', but give us none of the moment-to-moment twitches and starts of Carson's text. Just as Beckett once corrected an actress on the difference between a two- and three-dot ellipsis, the spacing before 'gone' gives us the helicopter's presence, suspended in the air, for the extra fraction of a second it takes to move across the double line-break to 'gone'. Similarly, the spaces around 'space' literalize its co-ordinates, just as the final couplet brings the washing-machine to a halt before our eyes while still ending on a note of movement ('shuddering') rather than arrest (the previous 'stops'). As Dónal Moriarty writes of two other poets concerned with rendering movement in the smallest detail of lineation, George Oppen and Brian Coffey, 'The pace of the poem is dictated by the mode of perception, form is dictated by the "ineluctable modality of the visible."'[5]

5 Dónal Moriarty, *The art of Brian Coffey* (Dublin, 2000), 41.

'I don't go in for long lines because of my nervous nature' William Carlos Williams declared,[6] and the nervousness on show throughout *Breaking news* may be reason enough to embrace the provisional, the gapped and the fragmentary over a more measured and leisurely utterance; as the narrator of Beckett's *Dream of fair to middling women* announced: 'The experience of my reader shall be between the phrases, in the silence, communicated by the intervals'.[7] The title 'Breath' offers another clue to the ways in which *Breaking news* tracks its 'mode of perception', synchronizing poetic vision with the respiratory system of the poem, its gaps, pauses and line-breaks. Among Charles Olson's prescriptions for Projective Verse is the demand that: 'ONE PERCEPTION MUST IMMEDIATELY AND DIRECTLY LEAD TO A FURTHUR PERCEPTION.'[8] 'That's not a direction for poetry', Michael Donaghy countered, 'That's instructions for being awake!',[9] but its applications to a reading of *Breaking news* are obvious and substantial, as so much of Carson's volume focuses on the sense of perception itself, the minute passage of time, and an Olson-like attention to breath, breathing and its connections to speech.

A smaller unit than the already tiny line is the individual word or letter, and throughout *Breaking news* Carson reflects on the materiality of the signifier on the micro-level. He writes of signs and shop fronts, missing words in radio conversations, the 'Braille' of a watch dial, the act of writing the poem we are reading, and of a Bible struck by a bullet 'stopped /at Revelation' (*Bn*, 33). Carson devoted sequences in *Opera et cetera* to the letters of the alphabet as well as the A–Z of the radio operator's code, and joins a long tradition in modern writing that finds the possibilities of language intimately tied up with their physical representation in the alphabet. Wisdom Hely's sandwich board men stalk the pages of *Ulysses* (apostrophe and all) like Saussurean updates of the human playing cards in *Alice in Wonderland*. Letters of Joyce's alphabet become detached and follow plot-lines of their own: in her *billet doux* to Leopold Bloom, also in *Ulysses*, Martha Clifford writes 'I called you naughty boy because I do not like that other world.'[10] 'For "world" read "word"', as a Paul Muldoon erratum might put it? Apparently not, on the textual evidence, but for those who worry about that possibly superfluous l Joyce redresses the balance several hundred pages later,

6 W.C. Williams (ed. Edith Heal), *I wanted to write a poem: the autobiography of the works of a poet* (Boston, 1958), 15.   7 Samuel Beckett, *Dream of fair to middling women* (Dublin, 1992), 137. 8 Charles Olson, 'Projective verse', in *A Charles Olson reader* (ed. Ralph Maud, Manchester, 2005), 43.   9 Conor O'Callaghan, 'Interview with Michael Donaghy', *Metre* 4, Spring/Summer 1998, p. 81. 10 James Joyce, *Ulysses* (Oxford: 1993), 74–5.

when the account of Dignam's funeral in the evening paper lists one 'L. Boom'. The linguistic sign is a site of constant instability, threat and siege, and the only guarantee against error may be to suppress the signifier altogether, as in Bloom's writing in the sand on Dollymount Strand ('I. AM. A.'), or when Lois interrupts the overheard words 'Lois is so – ' in Elizabeth Bowen's *The last September*, leaving her identity suspended at the end of a never-to-be-completed sentence.[11] The refusal of language is both self-protective but deathly too, in its denial of subjecthood. Bloom and Lois act of out choice, but in Carson's more violent world this is far from always the case. In 'Trap', the white noise surrounding a radio conversation seeps ominously into the poem. Carson tunes into the interference on the soldier's radio rather than its un-'read'-able communications, and ends with a rupturing of dialogue, as language collapses into crackle and hiss, the static that terminates the soundtrack of a soldier's life:

> backpack radio
> antenna
>
> twitching
> rifle
>
> headphones
> cocked
>
> I don't
> read you
>
> what the
>
> over (*Bn*, 15)

If we take our cue from another poem about linguistic incompletion, Beckett's 'what is the word', and assume the soldier has just been surprised by something unpleasant and possibly fatal, there are grounds for inferring that 'what the' should be followed by 'fuck'. With this in turn followed by 'over', the soldier has been comprehensively 'fucked over': one more expendable volunteer in the fight

---

11 Elizabeth Bowen, *The last September* (London, 1987), 60.

against terror, he is robbed of even his paltry last words and consigned to the white noise of forgetting.

Contemporary poetry abounds in examples of spacings, gaps and suppressions as signifying strategies. Tony Harrison has long exploited such devices, as when the coal-mine sign in *v.* is vandalized to read 'PRI CE O WALES', its missing letters (n and f) suggesting the handiwork of the poem's National Front-supporting skinhead.[12] In 'Winter wheat', from *Moy sand and gravel*, Paul Muldoon continually resorts to the filler 'something' for words he declines to spell out. The final section of Randolph Healy's poem 'scales' consists of the word 'Whereas' seven times amid twenty-six blacked-out lines, dwarfing the mere line and a half of blacked-out text in Justin Quinn's 'Last poem'.[13] Carson's 'News' too ends with an act of textual suppression, as '*The Belfast Telegraph* /sign reads //*fast rap*', coaxing the reader to make desperate sense of its message: upbeat hiphop? the energetic beating of some handy implement (not a baseball bat, one hopes)? a tightly wound skein of yarn, in this city of the linen industry? or even, remembering the eighteenth-century use of 'rap' for a bogus Irish halfpenny, some quick-spreading counterfeit? What is certain, if the meaning of '*fast rap*' isn't, is how quickly our readings of these slender poems threaten to overwhelm them: is it possible to subject these poems to the rigours of a critical reading without violating their spirit? This question goes to the heart of Carson's minimalist aesthetic, and the nature of his reaction against the fuller-throated lines of his previous work.

Literal violation of the spirit is a regular occurrence in *Breaking news*, and his use of spacing and line-breaks plays an important part in Carson's poetic intimations of mortality. In a translation from Sébastien Chamfort, Beckett uses mordant and dramatic line-breaks to counterpoint life and death:

> sleep till death
> healeth
> come ease
> this life disease[14]

As Christopher Ricks has noticed, it is unclear whether 'life disease' constitutes one or two entities, and whether it is disease that frees us of life, or death of 'this

---

12 Tony Harrison, *Selected poems* (London, 1984), 240.   **13** Randolph Healy, *Green 532: selected poems 1983–2000* (Cambridge, 2002), 128; Justin Quinn, *The 'O'o'a'a' Bird* (Manchester, 1995), 67
14 Samuel Beckett, 'Long after Chamfort', *Collected poems*, 166.

life disease.'[15] Carson exploits similar ambiguity in 'Last effect', describing an antique watch: 'hands /arrested //at the minute /and the hour //of his salavation /death //postponed /for years' (*Bn*, 48). It may be 'death' that has been postponed for years, but the couplet juxtaposition of 'salvation' and 'death' has a loosening effect of the tie between 'death' and 'postponed'. In typography, orphans and widows are small clusters of text that look abandoned at the foot or head of a page, but with its single-word lines *Breaking news* creates a world of orphaned meaning, each word cut off from the next, and revealing the latent 'death' behind 'death //postponed' at every step, and by extension the latent death of the lyric form itself.

Readings of Northern Irish poetry (in particular Edna Longley's) have privileged the lyric as a buffer against political violence and its brutal simplifications, but the abandonment of lyric plenitude in these poems puts in question not just the role of the artist in a time of violence, but the physical existence of his poems too, just as the sustained ventriloquism of Russell's journalism threatens to junk the concept of lyric 'voice'. How far in this direction can a lyric poem go before it ceases to be a lyric poem, and what takes its place when it does? Simon Armitage's introduction to the 1999 anthology *Short and sweet: 101 very short poems* raises germane questions about the proper boundaries of the poem when he deplores the 'stuff and nonsense' that bombards us daily from:

> billboards, branding, signposts, satellite TV, digital radio, telecommunication, the Web, the Net, e-mail, flyers, posters, slogans, strap-lines, skywriting, newspapers, magazines, fanzines, makers' names, subscriptions, junk-mail, free offers for the making of fortunes, fridge magnets for the making of poems … even poems. Most of it unsolicited, unavoidable, and garbage

– before harking back to a time 'when words were a valuable commodity, chosen carefully and painstakingly reproduced'.[16] Shorn of the raggedy grandeur of its advertizing slogans, graffiti and other detritus of language, however, Ciaran Carson's poetry would be nothing if not greatly diminished. Did not that connoisseur of the very short poem, A.R. Ammons, cultivate a whole book on just such a rubbish tip of language (*Garbage*)? Armitage does himself a further disservice when he describes the ideal, litter-free zone of poetry as a 'valuable

<hr/>

15 Christopher Ricks, *Beckett's dying words* (Oxford, 1993), 13–15.   16 Simon Armitage (ed.), *Short and sweet: 101 very short poems* (London, 1999), ix–x.

commodity' – collapsing Benjaminian 'aura' into the very debased commercialism he hopes to escape.

Carson's aesthetic, I wish to argue, forgoes any illusions of the lyric poem as a sphere of privileged transcendence or exemption from the signifying chaos of the contemporary world. On the contrary, he exults in it. If his use of gaps and suppressions counts as an anti-lyric strategy, another is his interest in dissident textual forms such as graffiti or found poetry, each of which feature extensively in Carson's work. Peter Ackroyd has noted the minatory nature of graffiti (something residents of mural-strewn Belfast will need no reminding of) with a quotation from Habakkuk: 'For the stone shall cry out of the wall.'[17] His fellow London psychogeographer Iain Sinclair celebrates graffiti at length in *Lights out for the territory*, their 'editorials of madness' and 'texts that nobody is going to stop and read',[18] while another writer again with similarities to Carson, Peter Reading, obsessively approximates to the texture and tone of graffiti. Sometimes Carson's poems present themselves as virtual found objects, as when 'Skip' describes being written on a bomb-damaged notebook, emphasizing their lowly, throwaway origins and disowning the conventional author function in their attempts to push the lyric poem to its limits and beyond.

A common bumper sticker admonishes the driver behind that 'If you can read this, you're too close.' As a text the sticker performs its own contradiction: anyone offering himself as a reader rules himself out in the same act; for it to have the desired effect no one will ever have been aware of its existence, yet we can only realize this after stumbling on and reading it. Context is all: found art provides the distorting, anamorphotic perspective from which we grasp the richer meanings hidden inside the language we think we know but don't. American poet Kenneth Goldsmith has taken this anamorphosis of the everyday to audacious heights in his books *Fidget* and *Soliloquy*, which form a record of every move he made and word he spoke over a one-week period. In other projects he has explored the effects of transposing words from one context (newsprint and magazine journalism) to another: in *Day*, which involved the retyping of an entire edition of *The New York Times*; *Week*, which did the same for an issue of *Time*; and *Month*, which completed the series with an issue of *Vogue*.[19]

17 Peter Ackroyd, *London: the biography* (London, 2001), 191.   **18** Iain Sinclair, *Lights out for the territory* (London, 1997), 3.   **19** Cf. Marjorie Perloff, 'A conversation with Kenneth Goldsmith', http://jacketmagazine.com/21/perl-gold-iv.html, and http://www.ubu.com for an invaluable archive of found and concrete poetry, or as it styles itself, a '4 dimensional space simultaneously expanding and contracting in every direction, growing "rhizomatically" with ever-increasing unpredictability and uncanniness.'

Carson's principle display of found poetry in *Breaking news* is his rewriting of
Russell's war journalism, but repetition and doubling had been in the air in
Carson's work before *Breaking news*, as in the mystic doubles and substitutions of
his 2001 odyssey, *Shamrock tea*. In 'The Irish for no' Carson's meditation on
sectarian difference in Belfast snags obsessively on conjoined verbal formations
such as 'mish-mash', 'hotch-potch' and 'yin-yang' (*Ifn*, 50), with the tiny but all-
important space of the hyphen standing in for the distance between one tribal
shibboleth and another. 'Spin cycle', from *Breaking news*, also hinges on a hyphen:

> here it comes
> again I said
>
> I couldn't
> hear
>
> myself
> speak for the
>
> thug-thug
>
> helicopter
> overhead
>
> I put in
> the ear-plugs
>
> everything went
> centrifugal (*Bn*, 39)

The hobbled line-breaks give the whole poem a centrifugal effect, with the
beginning of each new line qualifying what we thought the last line meant,
leaving us unsure whether to continue our movement down the page or to read
back upwards for a clearer picture of the sense (does 'again' qualify 'comes' or
'said'? – a saying that, three lines later, we learn he can't hear anyway). Only in the
onomatopoeically doubled-up 'thug-thug' at the poem's centre does the text
appear to come to rest, however precariously, like its hovering helicopter (with the
Indian etymology of 'thug', from the Hindi *thag*, a thief, providing a link to the

earlier poem 'The Indian mutiny'). In the four-word 'Spin cycle 2' that follows, the presence of a gun triggers an instinctive response of 'hear no evil':

gun-gun

ear-plugs in

blank-blank (*Bn*, 40)

The poem shuts down in a verbal white-out, firing a blank that might be the failure of poetic language to contain the full obscenity of war, or might be the embodiment of war itself, the gun-toting, ear-plugged soldier with no need of any other language than power. What is significant, however, is that this process is accompanied by Carson's taking refuge in verbal repetition, which acts as both theme and trope for so much of the writing and rewriting in *Breaking news*.

The question of difference and repetition has a long pedigree in postmodernist writing. Most celebrated of modern rewriters is Jorge Luis Borges's Pierre Menard, who produces a *Don Quixote* identical in all regards to, but bafflingly 'more subtle' than Cervantes' original: where the latter treats its chivalric theme in a 'clumsy' manner, the former uses the same words to point to 'a new conception of the historical novel'.[20] The Objectivist poet Charles Reznikoff's masterpiece, *Testimony*, is an epic found poem of stories he discovered while employed by a publishing firm to write up court records for legal reference books. Precisely in their closeness to their originals, these texts display an anxiety of repetition which affects not only their status but that of the originals too. Borges and Reznikoff reassign textual meaning from the author to the reader, from whence it is the shortest of steps to Roland Barthes' 'Death of the author'. But is a true repetition possible or not, and how, in examples like Menard's *Quixote*, do we tell the difference? In Kierkegaard's *Repetition* a young man, Constantine Constantius, travels from Denmark to Berlin to answer just this question. Attempting to recreate a memorable theatre trip, he is frustrated at every turn: the city has changed in numerous small ways, the coffee is no longer what it was, he fails to get his old theatre seat, and the performance itself falls flat. Where he does find a repetition it only annoys him further, as when he visits a restaurant and finds 'the same sameness' as on his last trip. Success brings not satisfaction but jadedness: 'The only repetition was the impossibility of a repetition.'[21] The apparent

20 Jorge Luis Borges, *Labyrinths* (London, 1970), 68.   21 Søren Kierkegaard, *Fear and trembling,*

impersonality and detachment of Carson's repetitions create an opposite effect from the eye-witness immediacy of Russell's texts, complicating the reader's response and forcing an interrogation of what might constitute an authentic or personal response to a war fought a century and a half ago.

Questions of narratology and time also enter into any consideration of literary repetition. The second part of Beckett's *Molloy* begins and ends with the words 'It is midnight. The rain is beating on the windows' – or almost.[22] Having closed the gap between narrative and diegetic time, bringing the narrative to the vanishing point of describing its own inception, Beckett explodes this tidy doubling with a final salvo of denials: 'It was not midnight. It was not raining.' Not only are narrative and diegetic time split asunder, but as the narrative starts all over again in Moran's act of writing, those 'nots' implicitly continue too, discrediting everything he says and that we have just finished reading. Frequently in *Breaking news*, Carson follows Moran in 'writing to the moment', approaching a condition of instantaneity at which experience or information can scarcely be processed: many poems' narratives find themselves overtaken by their own events. Though 'Edward Hopper: *Early Sunday morning*, 1939' describes a painting, the sense of split-second immediacy suggests the opening and shutting of a camera lens.[23] The painting's colours are weighed down by omnipresent shadow, so that 'beyond / the frame // immeasurably / long // another shadow / falls // from what / we cannot see // to what / we cannot see', drawing a thick blanket of invisibility over the eventual object of our gaze beyond the picture frame: 'dawn / before the War.'

In 'Blink' repetition and the camera lens link to that other ubiquitous theme of *Breaking news*, surveillance. Carson plays on military surveillance and its social counterpart in the sectarian feints and tics by which the inhabitants of Belfast determine one another's background and allegiances. The fact that contemporary surveillance often takes the form of optometric scans (as it also does in the narrative framing device of Paul Muldoon's *Madoc*) makes such information available in the literal blinking of an eye:

repetition, trans. Howard V. Hong and Edna H. Hong, Princeton, 1983), 170. For more on this theme, cf. John Kerrigan's 'Killing time: Nietzsche, Job and repetition' in his *Revenge tragedy* (Oxford, 1996), 267–89. **22** Samuel Beckett, *Molloy* (London, 1976), 189. **23** Carson gets the title of this painting slightly wrong; it is in fact dated 1930, not 1939.

everyone eyes
everyone

down to the cut
and colour

of their clothes
the pattern

of the retina
the fingerprint

the bits and pieces

being matched
as everyone

identifies
with this or that (*Bn*, 24–5)

This society obsessed with petty difference produces flattened-out, paranoid sameness: 'everyone is / watching everybody', 'everyone eyes /everyone.' The omission of a qualifying 'else' in these descriptions suggests a diseased self-perception, with the act of watching turned back on itself. A philosopher Carson features extensively in *Shamrock tea*, Wittgenstein, points out that the eye itself must be outside any field of vision ('you do *not* really see the eye'),[24] but these eyes operate under a distorted and distorting optic system.

A world in which 'everyone // identifies / with this or that' suggests leaderlessness or mass delusion: everyone copies everyone else, everyone assumes everyone else knows what they are doing, but in reality confusion reigns. Mutilated and dismembered bodies play an important role in Carson's earlier work, and bodily disarray features here too under the ghoulishly repeated form of slaughtered horses and decapitated bodies. 'War' provides a striking example of the latter:

---

24 Ludwig Wittgenstein, *Tractatus logico-philosophicus*, trans. C.K. Ogden (London, 1981), 151.

> Sergeant Talbot
> had his head
>
> swept off
> by a
>
> round-shot
>
> yet for half
> a furlong
>
> more
>
> the body kept
>
> the saddle
>
> horse and rider
> charging on
>
> regardless (*Bn*, 26)

Once again narrative and diegetic brush up against each other in that 'more', so like the repeated 'On's of Beckett's later work, as though the poem were forcing itself to narrate 'more' of its gruesome tale. Carson's constant return to wounded horses throughout the collection poignantly exemplifies a classical iconography of war at the moment of its collapse. To take a cinematic comparison, in Tarkovsky's *Andrei Rublev* horses are often the victims of barbaric violence, yet salvage enough poise and beauty to provide the film with its final scene of inexplicable visionary peace, just as the narrator of the final section of 'The war correspondent' rides unscathed through the battlefield on his 'crippled horse.' There is an intertextual dimension here too, if we hear an echo of Hopkins' 'Felix Randal' behind the 'great / blinkered drayhorses' of 'The Gladstone bar *circa* 1954', and note the correspondences with Michael Longley's own intertextual poem about the death of a horse, 'After Keith Douglas'. Carson's use of a painterly image in 'Francisco Goya: *The third of May, 1808*,' places its violence (a French firing squad executing a line of prisoners during the Spanish War of Independence) on the same fault-

line between the classically serene and the barbaric, in the Christ-like pose of one
of the victims:

> arms
> flung
>
> open
> to receive
>
> the volley
> offering
>
> the firing-squad
> his ghost (*Bn*, 47)

Writing on Goya's print *¡Grande hanzaña! ¡Con muertos!* ('Great feat! With
dead men!') from the series *Los desastres de la guerra*, which shows a mutilated
trunk and a severed arm and head tied to a tree, Robert Hughes finds a
'sickeningly effective play on the Neoclassical cult of the antique fragment [...] if
only they had been in marble and the work of their destruction had been done by
time rather than sabers, neoclassicists like Mengs would have been in esthetic
raptures over them.'[25] The classical fragment draws authority from the absent
whole for which it acts as metonym, but Goya dismembers form and content
with no such sanction, producing obscene images in the strictest sense: the prints
could not be exhibited during his lifetime and did not appear until 1863, 35 years
after his death. In 'Théodore Géricault: *Farrier's signboard*, 1814', a horse returns
to the iconography with equally disruptive effects: the subject matter spills over
from the paint to the board onto which the image is applied. When not falling
short of wholeness in his fragments, Carson is going beyond it in an art that
refuses all attempts at framing in preordained dimensions:

> this
>
> painted in oil
> directly on to

---

25 Robert Hughes, *Goya* (London, 2003), 295.

> roughly carpentered
> gap-jointed
>
> boards
> a door
>
> or shutter
> wood
>
> and nail heads
> showing through
>
> this the year
> before Waterloo (*Bn*, 42–3)

Here again the invitation to an intertextual reading is hard to resist. Coming after the Christ-like victim's pose in Goya's painting and the allegory of Christ's passion in 'Felix Randal' (if we allow the allusion to it in 'The Gladstone bar *circa* 1954'), the combination of a farrier and nails in wood here, and the timeline of the final couplet combine to suggest crucifixion-like agonies of war. Even the artwork, nailed through, shares in the crucifixion, as Carson turns high into found art, a Géricault canvas becoming what might be one more piece of battle flotsam from 'The war correspondent'. Nothing is exempt from makeshift recycling in war, as he shows in another equine poem, 'Some uses of a dead horse', with its grim puns on 'yield' and 'shot':

> the bones give
> buttons
>
> snuff-boxes
> and knife-handles
>
> the hooves
> yield
>
> a beautiful
> Prussian blue
>
> the shoes
> shot (*Bn*, 32)

As for the structure of 'The war correspondent', Carson divides the poem into seven sections. Although the poem has been described by reviewers (and the book's own blurb) solely in relation to the Crimean War, the final poem in the sequence, 'Sedan', deals with the Franco-Prussian war of 1870, which Russell also covered. But as Carson writes in that poem, 'What debris a ruined empire / leaves behind it!' (*Bn*, 71); and as images of decapitated soldiers and crippled horses again proliferate, the reader sees Carson's vision expanding to a larger history of nineteenth-century imperialism, and bearing down inevitably on the First World War to come. The theme of debris is signalled even before the beginning of the conflict in 'Gallipoli', with its protracted anaphoras and listing of the bric-a-brac of empire, from 'an Irish landlord's ruinous estate' to 'leaking ballast-laden junks bound for Benares' and the 'garlic-oregano-tainted arcades of Bologna' (*Bn*, 56). Given its borderline location between Christian Europe and the Middle East, the city makes an easy object of Orientalist fantasy, its horde-like population decked out in 'fedoras, fezzes, sashes, shirts of fine Valenciennes [...]' (*Bn*, 57), sexually and narcotically exoticized, and rife with infection, the soldiers lying 'dead or drunk among the crushed flowers.' After its extravagant reportage the poem ends as abruptly as a cabled despatch: 'I have not even begun to describe Gallipoli'.

Many of these poems follow Russell's text with extreme closeness. 'A stronger term than "allusion" is needed for this,' Sean O'Brien has commented, 'but it isn't "theft." '[26] I do not propose to perform an exhaustive comparison here of Russell's text and the entirety of Carson's sequence, but as one example here is Russell's account of the outbreak of fire in section two, 'Varna', with my parenthetical commentary on what Carson has chosen to include, omit and embroider:

> On the night of August 10th, a great fire broke out at Varna, which utterly destroyed more than a quarter of the town. [Carson inserts a description of 'tumbledown /wooden streets' on fire.] The sailors of the ships, and the French and English soldiery stationed near the town, worked for the ten hours during which the fire lasted with the greatest energy; but as a brisk wind prevailed, which fanned the flames as they leapt along the wooden streets, their efforts were not as successful as they deserved. [This sentence omitted by Carson.] The fire broke out near the French commissariat stores, in a spirit shop. The officers in charge broached many casks of spirits and as the liquid ran down the streets a

26 Sean O'Brien, 'Belfast and beyond' (review of *Breaking news*), *Times Literary Supplement*, 13 June 2003, p. 10.

Greek was seen to set fire to it. [Carson's pyromaniac Greek acts 'in a fit of drunken pique.'] He was cut down to the chin by a French officer and fell into the fiery torrent. [Carson's torrent is 'blazing'.] The howling of the inhabitants, the yells of the Turks, the clamour of the women, children, dogs, and horses, were appalling. [Carson adds 'prisoners in their cells'.] Marshal St. Arnaud displayed great vigour and coolness in superintending the operations of the troops, and by his exertions aggravated the symptoms of the malady from which he had long been suffering. [Subclause omitted by Carson.] The French lost great quantities of provisions, and we had many thousand rations of biscuit utterly consumed. In addition, immense quantities of stores were destroyed – 19,000 pairs of soldiers' shoes and an immense quantity of cavalry sabres, which were found amid the ruins fused into the most fantastic shapes. [Carson adds a long list of other destroyed items, from live pullets to polo-sticks, and extemporises on the image of the distorted sabres in the six lines beginning 'like an opium smoker's cityscape'.] To add to our misfortune the cholera broke out in the fleets in Varna Bay and at Baltschik with extraordinary virulence. The 'Friedland' and 'Montebello' suffered in particular – in the latter upwards of 100 died in twenty-four hours. [Russell's ending replaced by Carson with 'thousands of souls sail[ing] into Nirvana.']27

Carson's culling of the more fustian side of Russell's prose is minimal; what emerges from a comparison of the texts is less evidence of the poet bending the journalist's text out of shape for his own purposes than of how closely the original appears to have foreseen and accommodated Carson's Menardian ambitions for it. The description of the eviscerated Greek reads like a passage from Carson's version of Dante's *Inferno*, and the distorted sabres might be prototypes of the recycled bricks and 'fount of broken type' from the title poem of *Belfast confetti*. The question of overlap between Russell and Carson can all too easily become a distraction, however, since the aspects of Carson's style I have privileged in this essay – his use of lineation and spacing – are precisely what he cannot derive from Russell. Carson's borrowings from Russell could even be compared to a Hitchcockesque MacGuffin: where the naïve reader sees only plagiarism, the more instinctive will grasp how the apparent retreat from 'authored' content in 'The war correspondent' serves to foreground what is genuinely individual in the

27 *Russell's despatches from the Crimea*, 53.

poem, and which no amount of textual overlap can hope to account for. Here, by way of example, are the last three stanzas of Carson's, as opposed to Russell's 'Varna':

> A consignment of cavalry sabres was found
> amid the ruins, fused into the most fantastic shapes,
> looking like an opium-smoker's cityscape
> or a crazy oriental fairground –
>
> minarets, cathedral spires of twisted blades, blades
> wrought into galleries and elevated switchbacks,
> railroad sidings, cul-de-sacs, trolleyways, and racing tracks,
> gazebos, pergolas, trellises, and colonnades.
>
> Such were the effects of the great fire of Varna.
> Next day the cholera broke out in the British fleets
> anchored in the bay, then spread into the streets,
> and for weeks thousands of souls sailed into Nirvana. (*Bn*, 59–60)

'A Turkish war correspondent was recently caught red-handed babbling in his dispatches of "dove-gray" hills, or else it was "pearl-pale", I can not remember', Ezra Pound writes in 'A Retrospect',[28] and in section three, 'Dvno', and the bird-watching of section six, 'Tchernaya', we see Russell the naturalist at work. Hills are 'verdant', dells are 'shady', and 'dripping ferns' are 'shadow-dappled'. He imagines himself 'in Eden', but the reminder that the meadows are 'incandescent with poppies' is sufficient warning of the darker side of the landscape. As food supplies and animals are plundered (in section five, 'Kertch'), the soldiers prophetically decorate themselves with all manner of herbs and plants (in section four, 'Balaklava'), and soon enough are recycled as dead bodies planted on the battlefield or washed up at Russell's feet in the cholera-infected water ('Dvno'). In the earlier poem 'Waste not', it was 'women with shears' who preyed on the dead 'harvesting // gold braid / and buttons' (*Bn*, 34), recalling the thread-spinning Fates of classical myth, and here too scavengers are on hand to strip the dead bodies of their buttons and boots.

Writing on modern adaptations of Bach's music and the problem of musical authenticity, Theodor Adorno argued (in relation to Webern's orchestration of

28 T.S. Eliot (ed.), *Literary essays of Ezra Pound* (London, 1954), 5.

Bach's six-part *Ricercata*) that 'Perhaps the traditional Bach can indeed no longer be interpreted. If this is true, his heritage has passed on to composition, which is loyal to him in being disloyal; it calls his music by name in producing it anew.'[29] In writing about the Crimean War, Carson highlights the question of historical authenticity by cleaving to and reneging on the concept all at once – by cleaving so closely, that is, to someone else's authenticity in the act of discovering something radically new about himself. Led through and lost in the Carsonian maze of competing primary and original texts, composition becomes interpretation becomes composition again. If this seems to dissolve Carson's text away in an intertextual haze, leaving the author dead on the battlefield alongside the unfortunates of Inkerman and Sedan, it is important to ask in conclusion what separates the postmodern antics of *Breaking news* from an outright abdication of the lyric poem altogether.

In 'Ciaran Carson: beyond Belfast' Alan Gillis argues against readings which draw a simplistic equivalence between any 'poetic avant-gardism' on Carson's part and a 'radical politics.'[30] Despite the radical departure that *Breaking news* represents, at no point would I like to suggest that embracing Roland Barthes and Pierre Menard propels Carson into a postmodern hyperspace, blissfully awoken at last from the nightmare of history. Instead, Gillis insists, this is a poetry which 'remains knowingly and sceptically circumscribed within definite and oppressive historical horizons', a confinement intensified, he argues, by its commitment to privileging the symbolic over the semiotic. In Kristevan and Lacanian theory the Symbolic is the site of social conformity, binding the transgressive energies of the semiotic. Does this mean that Carson resigns himself to a world of never-ending violent nightmare and paralysis (as Carson famously claimed Heaney did in *North*)? Obviously not. Even as Carson's poems hover on the brink of extinction, or paint a picture of apparently unending bloodshed, they remain defiantly unreconciled to what they describe, or to disappearing into silence without at least the tiniest of protests first. As he writes in 'Exile', with its list of streets named for the Crimean campaign:

---

29 Theodor W. Adorno, 'Bach defended against his devotees', in *Prisms*, trans. Samuel and Shierry Weber, (Cambridge, MA, 1983), 146.   **30** Alan Gillis, 'Ciaran Carson: Beyond Belfast', in Nicholas Allen and Aaron Kelly (eds), *The cities of Belfast* (Dublin, 2003), 198.

Belfast
is many

places then
as now

all lie
in ruins

and
it is

as much
as I can do

to save
even one

from oblivion (*Bn*, 51–2)

Again in Lacanian theory, the unthinkable realm of full subjecthood known as the Real is excluded from the Symbolic, leaving a paradoxical void or oblivion as the basis of the subject's functionality. But as Elizabeth and Edmond Wright observe, 'it is this very void that distinguishes the subject from the results of the historical determinations that have made it what it appears to be.'[31] If Carson situates his poems within 'oppressive historical horizons', he leaves their supporting Symbolic order worm-eaten with interruptions, gaps and spacings, down to the smallest level of linguistic detail, disrupting any pretence that full subjecthood is possible under its tyrannical reign. The aim of *Breaking news* is less lyric transcendence than an interiorization of the violence of history, an embrace of broken and incomplete signifying strategies (moving 'from what / we cannot see // to what / we cannot see') over the delusions of aesthetic repletion. This may indeed mean that political reconciliation, as imagined by these poems, would take 'the paradoxical and ludicrous shape of continuing impasse', in Edna Longley's formulation,[32] but it is also a recognition that the lyric poem, as an imagined site

31 Elizabeth and Edmond Wright, 'Introduction', *The Žižek reader* (Oxford, 1999), 4. **32** Edna Longley, *Poetry and posterity* (Tarset, 2000), 314.

of reconciliation and balance between Northern Ireland's mythically familiar oppositions, can just as easily become an agent of mystification in its own right, if it presumes to stand apart from the breakdown and collapse it depicts.

The surest safeguard against this, and one that I have argued Carson adopts in *Breaking news*, is to extend this condition of breakdown to the functioning of the lyric 'I' and the very possibility of its staging, in ways that mark an unmistakable break with the previous generation of Northern Irish poets (Mahon, Longley and Heaney). Yet, given a choice between extinguishing its lyric impulse altogether and snatching it back from the oblivion invoked in 'Exile', with all the messy compromise that entails, it is the latter option that Carson chooses every time. Not only does the lyric 'I' consistently break down in *Breaking news*, the attempt to be rid of it does so too; the death of this particular author is, if not greatly, then at least significantly exaggerated. Within Carson's *oeuvre*, *Breaking news* came after a period of intense creativity that saw him publish a remarkable nine poetry and prose books between 1996 and 2003, since when there has been, by his standards, something of a hiatus (albeit punctured by his 2005 translation of *The midnight court*). Where the naïve temptation might be to hail *Breaking news* as a bold new departure, a more pessimistic view might be to see it as the end of a certain strand not only of Carson's work but of a whole tradition of Northern Irish lyric. Yet for all the casualties of *Breaking news*, improbable survival, tentatively, almost silently, finds a voice in these poems, just as for all his apparent desire to be shot of it, the obstinately enduring lyric poem remains Carson's first recourse in the face of the tragic, bloody waste of history. Slender though they be, the poems of *Breaking news* hold their own against the immense bloodshed, waste and violence they describe. As A.R. Ammons writes in defence of smallness: '[A] skinny thing / acquires great force / pushed next to nothing.'[33] Or as Carson himself writes, in his gleefully insouciant ending to 'The war correspondent', rediscovering the art of joy in the midst of so much cause for resignation and despair:

> I found a music-book
>
> with a woman's name
> in it, and a canary bird,
> and a vase of wild flowers. (*Bn*, 72)

---

33 A.R. Ammons, 'Immoderation', *Worldly hopes* (New York, 1982), 5.

'Walking in the city': space, narrative and surveillance in *The Irish for no* and *Belfast confetti*

JOHN GOODBY

Appropriately, for a Belfast postman's son, Ciaran Carson's *Irish for no* and *Belfast confetti* habitually trace and retrace the steps of a narrator who walks the city's streets. In this essay I shall try to unravel some of the implications of this in the light of some recent thinking about the way we make sense of the spaces of cities. In doing so I shall refer to the writings of the French critic and social theorist Michel de Certeau, and particularly to his essay in *The practice of everyday life* (1974), 'Walking in the city'.[1] In the first case, I shall argue that, for all its apparent 'backward look', Carson's work published in the late 1980s is very much of its time; that is to say, of the postmodern gentrification of cities, heritage and leisure industries, of brand marketing by transnational corporations, and of a politics of charisma (Reaganism, Thatcherism) – whose banal yet hyperreal aftermath is our own contemporary social, political and cultural landscape. In the second case, I will argue that Carson's work uses strategies which run counter to the more baleful effects of these trends, sometimes while seemingly mimicking them.

WALKING

I want to begin with walking, if only because the viewpoint of these poems is decidedly that of a walker (and from this point on I shall sometimes interpret 'walking', with the permission of the reader, in the most liberal way, to cover all forms of non-motorized motion – running, jumping, skipping, hopping, crawling (or pub-crawling, anyway), dancing, cycling, even lounging or, and this is a favourite Carson word, idling. The persona is almost invariably that of a pedestrian, frequently one reflecting upon the practice of walking in various forms, or analogues. There are several exceptions of course; so, in '33333', 'I found myself in the synthetic leopard-skin bucket-seat of a Ford Zephyr / Gunning through a mesh of ramps, diversions, one-way systems'. (*Ifn*, 39) But they prove

---

1 Many of the more general ideas underlying this essay can also be found in David Harvey's work on postmodernism in *The condition of postmodernity* (Oxford, 1990) and on cities in *Spaces of hope* (Edinburgh, 2000).

the rule. Even characters with names like 'Horse' or 'Mule' (in 'Dresden', *Ifn*, 11–16) rely on shanks's pony, and few speakers rise higher than the brief dignity of a bicycle ('Question time', *Bc*, 57–63).

Whatever the definition of walking, the persona is self-propelled and perambulatory, negotiating a path through Belfast of the Troubles. His, and his subjects' means of locomotion, are a major factor in shaping the encounter with the world and individual subjectivity, and our readerly encounter with these. The centrality of memory and the method of recall to this poetry, its pedestrian nature, means that the many past versions of the Carson persona are, almost invariably, walking too:

> ... Every time that Blue Grass
> Hits me, it is 1968. I'm walking with her through the smoggy early dusk
> Of West Belfast: coal-smoke, hops, fur, the smell of stout and whiskey ...
> ('Calvin Klein's Obsession', *Ifn*, 21).

So, too, are most of his subjects:

> The duck patrol is waddling down the odd-number side of Raglan Street
> ('Army', *Ifn*, 38)

Walking is both the clicking of the keyboard and punctuation in 'Snowball':

> ... The heels click off – another
> Blind date? ....
> ('Snowball', *Ifn*, 44)

The very way the subjects of these poems walk through the city tells us something about them, and about the someone who is doing the telling. While never precisely a moral judgement, the manner of locomotion is a kind of signature, a spoor, or 'enunciation', as de Certeau would say, as in

> Hen-stepping out of a pea-soup fog, he makes a shift for Cornmarket
> And pops up in Smithfield ..
> ('Box', *Ifn*, 43)

or

> *Your man*, says the Man, *will walk into the bar like this* – here his fingers
> Mimic a pair of legs, one stiff at the knee – ...
>
> <div align="right">('Bloody hand', <i>Bc</i>, 51)</div>

or

> ... the small boy trips over an extended tow-bar, picks himself up, giggles
> And pisses on a smouldering mound of Pampers.
>
> <div align="right">('Travellers', <i>Ifn</i>, 42)</div>

or

> Threading rapidly between crowds on Royal Avenue reading
>   Simultaneously
>
> <div align="right">('Linear B', <i>Ifn</i>, 33)</div>

or

> ... I knew Mule's step by now, his careful drunken weaving
> Through the tin-stacks.
>
> <div align="right">('Dresden', <i>Ifn</i>, 16)</div>

Small wonder perhaps, that in 'Whatever sleep it is', the speaker – albeit referring to a painting – claims 'the leg was giving me a problem' (*Ifn*, 26).

For it may be that, on the one hand, we take walking too much for granted to see it as unusual, and on the other, that we practice it very little, in the sense of negotiating a route through the city. How many of those in your workplace arrived by car? How many on foot? Outside working hours, we shop by car, go to conferences and take holidays by car, train, aeroplane. One of the few things it is difficult to do is to go for a drink by car, which is why cars in these collections by Carson are so often taxis. Only the young, the poor, serious drinkers, or army patrols have to walk any distance. It is, also, overwhelmingly urban; Heaney, for example, from early on, has a countryman's need to report on how the world looks from inside his car. In an era of mass car ownership, walking appeals only to the denizen of the city, one aware of the density of necessary locations (beyond these alternatives is the practice of organized 'leisure'). Walking, one way or another, is decidedly not what it was. Yet it remains, despite this, the first, and still definitively human, mode of locomotion; man is a primate who happens to have acquired a bipedal gait, and, in doing so, freed his hands, and his mind. Because it is so primary, walking is the least alienated, most phenomenologically engaged mode of moving through the world; there is relatively little between 'us' and 'out there' when we engage in it. As a result, like other loco-descriptive poetry in the English tradition (there is more of a link between Carson and Thomson's *The seasons* or Wordsworth's *The prelude* than we might imagine), Carson's exploits the links between the rhythms of walking, thinking and writing.

WRITING

He differs, however, from most earlier examples, in the extent to which he foregrounds an awareness of walking. This is seen in the way walking in the poems continually supplies terms for Carson's narration of his stories. 'He rambled on a bit', in 'Judgement', is an example of a class of words whose ambiguity covers either activity (we can also talk about prose being 'pedestrian', of course, or of 'being transported' by music, Carson's other great love), a metaphoric link which Carson elaborates by having Quigley, a character in Johnny's story, '[walk] the country – Ballinliss and Aughaduff, / Slievenacapall, Carnavaddy' (*Ifn*, 18). This is syntax as a stroll, the period as perambulation; syntactical repetitions, doublings-back, and general circumlocutoriness replicating the movements of the haphazard, but ultimately purposeful, Carsonian persona. Such narration resembles the walk described in 'The Irish for no', at the point when the narrator suddenly decides to 'turn into the dog's-leg short-cut from Chlorine Gardens / Into Cloreen Park'; he 'turns into' the short-cut', but also metamorphosizes the poem, 'turns' it 'into' a 'short cut', in this case a short cut to the 'Eglantine Inn' (*Ifn*, 49).[2]

---

2 Although he uses a public transport systems to make a similar point, de Certeau understands the link between narrative and movement. In his essay 'Spatial stories', he observes that in modern Athens the vehicles of mass transportation are called *metaphorai*, and that 'Stories could also take this noble name: every day they traverse and organize places; they select and link them together; they make sentences and itineraries out of them'. And since 'every story is a travel story – a spatial practice', they concern 'everyday tactics'. More than this, 'narrated adventures, simultaneously producing geographies of actions … do not merely constitute a "supplement" to pedestrian enunciations and rhetorics. They are not satisfied with displacing the latter and transposing them into the field of language. In reality, they organize walks. They make the journey, before or during the time the feet perform it.' (Michel de Certeau, *The practice of everyday life*, Berkeley and London, 1988, 115–16).

Like the movements of the dead Treacy in 'Narrative in black and white',
nobody can ever completely predict or 'account / For' the switch from strolling to
speaking. Elliptical, mooching, parenthetical, speculative, self-questioning and
self-correcting, full of tales-within-tales, sidetrackable, digressive, swift-moving-
and-suddenly-stopping, Carson's tales, and the lines they are written in, emerge
from a simultaneously walking and self-narrating consciousness, gingerly
investigative, and yet assured, moving, in so many poems, by taking 'One step
forward, two steps back', a phrase so characteristic of this form of movement that
it is used three times ('Calvin Klein's *Obsession*', *Ifn*, 23; 'Ambition', *Bc*, 27;
'Narrative in black and white', *Bc*, 102). For if walking is distinctively human, it
follows that it is a form of language, the human achievement we are told sets us
most apart from the animals. Carson, I suspect, would agree with Pierre Janet, in
The evolution of memory and the concept of time (1928) that 'Narration created
humanity'.[3]

Unlike most loco-descriptive poems, Carson's range across territory which is
dangerous even if it can be exhilarating. Threat (but also possibility) is a constant
in them, the contemporary Belfast equivalent of the eighteenth-century sublime
encountered by Thomsonian loco-descriptive wanderers. Destruction and
reshaping occur all around; furthermore, as Peter Barry reminds us, the narrative
mode in Carson 'is the correlative of a city in which the detour and the devious
route to a desired objective are not decorative or artistic flourishes, but an often-
necessary survival strategy'.[4] This is most vividly-realized in 'Question time', in
which the narrator, trying to make a map, is himself being surveyed, unknown (or
'unbeknownst') to him, by militant republicans. They seize and drag him into a
'hole-in the-wall taxi [place]' for questioning; in the process, 'The map is pieced
together bit by bit. I am this map which they examine, checking it for error,
hesitation, accuracy …' (*Bc*, 63) At this point the map of the vanished city has to
be accurate in a way that no map of the city of the present moment can be.

As a reader of the city, then, one is always being read, and therefore textualized,
just as the city is, by the city's other inhabitants. In this sense, the city reads those
who try to read it, and can only be described in terms of a text whose enactment
is realized by the multifarious activities of its populace. 'Night out' describes an
evening's drinking as 'the sentence of the night', and this – to use an old cliché
– is not only 'punctuated by drink' but by 'gunfire' (*Bc*, 77). At the worst, in
'Belfast confetti', 'All the alleyways and side-streets blocked with stops and

---

3 Quoted in de Certeau, 115.   **4** Peter Barry, *Contemporary British poetry and the city* (Manchester,
2000), 229.

colons.? … Every move is punctuated.' (*Ifn*, 31) The main point is that the process by which the city is read is a mutual one; like Nietzche's abyss, if you gaze into it it begins to gaze back into you. To ignore the reciprocity of the process, to imagine that it is possibly to simply stand outside the city and 'fix' it in a single, all-encompassing sweep, is an error, possibly a fatal one, for you or someone else.

This, of course, raises the issue of surveillance, a key theme of *The Irish for no* and *Belfast confetti*, of which more in a moment. So, in 'Last orders', the narrator notes

> … you never know for sure who's who, or what
> You're walking into. I, for instance, could be anybody. Though I'm told
> Taig's written on my face. See me, would I trust appearances?
>
> ('Last orders', *Bc*, 46)

Clearly, the menacing paramilitary 'readers' encountered in 'Question time' wouldn't agree that the speaker did have '[Taig] written on [his] face' – what are distinguishing marks for some are invisible to others. Context is all; this is a relativistic vision in which, as in particle physics, the observer affects the thing being observed.

TIME

But the 'exhilaration' I mentioned comes from the possibility that change will throw up something new (or a new combination of old things) which engages human creativity. In the poem that serves as a preface, 'Turn again', 'turn' is (again) used to mean 'change', and throughout, Belfast is seen as an indefinable, protean city of process, one which exposes the instability, impossibility rather, of any mapping system. This means that one may not be able, or want, to give straight answers to even the straightest questions:

> Someone asks me for directions, and I think again. I turn into
> A side-street to try to throw off my shadow, and history is changed.
>
> ('Turn again', *Bc*, 11)

Similarly, this being a relativistic vision of the universe, we can expect a blurring of barriers between those usually discrete entities, space and time. The low may be exalted and it is possible that the digression will become the main narrative.[5] Time is the medium of all narrative, like music – however distorted, sped up, slowed down, even frozen – and it, too, demands to be viewed, like the narratives in which its possibilities are realized, as urban terrain to be walked:

> For if time is a road,
> It's fraught with ramps and dog-legs, switchbacks and spaghetti; here and
>   there,
> The dual carriageway becomes a one-track, backward mind.
>
> … And if time is a road, then you're checked again and again
> By a mobile checkpoint.

('Ambition', Bc, 27–8)

Temporal dislocation, like narrative and spatial dislocation, is therefore not unusual in Carson's Belfast: so, in 'Hamlet', 'As usual, the clock in The Clock Bar was a good few minutes // fast: / A fiction no one really bothered to maintain, unlike the story / The comrade on my left was telling …' And having once become a fiction, it doesn't matter if the clock is corrected to tell the right time 'everyone will still believe it's fast.' ('Hamlet', *Bc*, 105, 108)

There is, in other words, a fundamental (though I use that word provisionally) human need to disbelieve in order that disbelief may be suspended. When this can be done, fictions can be told. In other words, if everything were an agreed 'truth', or 'fact', wholly believed by us, fictionalizing would be impossible and the imagination would die. This is the sense in which the 'turning' metamorphousness of the city-as-writing takes on a more positive aspect. It draws in the walker-narrator to read its signs, and it problematizes his fixed sense of self (unravelling place and time, the co-ordinates of identity). The change it offers can be a renewal, not merely destructive. Against the violence of the city is the insistent vibrancy and process of it; continually changing, continually reinventing

---

5 Of course, the figure usually invoked to explain all such 'procedures', to use Carson's own word, is the *seannachie*, and the point is usually also made that, in breaking with the more 'literary' qualities of an earlier generation of Northern Irish poets – Seamus Heaney, Derek Mahon and Michael Longley – Carson celebrates the oral as against the written. But this is only true up to a point, and easily turns into an idealization of the oral, or (worse) an essentalization of the Irish as innately oral. (Stephen Matthews is guilty of this; see his *Irish poetry: politics, history, negotiation*, London, 1997), 186–206.) This poetry is very *written*, and conscious of its status as words on the page, of the way verbalization must always lag behind conception, like footsteps echoing in some city alleyway.

itself. That hoary old trope, resurrection of the dead into life, may be concealed within it:

> … Turning into Tomb Street, I began to feel a new man.
> Perfume breathed from somewhere, opening avenues of love, or
>   something déjà-vu.
>
> ('Queen's gambit', *Bc*, 40)

MICHEL DE CERTEAU

Michel de Certeau's essay 'Walking in the city' is in that section of *The practice of everyday life*, titled 'Spatial practices'. It begins, eerily in our post-9/11 world, with a description of Manhattan island as seen from the 110th floor of the World Trade Centre.[6] The all-embracing 'geometric' or 'geographic' vision of the city below, for whom the ant-like individual is an abstract subject, or 'citizen', is associated by de Certeau with town planners and politicians. He goes on to argue how this vision can be, and is often, challenged; and to elaborate a theory of, or rather an ideal for, the city, against those of authority, one 'Escaping the imaginary totalizations produced by the eye'.[7] In order to do so, he argues, it is necessary not to look down at the city as from the WTC, but to walk in it.

> The ordinary practitioners of the city live 'down below', below the threshold at which visibility begins. They walk – an elementary form of this experience of the city; they are walkers, *Wandersmaenner*, whose bodies follow the thicks and thins of an urban 'text' they write without being able to read it. These practitioners make use of spaces that cannot be seen [from above]; their knowledge of them is as blind as that of lovers in each other's arms. The paths that correspond in this intertwining, unrecognized poems in which each body is an element signed by many others, elude legibility. It is as though the practices organized by a bustling city were characterized by their blindness.

---

6 Even the language of the essay seems ominously prophetic: 'Unlike Rome, New York has never learned the art of growing old. A city composed of paroxysmal places in monumental reliefs. The spectator can read in it a universe that is constantly exploding … the tallest letters in the world compose a gigantic rhetoric of excess in both expenditure and production.'   **7** 'Surveys of routes miss what was: the act itself of passing by' (de Certeau, 93). Or, in Carson's words: 'Maps and street directories are suspect. No, don't trust maps, for they avoid the moment.' (*Bc*, 58)

In de Certeau's updating of Walter Benjamin (from whom Carson takes the epigraph for *Belfast confetti*) walking in the city turns out to gift us with powers of resistance and re-imagining; recreation as re-creation, so to speak. Walking, it transpires, has a logic, or 'enunciatory' rhetoric of its own. The walker, choosing his or her own route, time(s), use of space, observance (or transgression) of boundaries, is able to individuate and make ambiguous the 'legible' order imposed by planners on cities. And this can be compared to the speech act; the city thus becomes a text, as we have seen Belfast does for Carson, one which the walker is empowered to realize in his or her own way.[8]

The refuting of the total vision is truly postmodern in its suspicion of metanarrative, of course. But this does not make it any less convincing. We all know, from personal experience, how cities die because the possibilities for the public use of space have been drained from them; blocked roads left to die; paths in the wrong places; pelican crossings obedient to the imperatives of traffic rather than of pedestrians; concrete soullessness; windswept piazzas monumentalizing the scope and power of the multinational, the council and award-winning university architect. In Belfast, all of this has been intensified and complicated by the Troubles. An article of 1994 by Damien Smythe makes the points that Belfast in the 1970s and 1980s was planned 'explicitly as a "neutral ground" ... the purpose has not been "urban renewal" but urban sterilization'. It also points to the way that the sectarian divide has been 'institutionalised in the very streets of the city':

> More tangibly than the 'peace line', the perverse strategies whereby the
> centre has turned its shoulder to the west and north reflect the norms of
> sectarian division. Streets leading from the west to Royal Avenue have
> been systematically closed off. The little fenian bolthole of Smithfield ...
> is non-negotiable. Like the 'peace line', which is anything but, the
> Westlink is a bizarre contradiction [in terms], separating ... rather than
> linking.[9]

In words which may echo those of Carson's labyrinth-like 'Smithfield market', Smythe writes of the reconstructed markets looking like 'a circle of wagons – one way in, one way out' of a 'corralled living space' chopped up by 'wide, tank-

---

8 Thus, de Certeau contrasts 'place' with 'space': 'The law of the "proper" runs in the place', he says. 'Space', on the other hand, is 'a practiced place'. He illustrates this by claiming 'Thus the street geometrically defined by urban planning is transformed into a space by walkers. In the same way, an act of reading is the space produced by the practice of a particular place: a written text' (117).
9 Damien Smythe, 'Being unkind to Belfast', *Fortnight*, 325 (February 1994), 43.

friendly roads'. In another possible echo, a negative one, he also mentions the city's literature 'which cannot conceive of a city to which anyone but a victim can belong, which substitute[s] the crassest "against-all-odds-we-can-still-laugh sentimentality for the human feeling of a population', but which still receives 'the massive subsidy one would expect from an administrative ethos committed to institutionalising division.' Finally, Smythe concludes that the '"Troubles" are no excuse for this. There has always been trouble in Belfast …' The point is that the city has itself come to 'mirror constitutional violence in its very fabric … we are building the city according to the "troubles" and thus are begging them.'

It is these spaces, progressively drained of human meaning and sectarianized, that the walking consciousness resists – as far as it can. And yet there are other ways of describing Belfast in the 1980s. Glenn Patterson's novel *Fat lad* (1992) describes a city well poised to take advantage of the warehouses-into-flats, loft conversions, Waterstones-style bookshop and myriad coffee outlets. *The Observer*, in 1984, reported that '[Belfast's] poverty is ancient and ingrained', but even as these impressions were being written, transformation had begun. To some extent it flowed, bizarrely, out of the Thatcher government's willingness to treat Northern Ireland as a special case (we might recall, in this context, that at the end of the decade the Tory government felt it was too risky to even consider introducing the Poll Tax to Northern Ireland). Cutting public expenditure elsewhere, as part of a strategy of mollification and containment of Sinn Féin, the Thatcher government spent the 1980s boosting the infrastructure of Northern Ireland, and especially Belfast.[10] A *Belfast Telegraph* article in May 1985 enthused that there was 'a new buzz and bustle about a city that looks better, smells better and smiles better'. The city council's advertising campaign used the phrase 'Belfast's got the buzz'. And '[b]etween 1982 and 1985 some 41 restaurants, 38 cafes and 55 hot food bars opened, while around £86 million was invested in the inner-city area.'[11] All of which is perhaps to say no more than that Belfast's experience is a heightened version of the British experience of postmodern urban gentrification.[12]

---

10 Public spending grew by 1.3% p.a. in real terms in the late 1980s, where in Leeds, London or Liverpool it was being cut by 0.5% p.a. 'By 1989, government employment schemes accounted for a quarter of all jobs in industry while the employment of the remainder in manufacturing was heavily dependent on government subsidy … service[,] accounted for nearly two thirds of Northern Ireland's jobs by 1985', 60% of which were public sector jobs – education, health, social services, etc. (Jonathan Bardon and David Burnett, *Belfast: A pocket history*, Belfast, 1996, 146). Massive subventions meant a 'workhouse economy'. **11** Bardon and Burnett, 143–4. **12** 'Nevertheless, the heavily fortified army and police bases which continued to mar the Belfast landscape stood as stark reminders that this was no ordinary city … Castlereagh holding centre in east Belfast … was alleged to torture

Can sites of blight be recovered, if only temporarily, by being strung onto what de Certeau calls the necklace-like narrative of our progress through them? Belfast's dystopia, graphically outlined by Smythe, makes the struggle to transform voyeurs into walkers a difficult one. Its makeover, as illustrated by the figures of investment, points to a consumerist, service industry-based society which need ask no questions. Yet a utopian vision, a plea even, for something more than just further pedestrianization or better shopping outlets, lies at the heart of Carson's vision, just as it does of de Certeau's. If we take that line from 'Ambition' as a cue as to how Carson sees it: 'here and there, / The dual carriageway becomes a one-track, backward mind'.[13]

ENTRAPMENT, MAPPING AND SURVEILLANCE

De Certeau's concern with surveillance is Carson's too, although manipulation is more malign in Carson, and his utopianism is weaker – as we would expect. Carson describes surveillance even as, through manipulations of walking – narrative, memory and time – he attempts to ambiguate and elude it. Famously, in his work, 'The city is a map of the city' (a refrain phrase which, like a musical leitmotif, reappears throughout). No map ever can be an accurate representation of the city, because they are gapped (they are not permitted to reveal the details of military installations, prisons), or to include items which are either incomplete, or have disappeared, or which never were. 'Mapping' is Carson's version of de Certeau's 'geographic' vision from the WTC, and he shares the desire to challenge its claims to power with recent Northern Irish literature, from Brian Friel's use of the 1833 Ordnance Survey in *Translations* to the 'not yet accurate linen / Map of the world' symbolizing imperial power in Derek Mahon's 'Courtyards in Delft'.

detainees and was investigated by Amnesty International' (Bardon and Burnett, 145). In March 1988 *The Economist* claimed that one Northern Ireland minister 'used to escort parties of English MPs round the province to show them its problems' but he 'found them so envious of his baliwick's housing and health that he stopped inviting them'. Spending per head on housing was 3 times more than in England and Wales; 10% of GDP was being spent on health compared with 6% in England; real expenditure on education rose in the 1980s as it fell elsewhere.   **13** The equation of dual carriageway with 'backward' mind isn't merely, if at all, reactionary; rather, it is a moral gesture which asks just how do we live in, know, and *see*, the city? How do we understand urban spaces? Or, to put it more gallically, more evocatively, in the words of de Certeau: 'To what erotics of knowledge does the ecstacy of reading such a cosmos belong? Having taken a voluptuous pleasure in it, I wonder what is the source of this pleasure of "seeing the whole", of looking down on, of totalizing the most immoderate of human texts.' (*The practice of everyday life*, 92.)

Maps, whoever they are made by, and for whatever reasons, have a tendency to stand in for territory, and to serve dominance and even destructive agency, over it.[14]

The difference between Carson's and Friel's working out of the implications of this lie in the different context of the continually shattering and re-forming city of the Troubles. For of course (to be Foucauldian about it) the flaw which is innate in the mapping impulse does not suspend or stifle it; indeed, it may well encourage still further extensions of the power of information-gathering, inciting the drive of discursive power towards the ever-greater mastery it desires. The struggle, then, between those who would elaborate alternative narratives of the city and the master-narrative of the mappers and planners is constant. But the oppositions are not simple ones. In the early 'The insular Celts', spiral designs on a brooch symbolize the violent introversions of a pre-British Irish past, and *The Irish for no* and *Belfast confetti* develop this image of internal division further. The brooch becomes a labyrinth, emblem of confinement, echoing Smythe's description of the circle of wagons with 'one way in, one way out':

> Since everything went up in smoke, no entrances, no exits.
> But as the charred beams hissed and flickered, I glimpsed a map of Belfast
> In the ruins: obliterated streets, the faint impression of a key.
> Something many-toothed, elaborate, stirred faintly in the labyrinth.
>
> ('Smithfield market', *Ifn*, 37)

The minotaur hinted at is a symbol of the Troubles; the beast of violence animated or goaded by state and paramilitary forces. Nevertheless, it would be a mistake to see it as only this. Confined by Dedalus (as Carson's city-walking persona lives under the Joycean shadow of Stephen Dedalus, perhaps), the minotaur is also a figure for the writer, skulking alone in the labyrinth of his lair of words (the later rather than the early Joyce), doomed by his gift-cum-curse to 'elaborate' texts to which other will try to find a 'key'[15] For as Carson has observed in an interview with Frank Ormsby, 'For a map to work, it has to use shorthand, or symbols, or metaphor, and in this it resembles poetry'.[16] Likewise, in 'Hamlet', a fanciful etymology for the 'Falls', the main Catholic area of Belfast is brought

---

14 It is, after all, a *map* of Dresden which is bombed in the poem of the same name (the bombers, flying by night, rely totally on maps to target the inoffensive city): 'All across the map of Dresden, store-rooms full of china // shivered, teetered / And collapsed ...' (*Ifn*, 15)   15 We might remember Joyce's father's comment that if his son were dropped in the middle of a desert, the first thing he would do would be to make a map of his surroundings.   16 'Ciaran Carson interviewed by Frank Ormsby', *Linen Hall Review* (April 1991), 4–8, 5.

into conjunction with 'pound', as in sterling and animal 'pound', to produce a riff on just this theme of containment and enclosure, a compounding of English and Irish words:

> For pound, as some wag
> Interrupted, was an off-shoot of the Falls, from the Irish, *fál*, a hedge;
> Hence any kind of enclosed thing ...
>
> ('Hamlet', *Bc*, 105)

Does the fact that the monarch's head is emblazoned on the money slapped down on the bar compromise or confirm the allegiances of those who use it? That way the madness of a totally sectarianized environment lies, of course, although it is one which is not so far from the truth in a place where the slightest slip of the tongue can provoke lethal displays of intolerance. What can be said is that if mapping tends towards a kind of entrapment, an attempt, always doomed, to grasp the totality of the city, there is a sense in which we are still all forced construct provisional maps, to be complicit in the map-making process. Danger therefore lies in the impulse to replace the oppressors' map with your own mirror-image of it; this may merely replicate, and so confirm, the original labyrinthine entrapment. In 'Slate Street school', the trapped child envisages a time when he will visit the grim constraint of the city back on it in an act of revenge:

> And I am the avenging Archangel, stooping over mills and factories and barracks.
> I will bury the dark city of Belfast forever under snow: inches, feet, yards, chains, miles.
>
> ('Slate Street school', *Ifn*, 46)

Justified though this viewpoint might be, it is not necessarily the poet's. Indeed, the Archangel looks down on the offending city much as the imaginary observer from the WTC in de Certeau's essay; the child has in one sense merely inverted the vision of dominance and control, remaining trapped by its high-low, superior-inferior logic; to truly exorcise it will require more than this. This is why in his writing Carson has, after all, not so much 'buried' Belfast as the opposite, disinterring it, showing the 'avenging' vision to have been warped, a product of violence.

More than this, particularist listing can lead to synoptic overview; following the list of buildings on a 1920 Ordnance Survey map of Belfast, in 'Intelligence':

> … a camera pans down from some aerial vision (the VTO craft pioneered by Shorts?) into a mass of chimney stacks … suddenly I have just climbed the Whiterock Loney to Black Mountain, and my father and I are sitting in the Hatchet Field as he … points out, down in the inferno, Clonard Monastery … and the tiny blip of our house that we both pretend to see …
>
> ('Intelligence', *Bc*, 81)

This reminds us that Carson's world is continuously surveyed, the technology which produced the (however inaccurate) Ordnance Survey map now multiplied in 'peep-holes, one-way mirrors, security cameras … this helicopter [which] chainsaws overhead … this 30,000,000 candlepower gimbal-mounted Nitesun by which the operator can observe undetected …' (*Bc*, 78) Its culmination is Jeremy Bentham's Panopticon, the design for a radial prison with a central, all-seeing observer at its hub. Though few were built, one of the best-preserved is in Ireland (the Women's Prison in Cork), and the implications for the development of the modern state attitudes to surveillance is discussed at chilling length in Foucault's *Discipline and punish* (1975). The panopticon is described at length and discussed in 'Intelligence' (*Bc*, 79–80), as an ultimate nightmare; the city as a prison made totally transparent, and accessible, to power.

It is opposed by Carson in terms of different remembering, and therefore remapping, through speculative local and family history. These appear in the panorama of Belfast described in the Milltown Cemetery chapter of *The star factory*, as well as in *The Irish for no* and *Belfast confetti*:

> Snags of greyish wool remind me of the mountain that we climbed that
>   day –
> Nearly at the summit, we could see the map of Belfast. My father stopped
> For a cigarette, and pointed out the landmarks: Gallaher's tobacco-factory,
> Clonard Monastery, the invisible speck of our house, lost in all the rows
> And terraces and furrows …
>
> ('Patchwork', *Ifn*, 59)

Later, in *Belfast confetti's* 'Ambition', the same episode is recounted, but this time the view is obscured:

> But smoke obscures
> The panorama from the Mountain Loney spring. The city and
> the mountain are on fire ...
>
> ('Ambition', *Bc*, 27)

Humanization of, and ultimately resistance to, the panoptic vision of surveillance, relies on walking, local observation, the intimate, ground-level view, constructed by non-invasive, provisional, self-questioning narrative which, in its writerly procedures, is a part of what it defends. For, in de Certeau's phrase, the story of these 'multiform, resistant, tricky and stubborn procedures' 'begins on ground level, with footsteps'.[17]

MEMORY, THE PAST AND NOSTALGIA

I'm bound to be corrected, but of all the synonyms for 'walk' in the poetry I've referred to so far, I don't think I've once come across the word 'dander'. This might seem a surprising omission; Belfast's very own word for a 'walk', meaning, according to the *Concise Ulster dictionary*, 'to stroll, saunter', or 'a stroll, a leisurely walk', is precisely what I'm talking about in this paper.[18] My guess is that it doesn't occur precisely because it is too obviously an Ulster word. In the sense that Pierre Macherey would understand it it is the silence which speaks – or, closer to home maybe, Sherlock Holmes' dog which didn't bark. The point about 'dander' is precisely that it is too easy, too redolent of 'Ulster' identity, too predictable and sentimental, too easy a gesture towards an identifiable identity rooted in a singular, self-identical place.

For Carson's work is, perverse though such a claim might seem, more anti-foundationalist, anti-rooted, even anti-belonging, than otherwise.[19] While, as Peter Barry notes, his poems always tie up their loose ends – unlike, say, a more wholly postmodern text, such as a poem by John Ashbery – and although they 'seem located in the idea of residency and the negotiations of rootedness', Belfast

---

17 de Certeau, 96–7. Or, according to Oscar Wilde, 'A Map of the world that does not include Utopia is not even worth glancing at.' Quoted in David Harvey, *Spaces of hope*, 133.   **18** C.I. Macafee (ed.), *A concise Ulster dictionary* (Oxford, 1996), 91.   **19** Carson does fish for amber, that well-known preservative. But he eschews the symbolic, transcendental signifier of the symbol, or the fetishization of the past. The members of 'The exiles' club' resurrect their memories in a way which, as well as being surreal-comic in its impossibility ('the entire contents of Paddy Lavery's pawnshop') is also 'slightly-mouldy', like the 'batch of soda farls' they've bought in for their get-together, along with the 'Red Heart Stout, Park Drive // cigarettes and Dunville's whiskey' (*Ifn*, 45).

is often not so much a place to embed in (when does the Carson persona divulge where he lives in the present tense of the narration, as opposed to the past? Or who with? Or what he does for a living?) as an activity to observe, a set of memories and possibilities located not 'in here' (the subjective self) or 'out there' (the cherished locale) but the tension between these which is productive of an endless distancing, narrative energy. When we talk of Carson's orality, his use of tradition, we have, I think, to remember the Derridean point about the illusoriness of the presence promised by voice, of the oral as more real, more true, than the written.

On the one hand, the very look of a Carson poem reveals that it has visual, as well aural, designs on us. Those trademark long lines, although they seem to spill back on themselves of necessity, could quite easily be laid out singly, and un-enjambed. Why aren't they? Because the breaking-off of the end of the line trips up its flow, reminds us of the materiality of the language on the page, interrupts the flow of storytelling into continual hesitations, asides, turn-abouts. The mimeticism valued by F.R. Leavis ('And sometimes like a gleaner thou dost keep / Steady thy laden head across a brook'), is not the point I'm making here, however. That is based on a naïve belief in the transparency of language; its subservience to communication, the 'enacting' of something else, namely the famous 'concrete' image. Which isn't to say this kind of enjambement doesn't happen occasionally in Carson, too; think of

> ... and we'd climb the narrow stair to where she lay, buried
> Beneath the patchwork quilt.
>
> ('Patchwork', *Ifn*, 62)

But even in this instance the differences are more striking than the similarities; the device is being put at the service of a slightly black joke; and generally in Carson's poems, the line-break is arbitrary, as if challenging notions of poetic language as merely instrumental, a means to an end. The breaks, then, signal precisely the artificiality of the verse, its 'always already' written quality, and this is very necessary in writing which can so easily be taken as being straightforwardly realist. That goes also for Carson's reliance on memory, his framing (in the sense of 'implicating', as well as 'demarcating') of reminiscences. Neil Corcoran partly describes this when he writes of him 'playing the oral against the literary, the long lines of his poems [having] something of the sustained, improvisatory panache of the ... *seanachie*', yet adding that they 'in their sustained syntactical ebb and flow', they also '[maintain] a control of uncommonly sophisticated writerly resource-fulness'.[20]

Another explanation for Carson's avoidance of nostalgia, kitsch and 'heritage industry' writing, although he is a writer utterly dependent on memory – and largely childhood memory at that – grows out of these 'mere' devices. The arbitrariness of line break, mimetic of the weird associative leaps of memory more than of physical action, establish one kind of authenticity but may undermine another, more unimpeachably lyric, variety. For the image of the past and identity in Carson is not that of the *omphalos*; rather, it is the patchwork quilt, or the endless, and endlessly self-revising, story. The nature of memory means that the past is always being provisionally constructed in the present; this, in fact, is what memory is, in Carson's work, rather than the establishing of a pure source, or origin. Hence, everything potentially falls inside poststructuralist quotation marks: 'A dreadful mistake, I hear one of them saying, has been made, and I get the feeling he is speaking in quotation marks, as if this is a bad police B-movie and he is mocking it, and me, and him' ('Question time', *Bc*, 63).

Of course, one downside of this is that it is can run together with late capitalism's less than disinterested interest in the evacuation of depth, namely its selling of brands (in order to sell products), as memorably indicted by Naomi Klein in *No logo*.[21] Carson's remembered world may appear to be largely a 1950s steam-driven, bricky and soot-darkened one, but the 'crackling // see-through / Cellophane' around the Lucozade bottle in 'Patchwork' (*Ifn*, 60) is not the standard amber-shading-to-sepia glow of autobiographical reminiscence; rather, it has distinct affinities with what Frederic Jameson once called 'the cellophane wrapped paradise of postmodernity'. Carson's insight into this, into the hows and whys of commodification, the ways we are caught up in it, are apparent in his listing of brand-names – Corcoran lists forty-seven in only a selection from *The Irish for no*'s twenty-four poems.[22] The self-knowledge by which we may – perhaps – resist commodification ourselves is best exemplified in the knowingly italicized final line of 'Calvin Klein's *Obsession*':

20 Neil Corcoran, 'One step forward, two steps back', in Neil Corcoran (ed.), *The chosen ground: essays on contemporary poetry of Northern Ireland* (Bridgend, 1992), 217. **21** Naomi Klein, *No logo* (London, 2000), 3–61. **22** Corcoran, 223.

> ... There is talk of money, phrased as talk of
> Something else, of how there are some things that can't be bought.
> *Or maybe it's the name you buy, and not the thing itself.*
>
> ('Calvin Klein's *Obsession*', *Ifn*, 24)

DREAMS (AND NIGHTMARES) AND RESPONSIBILITIES

In his 1991 interview with Frank Ormsby, Carson sets his movements within the context of a series of remembered dreams of wandering in a Belfast of the mind subtly different from the real one (but what is the 'real' one when there is no such thing as a true map of the city, when its totality is ungraspable?). Ormsby is referring to *Belfast confetti*'s epigraph from Benjamin:

> Not to find one's way in a city is of little interest ... But to lose one's way in a city, as one loses one's way in a forest, requires practice ... I learned this art late in life: it fulfilled the dreams whose first traces were the labyrinths on the blotters of my exercise books.

Carson comments: 'For years I've had a series of recurrent dreams about Belfast – nightmares, sometimes, or dreams of containment, repression, anxiety and claustrophobia ... often I'm lost in am ambiguous labyrinth between the Falls and the Shankill; at other times, the city is idealized and takes on a Gothic industrial beauty'. The shift is between the gothic as conceived by Piranesi or by Ruskin (Ruskin's vision being shown as collapsing into something like that of the former in 'John Ruskin in Belfast', *Bc*, 96–8). This dream city is, for Carson, 'a landscape I know almost better than the waking city'. Dreams, as well as music, work by repetition – nowhere more so than in Carson's father's twenty-year dream of never being able to catch a tram carrying his dead father (*Tsf*, 27–9). As de Certeau puts it, 'Haunted places are the only ones people can live in – and this inverts the schema of the Panopticon'[23]. Dreams, too, are the source of 'certain phrases or images which are repeated in the poems'[24] and many of them proceed according to an abrupt, quasi-surreal dream-logic.

Yet 'The similarity between "discourse" and dreams has to do with their use of the same "stylistic procedures"; it therefore includes pedestrian practices as well'.

---

23 de Certeau, 108.   **24** Ormsby, 5.

The rhetoric for discourse and dreams is adequate for walking; if there is parallelism, it is because the development of all three 'is organized as a relation between the place from which it proceeds (an origin) and the nowhere it produces (a way of "going by")'. To walk, that is, is by definition to lack a place, and 'Memory is a sort of anti-museum: it is not localizable'.[25] On the other hand, 'The memorable is that which can be dreamed about a place'.[26] Place is displaced by this kind of dream-memory proceeding by association, unchecked, without a preset destination, but operating within the stringent rules of dreaming, or walking, or narrating a story, or, it may be, of music.

THE MUSIC OF WHAT HAPPENS

Music has always been central to Carson's work, and it's a good place to conclude a discussion of it. Together with the *seanachie* explanation, and the obligatory nods to George V. Higgins and C.K. Williams, Irish traditional music has often been seen as being central to the poetic of the two Belfast collections. In a sense, the best explanation of why this is so is to be found in *Last night's fun*, a personal study of Carson's association with the traditional music scene; and various interviews have matched the poetry with the music's melodic phrasing, aesthetics of improvisation (and hence unrepeatability), variation within strict parameters and eschewal of the authenticating indicators of 'art music' (vibrato, tremolo, (de)crescendo, etc). Nevertheless, and invoking here that other part of the title of de Certeau's book, *everyday life*, I'd like to suggest a further parallel. This is offered by what I feel is one of the key passages in Carson's first book on music, the *Appletree guide to Irish traditional music*. It's not by Carson himself, but a quotation from John Cage, the avant-garde American composer:

> When we separate music from life what we get is art (a compendium of masterpieces). With contemporary music, when it is actually contemporary, we have no time to make that separation (which protects us from living) and so contemporary music is not so much art as it is life and anyone making it no sooner finishes one of it than he begins making another just as people keep on washing dishes, brushing their teeth, getting sleepy and so on. (*Itm*, 8–9)

25 de Certeau, 108. **26** de Certeau, 109.

Given his claim that this book was a template for *The Irish for no*, this is significant in indicating a major aim of Carson's art, namely the breaking down of the barrier between art and life. Traditionally this is associated with avant-garde practice, and I don't wish to suggest that Carson is an avant-garde writer in any obvious sense (Irish avant-garde, or 'linguistically innovative' poetry is another essay; suffice it to say that Carson is the only Irish 'mainstream' poet, to my knowledge, to have been invited to read at the Prynnean Cambridge Conference for Contemporary Poetry). Nevertheless, it is fair to say that there are some radically unlyrical and anti-essentialist implications to his writing and his treatment of memory, heritage, history, surveillance, language, the self and – ultimately – identity. In Carson's work, for example, dream-logic, or dream scenarios and narratives, are used not merely as a setting, as in the 'private waking from a dream of death – Jerking his head spasmodically as he is penetrated by invisible gunfire …' in 'Night patrol' (*Ifn*, 34). Rather, they tend to occur as ways of complicating the topography of the city, as palimpsests (another recurring image is that of the children's carvings over and over on a school desk). In this as in other aspects of their working, a kind of blurring takes place, but one which has this intent (a powerfully political one, in many ways) of abolishing the art/life distinction. Walking, to return to this essay's point of departure, is a form of continuity with everyday life through the body, and in the absence of technology; it is to be immersed in the quotidian, the banal, the everyday. There is no Heideggerian 'earthing' in this; Carson's balancing of traditional and contemporary is tactical, not strategic, and it moves through its acceptance of un-location and dissenting from essentialism. Nevertheless, there is in it the kind of 'heroism [which lies] in surviving the disorienting space, both labyrinthine and agoraphobic, of the metropolis. It lies in the ability to discern among the massed ranks of anonymity the outline forms of beauty and individuality appropriate to urban life'[27] – one which has also redefined the 'traditional' as something which belongs, with no sense of incongruity, to its wanderings: '[Y]ou descended to the mundane busy street. Absorbed in the crowd, you let yourself be taken by its flow, and became another corpuscle in its bloodstream.' (*Lnf,* 21)[28]

---

27 James Donald, 'This, here, now: imagining the modern city', in Westwood, S. and J. Williams. (eds), *Imagining cities: scripts, signs, memory* (London, 1997), 197.   **28** I detect in this an echo of Stephen Dedalus's definition of God as 'a shout in the street'; it may be no coincidence that at this point, in 'Nestor', he is demurring at the claims of the Orangeman Mr Deasy. There are, of course, numerous echoes of Joyce's experimental, democratic and urban aesthetic in Carson's writing (and the linguistically playfulness of *First language* (1993) and *Opera et cetera* (1996) immediately followed the relatively realistic Belfast collections).

'The mouth of the poem': Carson and place

EAMONN HUGHES

Ciaran Carson has, it is now a commonplace to say, established himself as the poet of Belfast not just as a specific city but as a paradigm of the urban. Equally, and to a degree, which I wish to consider here, contradictorily, he is a writer much influenced by traditional forms and practices from both music and narrative. The standard account of Carson's work involves a conventional beginning in the 1970s, a long period of poetic silence during which he worked with traditional arts, and his eventual emergence as an urban writer with *The Irish for no* and *Belfast confetti* in the late 1980s. This narrative suggests discontinuities and disguises contradictions which need some examination. According to it the early, conventional writing is not influenced by traditional forms and practices, while the later writing turns to urban modernity under their influence. It is worth returning to the early work to consider the path taken to the urban.

When *The new estate* was published in 1976 Carson was described as:

> a writer who finds poetry everywhere: in the past and the present, in the landscape, in family relationships, in the intricacies of craft – whether it is linen weaving, the casting of a bell, or a bomb disposal – and in the great heritage of Irish culture.[1]

This represents him as a rather conventional writer but omits the fact that he was also a poet oddly wary of both written and spoken language. Two early poems, 'St Ciaran and the birds' and 'St Ciaran's island', are necessarily self-reflexive, partly because of the use of 'Ciaran', and partly because the first of them derives from the *Buile Suibhne* sequence used variously by Flann O'Brien and Seamus Heaney as a narrative of the poet. There we find 'For my voice, / The tongueless bell, / For my silence / No tongue can tell' (*Tne*, 4), while the ambition of the manuscript-illuminating monk in 'St Ciaran's Island' is 'To lose the written word/In the

---

1 Ciarán Carson, *The new estate*, back cover blurb. 2 Both poems, along with 'St Ciaran in the trees', had appeared in Carson's first pamphlet *The insular Celts*, 6, 7, 8–9. These three poems and 'Tuaim inbir' (*Tne*, 30) derive from Gerard Murphy (ed.), *Early Irish lyrics: eighth to twelfth century*. (Oxford, 1956).

appearance of art' (*Tne*, 5).² Despite the conventional description of the work and this muted anxiety about language, *The new estate* contains much that is recognizable as what we have come to regard as typical of Carson: 'the flight//Of one thing into the other' in 'the spirals / Of [the Insular Celts'] brooches' (*Tne*, 3) is echoed by the ravelling and unravelling of both textiles and voices in 'Linen' and 'An early bed' (*Tne*, 11, 12–13). There is even a 'Belfast' poem in 'The bomb disposal' (*Tne*, 21), which, apart from some earlier domestic interiors, is the first poem located securely, if that is the right word, in Belfast. This is a Carson poem, as we have come to know those poems, and looks forward to much of the later work. The title phrase is itself rather odd because of its definite article: bomb disposal is one thing, 'the' bomb disposal another. There is then a riddling quality to the poem not least in the fact that the first two stanza-sentences are questions, and the deliberate juxtaposition of 'answer' with a question mark draws attention to other oppositions: 'deliberation' and 'hesitation', 'I … myself' and 'crowded', the idea of 'find[ing] oneself' while 'deviat[ing] from the known route', 'breaks out' as against the sense of imprisonment in the 'cul-de-sac' and 'the boarded windows'. Such features send us back to the first two stanzas as being less to do with bomb disposal and more to do with 'picking [the] lock' of this poem, 'the message of [whose] threaded veins [is] print'. The poem picks up on the interest of earlier poems in a convoluted art about 'the flight of one thing into another' giving some warrant to a reading which sees it as a poem about how one might read it and its turn from the one thing of bomb disposal to the other thing of a taxi ride. The taxi ride has a MacNeicean quality: to 'deviat[e] from the known route' and end 'in a cul-de-sac' has a particular symbolism considering the funeral of the first stanza; the 'drawn blinds' become a mark of respect for a funeral cortege. The poem is then potentially about bomb disposal, about poetry or about death by bomb blast (when all areas of the city become 'forbidden areas'). Belfast may have appeared but, despite the central emblematic line 'The city is a map of the city', the closing voice is still muted ('whispers') and the poem can only reach a dead end. What is striking about the poems after 'The bomb disposal' is that while they are often urban (in line with the collection's title) they are most commonly set in domestic interiors, versions of home. Such spaces in Carson's work are not safe or happy: 'An early bed', 'House painting', 'Soot' (*Tne*, 12–13, 37, 38) and poems from the later pamphlet, *The lost explorer*, such as 'Twine' (*Tle*, 10) and 'The patchwork quilt' (*Tle*, 13–14) all figure home as a place of childhood fear, violence, decay or defilement. Rather than a refuge, home is nearly always a trap, set on a level with those dead ends and cul-de-sacs which are to be avoided from their first mention in 'The bomb disposal'. The only alternative in these 1970s writings is a set of poems which make Muldoon-like gestures to travel ('The great Fitzpatrick', 'Africa', 'East of Cairo' *Tne*, 4–5, 6, 11). The cul-de-sac of 'The bomb disposal' is indeed a dead end, leading only into the mutedly domestic, rather than enabling the poet to range the city.

When Carson revises this earlier writing as *The new estate and other poems* in the wake of *The Irish for no* he does so in ways which no longer simply indicate an unfocused allegiance to tradition within which various 'crafts' are analogues for poetry and isolated monks are models for the poet. If anything tradition is more grounded in both the new and the revised collection and the juxtaposition of the urban with Irish oral and musical traditions (along with similar juxtapositions) instead of being potentially contradictory is made thematic. The city, the site of modernity, is the location for a poetry which, as the acknowledgement to John Campbell in *The Irish for no* makes clear, is based firmly in traditional oral and musical forms. It is also a poetry which is energized by urban demotic speech,[3] often the speech of the father whose words and presence are riddled through so many of the poems in the early volumes. That same speech and presence is, however, balanced by the father's job as a postman, a vital cog in the machinery of print capitalism, which points to the material textuality with which the poems are equally obsessed. Such oppositions and contradictions can be almost endlessly elaborated from within the poetry: a commitment to the here and now as against an obsession with history and memory; an almost pedantic attention to detail and fact as against frequently phantasmagorical narratives and an acknowledgement of the power of imagination; images of imprisonment and closure as against the endless voyage of the *flâneur*; the city as known territory as against the need to be lost; the city as site of alienation as against its lively speech community (while Carson's citizens frequently look at each other sidelong or through mirrors, they also talk endlessly to each other); the city founded on unstable sleech is made of solid brick and so on.

Both the urban and the traditional are then self-evidently present in Carson's work; this is a poetry which introduces John Campbell of Mullaghbawn to Walter Benjamin of Berlin. What is new is that the urban is given the convoluted form previously associated with the traditional; the urban has become, like the traditional, self-inwoven and recursive. The explicit use of Belfast as setting is

---

3 See Steven Matthews, *Irish poetry: politics, history, negotiation, the evolving debate, 1969 to the present* (Basingstoke, 1997), 189; Neil Corcoran, *Poets of modern Ireland: text, context, intertext* (Cardiff, 1999), 216.

matched, that is to say, by the self-conscious incorporation of references to both creative and theoretical writing of the urban. The standard critical tactic of referring to such theorists of the urban as Walter Benjamin or Kevin Lynch is anticipated and even mocked by such writerly procedures.[4] Like Benjamin or Jorge Luis Borges (also never far beneath the surface of the writing), Carson's writing is self-evidently predicated not just on observation of the cityscape but also on reading about it. Reading, just as much as the demotic and traditional forms and practices, is a crucial factor in the writing, to the degree that it is thematized in Carson's work from *The Irish for no* and *The new estate and other poems* onwards.[5] As well as considering the allusions that give so much texture to the work – William Shakespeare, John Keats, Thomas De Quincey, Arthur Rimbaud, Robert Frost and Wallace Stevens as well as Benjamin and Borges are perhaps the most obvious presences[6] – we should also attend to the epigraphs, acknowledgements, permissions, reading lists and lists of books purchased or consulted in libraries, sources for translations and found poems which are so common in Carson's work.[7] A typical moment occurs in *The star factory* when he offers us a list of books bought 'about four hours ago' (*Tsf,* 26) with some book tokens from a named bookshop in Belfast city centre. As with his references to urban theorists, there is a teasing relevance to the named texts: *Roland Barthes* by Roland Barthes (re-issued 1994) is as much meditation on autobiography as it is

4 *Belfast confetti* has epigraphs from both Walter Benjamin, *A Berlin childhood around the turn of the century* trans. Howard Eiland (London, Cambridge, MA), 53–4 (*Bc,* 14) and Kevin Lynch, *The image of the city* (London, Cambridge, MA), 126 (*Bc,* 84). The recursive aspect of the writing is reinforced by the fact that Lynch is citing the Italian neo-realist Vasco Pratolini's, *Il quartiere* (1947). The epigraphs are, of course, contradictory: Benjamin's is about the need to be lost in the familiar while Lynch's is about how the citizens of Florence insist on following familiar but no longer existent paths in a bombed city. **5** Neil Corcoran has written on reading in contemporary Northern Irish poetry, specifically in the work of Seamus Heaney, Paul Muldoon and Tom Paulin; his chapter ends by quoting 'Belfast confetti'; see 'Strange letters: reading and writing in contemporary northern Irish poetry', in his *Poets of modern Ireland,* 77–94. **6** Patricia Horton, 'From romantic to postmodern: imagining the real in the work of Ciaran Carson', *Canadian Journal of Irish Studies,* 25, 1 & 2 (2000), 337–51 identifies Keats, de Quincey, Rimbaud and Borges as presences; Shane Murphy, 'Sonnets, Centos and Long Lines: Muldoon, Paulin, McGuckian and Carson' in Matthew Campbell (ed.) *The Cambridge companion to contemporary Irish poetry* (Cambridge, 2003), 189–208, 206, identifies Wallace Stevens as source for 'Ark of the covenant' (*Fl,* 55–8); Neil Corcoran, *Poets of modern Ireland,* 193–6 identifies Robert Frost's 'After apple-picking' in 'Whatever sleep it is' (*Ifn,* 26–8). Frost was a key subject of Carson's inaugural lecture as Director of the Seamus Heaney Centre for Poetry: '"Whose woods these are …" Some aspects of poetry and translation', inaugural lecture, Queen's University of Belfast, 4 May 2005. **7** Carson's work as translator and adapter adds various early Irish and Welsh sources as well as Baudelaire, Dante, Stefan Augustin Doinas, Mallarmé, Brian Merriman and George Seferis to the list of his intertexts.

autobiography; Benjamin's *Selected writings, vol. 1: 1913–1926* (1996) contains a number of potentially pertinent pieces including 'One-way street', which is both autobiographical and urban, and from which Carson quotes in the next chapter of *The star factory* (*Tsf,* 30–1); the *Encyclopaedia Acephalia* (1995) invokes surrealism and other possible intertextual relationships with writers such as Georges Bataille and Michel Leiris, as well as gesturing towards the dismemberment and mutilation in poems such as '33333', 'Cocktails' (*Ifn,* 39, 41), 'Bloody hand', 'Jump leads' or 'The mouth' (*Bc,* 51, 56, 70), and *A nostalgic look at Belfast trams since 1945* (1994) by Mike Maybin, to which we will return.

This moment does not just introduce a set of allusions, however. It foregrounds reading as an activity and what is more as an activity necessarily implicated in structures of production, distribution and exchange: the book tokens, the named bookshop, the fact that three of the books are translations, and that all of them were newly published when *The star factory* first appeared are details which remind us of 'the elaborate / Machinery of books, where I materialized' ('Latitude 38°S', *Fl,* 68). Carson makes use of such moments and of paratextual apparatus to play consciously with the book as object. This is evident from *The new estate and other poems* which does more than simply gather most of the previous work; alongside its revisions, excisions and re-orderings the 'revised version' begins with what we have to assume is a poem:

Advertisement
This ink
Prevents gumming, clogging, metal corrosion and rubber-rot.

It dissolves sediment.
It cleans your pen as it writes.   (*Tneop,* 10)

'Advertisement', laid out as a poem and listed on the Contents page, differs from the other poems in the collection by being set in italics (a common indicator of quotation) and for this and other reasons, we assume that it is a 'found' poem (Carson returns to Quink blue-black ink and pens later in his work)[8], and while it is tempting to tease out its possible meanings ('corrosion' and 'rot' could refer to politics; the geology of Belfast may be indicated by 'sediment'; the clean pen

---

8 See, for example, 'Loaf' (*Bc,* 15), in which Carson plays with the idea that one cannot live by bread alone by noting his habits of consuming and thus being sustained by the materials of writing: paper, print and chalk.

might symbolize some form of elucidation) it is more fruitful to think about how this text invokes a material world not least in its reference to the long-standing practice of printers, publishers, editors and authors of placing 'Advertisements' at the start of printed texts.[9] 'Advertisement', however we interpret it, challenges our use of 'text' and its displacement of the written word from the pages of a book into the weave of language. Critics are inclined to notice and use 'front matter' for contextual purposes: place and date of publication, epigraphs and dedications can all yield useful information *about* the text, but are rarely considered as a constitutive part of it, but they are undoubtedly part of the book.[10] Here and elsewhere Carson prompts us to ask where the text begins. 'Advertisement' can be considered as a poem, a comment on consumerism (a parodic 'word from our sponsors'), a wry ironizing of all that follows, or as a reminder of a world beyond the text which consequently foregrounds thresholds, boundaries and limits and their place not just in the thematics of the revised collection (which in its movement from 'The insular Celts' to 'The patchwork quilt' is preoccupied with both the making of material objects – bells, textiles, pottery, quilts and illuminated manuscripts as well as their marginal poems[11] – and the concepts of boundaries, horizons, connections) but also in the book as object. Just as Laurence Sterne's marbled pages in *Tristram Shandy* play with readers' expectations about the conventional outer limits of a text, so Carson's revisions and additions to *The new estate and other poems* signal the importance of thresholds and boundaries, beginnings and endings, and the fact that these are not just conceptual but also apply to the book we hold in our hands. Subsequent collections keep this idea in front of the reader. 'Acknowledgements' (conventionally used to refer to printed sources in later collections) are, in *The Irish for no*, made to oral and musical sources; like *The Irish for no*, *Belfast confetti* is divided into three parts which are preceded by 'Turn again', an arrangement that makes one wonder (as with 'Advertisement') if the poem is somehow separate from the rest of the collection

9 This goes back to at least the eighteenth century when the 'advertisement' could vary from explanations of how the text came into the hands of the printer, publisher or editor (and thence into the reader's hands) through variously modest, apologetic or aggressive statements, to attempts to raise subscription lists for future volumes. Over time this mutates into something more akin to modern advertising and the common, but rarely considered, practice of advertising other books from the same author or publisher (http://galenet.galegroup.com/servlet/ECCO, 30 June 2007). I am grateful to my colleagues Moyra Haslett and Shaun Regan for their advice and comments on this issue. **10** The obvious exception to this generalization is Gerard Genette, *Paratexts: thresholds of interpretation*, trans. Jane E. Lewin, foreword Richard Macksey (Cambridge, 1997); originally *Seuils* (1987), to which I am indebted. **11** The title of 'The insular Celts' may also be a reference to the 'insular' style of script used in Irish and English monasteries.

and, in turn, if the dedication to Carson's father applies just to the first poem or the collection as a whole; either way, this dedication itself is arguably his first (though it is doubled by being made in both Irish and English) since 'Advertisement' displaces the former dedication of *The new estate*. Each part of *Belfast confetti* has its own epigraph, Part Two switches between prose and verse, and the whole collection is interspersed with versions of *haiku*, each attended by a floral symbol. *First language* finds more ways of making us think about book design and layout from the explicit ('"Let me know the details, including Designer, Printer, and the length of run including variables."' 'Sonnet', *Fl*, 44) to the more playful. 'Opus 14' is in fourteen parts and is the fourteenth poem in the collection (counting 'Four Sonnets' as four poems rather than one sequence) and is linked to '*Tak, tak*' since their stanzas are marked by the quill symbol that also appears on the title page. In addition, the collection's versions of sonnets, with their intertextual nod to Paul Muldoon's own games with the look as well as the structure of the sonnet,[12] exemplify John Goodby's comment about Carson's long, wrapped-around lines troubling the eye of anyone used to the conventional layout of lyrics surrounded by clean white margins.[13] *Opera et cetera* has four named parts (and again a first poem, 'Eesti', which is separate from the rest of the collection and enjoins us to 'Listen' rather than to read *Oec*, 8), multiple dedicatees and notes and acknowledgements. While the short line in *Breaking news* is obviously a radical departure for Carson, we should not overlook the shock value of *The twelfth of never* (following on from *The Alexandrine plan*'s 'versions of sonnets by Baudelaire, Mallarmé and Rimbaud') in which the reader of Carson would have found an unfamiliar conventionality, though Carson's habits of revision and repetition – his intra-textuality – are so pronounced here that the reader must constantly flick back and forth through the book to follow words, phrases and characters as they recur.

Carson's most explicit statement about the readerly aspect of his writing appears in *Fishing for amber*:

> As will be clear from the list of sources which follows, *Fishing for amber* is as much about reading as it is about writing. All the books mentioned afforded some inspiration to the writing of my own book: sometimes a mere turn of phrase, or a snippet of information, sometimes significant trains of thought; sometimes whole stories. (*Ffa*, 352)

12 'Muldoon clutched the wheel of a convertible Hillman Imp with the canopy rolled back' ('Sonnet', *Fl*, 44). For Muldoon's games with sonnets, see 'The more a man has the more a man wants', *Quoof* (London, 1983). 13 John Goodby, '"That's another story": Carson redivivus', *Irish*

This statement could, with little amendment, be included in any of his books. Emphasizing the bookish aspects of his work (in both content and appearance) balances the stress that has been placed on Carson's debts to the oral and folk traditions. While those traditions are unquestionably important, the material cultures of literacy and print upon which the design and layout of his collections, just as much as their thematics, also insist are equally important. *Last night's fun*, Carson's brilliant account of traditional music, gives full weight to what we might call the paratextual elements of music-making – from 'the Talk … the Grip … the Truckly-How', through the 'kind of poker' played between musicians on first meeting, the setting for sessions, the instruments used, to the rituals of cigarette smoking[14] – thereby grounding the etherealities of music and talk in material (albeit irretrievable) social particularity. The potential ethereality of 'text' must be similarly materialized in the particularity of Carson's books, something that Carson himself stresses: 'This is the beauty of a text. It is a textile thing, a weave.'[15] In this essay Carson dwells on the smell of books and also on the making of paper. A section on the uses of mummies as torches, as fuel for steam trains, as a source of pigment and ultimately as material for papermaking ensures that no reader of Carson can ever doubt his sense of the material, even bodily nature of text. This aspect of his writing is brought to what is probably its highest pitch in 'The display case':

> 'Take down these words,' she [Hibernia] said, 'that all might
>   know my claim.'
> I opened up a vein and drew my blood for ink –
>
> I'd no accoutrements of writing, save the knife;
> The pen she gave me was a feather from her plumage,
> And my arm the parchment where I'd sign away my life…
> Her full speech is tattooed for all time on my mummied arm,
>
> A relic some girl salvaged from the scaffold
> Where they quartered me. *God keep the Irish from all harm!* (Ttn, 74)[16]

poetry since 1950 (Manchester, 2000), 290–5, 290.   **14** 'the Talk … the Grip … the Truckly-How' is quoted from a piece attributed to Séamus Ennis which appears before the Contents page of *Lnf*, while the phrase 'the rituals of cigarette smoking' is on p. 75.   **15** Ciaran Carson, 'This is what libraries are for' *Dublin Review*, 4 (Autumn 2001), 26–40, 38.   **16** Given the collection's references to transubstantiation as well as this writing on the body, this is strongly reminiscent of *Finnegans wake*: '… this Esuan Menschavik and the first till last alshemist wrote over every square inch of the

This reminds us that bodies and their representations are also readable and Mike Maybin's book, referred to in *The star factory*, has a 1952 photograph of Castle Place (mere yards from the bookshop) in which Carson thinks he recognizes his father, who has been strongly identified with the oral at the start of *The star factory*: the 'realm of [the father's] voice ... extends ... into the space of memory and narrative' *(Tsf,* 1). Unsure about the photograph, Carson phones his brother who, also unsure, then checks it with the father (in Cushendun) and when ('Now, "tomorrow" has become "today"') the father's verdict is returned ('the postman is not him') the photograph 'becomes all dots and chiaroscuro' (*Tsf,* 29).[17] From this it should be evident that 'reading', as well as referring to a specific print-based activity, also encompasses, in Carson's work, all forms of sensory apprehension. Carson could borrow the motto of Irish literature's other great pedestrian, Stephen Dedalus: 'Signatures of all things I am here to read',[18] though Dedalean confidence is frequently undercut, as in this passage, when potential patterns dissolve into 'dots and chiaroscuro' in a Pynchonesque recognition that interpretation can be a paranoid yoking together of unrelated things. We should note, however, that while the father's figure dissolves, what is left is still a postman, and, again following Pynchon, this is a figure of both actual and symbolic import within systems of communication, an anti-*flâneur* whose job is to provide important links in the material culture of print and literacy: 'I am like a postman on his walk, / Distributing strange messages and bills, and arbitrations with the world of talk' ('Second language', *Fl,* 12). Carson's inheritance, his tradition, is therefore (as those 'arbitrations with the world of talk' suggest) both realms: orality and literacy; speech and print; Bélfast and Belfást.[19] Boundaries in Carson's

---

only fools-cap available, his own body, till by its corrosive sublimation one continuous present tense integument slowly unfolded all marry-voising moodmoulded cyclewheeling history (thereby, he said, reflecting from his own individual person life unlivable, trans-accidentated through the slow fires of consciousness into a divi-dual chaos, perilous, potent, common to allflesh, human only, mortal) but with each word that would not pass away the squid-self which he had squirtscreened from the crystalline world waned chagreenold and doriangrayer in its dudhud.' James Joyce, *Finnegans wake* (London, 3rd edn, 1964), 185–6. **17** The stress on time here is worth noting: in an interview with Frank Ormsby on the publication of *Belfast confetti*, Carson noted that 'all the longer poems begin in the present tense, suggesting that their stories are being told *now*' (Frank Ormsby, 'Ciaran Carson interviewed', *Linen Hall Review* 8:1 (Spring 1991), 5–8, 5. Emphasis in original) but the difference between the present tense used by the oral storyteller and its use by a print storyteller is precisely in the reminder in the latter case that there is a significant time lag between the 'now' of telling and the 'now' of reading, a lag necessarily introduced by the 'machinery of books'. **18** James Joyce, *Ulysses* (Oxford, 1993), p. 37. **19** See Patricia Horton, 'From romantic to postmodern', 344–6 on the variations and doublings of Belfast.

work are often uncertain and shifting, so a painting can become a poem ('Whatever sleep it is', *Ifn*, 26–28), and stories, Disney films and dreams can merge into each other ('Bed-time story', *Bc*, 86–88), but the distinctions between these realms remain: listening is not reading, speech is not print, the postman is not a *flâneur*. The result is that, as Stan Smith has put it, Carson is ambilocated: '… always in neither place … between places … in one place which may be Belfast, but always at the same time in many other places, dis-located, relocated, mis-placed, displaced, everywhere and nowhere.'[20]

There is a continuity in Carson's writing which links *The new estate and other poems* to his translation of *The inferno* or *The midnight court*:[21] Just as translation requires a source on which to work, so all writing, Carson's work affirms, is traceable to and a reworking or re-imagining of previous writing (or narrative, or music, or painting, or film, etc). It would be overstatement to see Belfast as a metropolis in the way that Raymond Williams describes it:

> The metropolis housed the great traditional academies and museums and their orthodoxies; their very proximity and powers of control were both a standard and a challenge.[22]

However, what Williams touches on here is the way in which printing and publishing (themselves foundational of the 'great traditional academies and museums and their orthodoxies') have always been urban-centred, have become the tradition of urban life as much as orality is considered as the tradition of rural life.[23] Paradoxically, it is this aspect of the work which gives Carson's writing its authority as something which has never quite been done before. His work, like that of his contemporaries Paul Muldoon and Medbh McGuckian,[24] engages in a deliberated intertextuality, often for the purposes of parody and pastiche, and, while establishing new forms of connection, also challenges established

---

20 Stan Smith, 'Cruising to the podes: Ciaran Carson's virtual realities', in this volume, 107.　**21** Paul Muldoon's teasing intertextual relationship with Heaney is now well-known, but Carson seems to have a relationship with Heaney through translation: both writers have made versions of *Buile suibhne*, Dante and Merriman.　**22** Raymond Williams, *The politics of modernism: against the new conformists* (London, 1989), 44–5.　**23** See Lucien Febvre and Henri-Jean Martin, *The coming of the book: the impact of printing, 1450–1800* (1958) trans. David Gerard, eds. Geoffrey Nowell-Smith and David Wootton (London, 1984), 170–80; and Donald Sassoon, *The Culture of the Europeans from 1800 to the present* (London, 2006), passim, but see especially 'Books were produced and read in cities while the rural classes, rich and poor, remained culturally deprived until the advent of radio and television' (54). Sassoon overstates the case, but seems to have Marx's rural idiocy in mind.　**24** See Shane Murphy, 'Sonnets, centos and long lines, 189–208.

distinctions, most trickily that between the creative and the critical. If a standard critical tactic is to use some critical or theoretical source as a fixed predicate by which to analyse a text, then what happens, this trio seem to ask, if those possible sources are already incorporated into the work in question? Authority is questioned by such tactics and the distinction between the creative work (authored) and the critical work (authoritative) collapses. It is easy, indeed probably glib, to see a connection between such an attitude and the formation of these writers in Northern Ireland during the Troubles, surrounded by uncertainty and violence and yet bombarded by always supposedly authoritative voices – political, journalistic and scholarly: to return to Williams, 'their orthodoxies; their very proximity and powers of control were both a standard and a challenge'. As Carson puts it in another context 'every inch of Belfast has been written-on, erased and written-on again' ('Schoolboys and idlers of Pompeii' *Bc*, 52). In 'Queen's gambit', one of those narrative poems which can never quite be unravelled into its separate strands (despite the best efforts of Alan Gillis)[25], Carson both comments on his own habits of reading and quotation and challenges the authority and orthodoxy of 'commentators' who must equally engage in reading and quotation, by suggesting that everything can ultimately be placed in quotation marks both as acknowledgement of source and as a recognition that history itself can be seen as an ever more ironical set of quotations:

> Making 69 – the year – look like quotation marks, commentators
>   commentating on
>
> The flash-point of the current Trouble, though there's any God's amount
> Of Nines and Sixes: 1916, 1690, The Nine Hundred Years' War, whatever.
>   ('Queen's gambit', *Bc*, 35)

Creative writing, poetry especially, is not and cannot be seen as distinct, as immune to this process, especially as the only alternative is the ultimate full stop: 'Or maybe we can go back to the Year Dot … the Big Bang, releasing … everything into oblivion' ('Queen's gambit', *Bc*, 35).

---

25 Alan Gillis, 'Ciaran Carson: beyond Belfast', in Nicholas Allen and Aaron Kelly (eds), *The cities of Belfast* (Dublin, 2003), 183–98, 188–90. I do not mean to disparage this very helpful reading, so much as to say, in an image from Carson, that the unravelled stories are no more the poem than the strands of a rope are the rope.

Carson's attack on Seamus Heaney's *North* because of its myth-making is well-known, but what is overlooked is that part of the attack on the collection is also an attack on its first readers on the grounds that they thought it could be distinct and immune:

> Everyone was anxious that *North* should be a great book; when it turned out that it wasn't, it was treated as one anyway, and made into an Ulster '75 Exhibition of the Good that can come out of Troubled Times.[26]

The attack on Heaney on the grounds that one cannot escape from the massacre, as Alan Gillis has made clear, calls into question ideas of history and historicity in such a way as to challenge the distinctiveness of poetry.[27] For Carson the aim was never to achieve the (necessarily false) overview that Heaney aimed for: Peter McDonald has pointed out he may be a narrative poet but he is suspicious of the tendency towards coherence generated by narrative.[28] Carson's aim was to set down another version in full knowledge that no one version could ever be adequate:

> But my aim was, in that work which deals with the 'Troubles', to act as a camera or a tape-recorder, and present things in a kind of edited surreality. An ear overhearing things in bars. Snatches of black Belfast humour. If there's one thing certain about what was or is going on, it's that you don't know the half of it. The official account is only an account, and there are many others. Poetry offers yet another alternative. It asks questions, I think. It asks about the truth which is never black-and-white.[29]

This questioning of history and historicity has consequences for ideas of place in Carson's work, especially his poetry. One aspect of his condemnation of Heaney was that the latter suggested that there was another place, or another kind of place to which one could escape. A reading of Carson's work obviously requires an understanding of the place of his writing: the 'mouth of the poem' ('Farset', *Bc*, 49). Many commentators have noted that the urban is itself unusual in the context of the more normal rural places of Irish writing; places which are always ready to slip

---

26 Ciaran Carson, 'Escaped from the massacre?' *The Honest Ulsterman*, 50 (Winter 1975), 183–6, 186.
27 Alan Gillis, 'Ciaran Carson: beyond Belfast', 183–98.   **28** Peter McDonald, *Mistaken identities: poetry and Northern Ireland* (Oxford, 1997), 60–4.   **29** Ciaran Carson in John Brown, *In the chair: Interviews with poets from the North of Ireland* (Cliffs of Moher, 2002), 141–52, 148–9.

metonymically into representations of the authentic nation. If metonym can be described as a way of having the same again (here is a cottage kitchen, the 'West', or a stretch of bogland which is actually the nation itself), Carson's writing (like Muldoon's and McGuckian's) is always interested in the possible something else of metaphor with its interest in both connection and distinction: 'the flight of one thing into the other' ('The insular Celts', *Tne*, 3), or 'changing something into something else' ('Queen's gambit', *Bc*, 36), until eventually 'Everything was neither one thing nor the other' ('Opus operandi', *Fl*, 60). Where metonymic writing assumes that there is a fully knowable entity, a consensual reality, to which one can gain access, metaphorical writing like Carson's is aware of the always absent totality which one is attempting to delineate:[30] his etymological excursus on the Falls Road exemplifies this in that it cannot, with authority, decide on whether the Falls is an enclosure, a limit or a thoroughfare:

> ... the Falls, from the Irish, *fál*, a hedge;
> Hence, *any kind of enclosed thing*, ...
> ... For *fál*, is also *frontier, boundary*, as in *the undiscovered country*
> *From whose bourne no traveller returns*, ...
> ... in other versions of the Falls:
> *A no-go area, a ghetto, a demolition zone.*
>
> ('Hamlet', *Bc*, 105, 106, 107)

The urban in Carson's work is an always absent totality (and its doubled nature – traditional and modern, oral and print, Irish and English, Bélfast and Belfást – is a gesture towards that totality): his details, digressions, revisions and repetitions are a way of coping with the ultimate impossibility of encompassing that totality. The figures who make up 'The exiles' club' (*Ifn*, 45) and who re-appear revised in 'Schoolboys and idlers of Pompeii' (*Bc*, 52–4) are deluded nostalgic obsessives, pedants of place, but also analogues of the poet whose poem and prose piece enact what the exile's club is attempting, in the delineation and cataloguing of place. Such an exercise, the two pieces strongly suggest, is futile since regardless of one's distance from or nearness to, in both a geographical and a historical sense, the places that one is trying to recapture, such a recapturing is itself impossible, not least because of the metamorphic nature of the city.

30 The argument at this point draws upon David Lodge, *The modes of modern writing: metaphor, metonymy, and the typology of modern literature* (London, 1977); and Frederic Jameson, 'Cognitive Mapping', in Cary Nelson and Lawrence Greenberg (eds), *Marxism and the interpretation of culture* (Chicago, 1988), 347–60.

If this seems to be the condition of urban modernity, we should note that the city is also a traditional place. Any performance, musical or narrative, combines the formulaic with the improvisational and can only ever be a gesture towards all the other performances which enable it but the irretrievability of which are also indicated by it as is made clear in *Last night's fun*. Carson's city is both a familiar and a strange place. His city, and his work in general, absorb qualities and features familiar from a Catholic nationalist, and therefore most frequently ruralist, position which is most often seen as traditional.[31] In Carson's writing the juxtaposition of city and tradition leads to consequences for each. Located in the city, Irish traditional culture appears to move from primitivist authenticity to post-modern contingency. By seeming to fit so well into the urban, the claim that tradition is rooted and timeless is challenged and its truer identity, at least for Carson, is revealed. Edna Longley summarizes well the views that Carson elaborates in many places, most notably in *Last night's fun*: 'Carson views "tradition" as always contemporary, always improvised in the present on a unique occasion, yet transmitted down long, multiple, intricate chains from the past'.[32] Rather than tradition appropriating or authenticating the city, its urban existence is used to show the falsity of other definitions of tradition. (This I think settles the argument about whether or not Carson is a post-modernist: he is a traditionalist who insists that we have misunderstood tradition.)[33] In turn the city, represented in and by traditional forms and means, is rendered as a strange place: John Campbell of Mullaghbawn one might say is teaching Walter Benjamin how to get lost in the city. As a strange place and a place of strangers, the city is then an affront to such nationalist predicates as familiarity and the organic community. The city can sustain Irish tradition but as Carson's poetry demonstrates, that tradition will find itself in a shifting equilibrium with literacy, print and capital.

The city in Carson's work cannot therefore be seen as organic or coherent: known places are returned to until such time as the repressed is recalled. Words, phrases and sometimes even whole poems recur and return in Carson's work, either revised or recontextualized. The pairing of 'The exiles' club' and

31 Richard Kirkland, "'The *shanachie* of Belfast and its red-brick Gaeltacht": Cathal O'Byrne', *Bullán* 4:2 (Winter 1999/Spring 2000), 67–82, 72; Richard Kirkland, *Literature and culture in Northern Ireland since 1965: moments of danger* (London, 1996), 38–40. Kirkland makes astute connections between Carson, Cathal O'Byrne (whose *As I roved out* is a foundational text for Carson) and Gerry Adams in this regard. **32** Edna Longley, *The living stream: literature and revisionism in Ireland* (Newcastle upon Tyne, 1994), 60. **33** See Neil Corcoran, *Poets of modern Ireland*, 177ff; Edna Longley, *The living stream*, 52; John Goodby, *Irish poetry since 1950*, 290–5; and Richard Kirkland, *Identity parades: Northern Irish culture and dissident subjects* (Liverpool, 2002), 119.

'Schoolboys and idlers of Pompeii' is such a revised return and many others exist: 'The patchwork quilt' (*Tle*, 13–14) and 'Patchwork' (*Ifn*, 59–63); 'Belfast confetti' (*Ifn*, 31) is the title poem of a collection in which it does not appear except as the related prose piece 'Question Time' (*Bc*, 57–63). *The twelfth of never* (its title already predicted in 'the Twelfth of Nevuary' ('Four sonnets, 2', *Fl*, 23) loops around and between settings (Tokyo, Belfast, France), motifs (the poppy, cigarettes, alcohol), characters ('Of maidens, soldiers, presidents and plants I've sung', 'Envoy', *Ttn* 89) and other connections. Carson's intratextuality is the formal equivalent of those narratives which revisit and return to supposedly known places until such time as they become altered and unfamiliar. The menacing interrogation of 'Question time' (*Bc*, 57–63), for example, follows from a revisiting of past and familiar places which are rendered *unheimlich* through the process of one's knowledge of and familiarity with them being tested. If the bicycle ride of 'Question time' is a return to an originary place, the interrogation makes clear that such a return is impossible for as the litany of place names is repeated so those places become revised versions of themselves, their significance altered irrevocably: what were once the scenes of childhood are now markers of political allegiance. The interrogators proceed on a false principle: by testing the narrator's supposedly organic rootedness in these places, by making him proclaim his familiarity with what they regard as home, they reveal the precariousness of such concepts, and the very effort to hold to the familiar makes it *unheimlich*. The interrogators are appealing to an idea of dwelling, a natural connection between identity and place,[34] which the piece itself challenges: the truly rooted figure, the figure dwelling in a familiar place, could never be subjected to such an interrogation. Consequently, they are actually exhibiting what Manuel Castells has called the 'tribalism of local communities, retrenched in their spaces that they try to control as their last stand against the macro-forces that shape their lives out of their reach'.[35]

The problem for the interrogators is that they think that their map of the city tells the whole story, but the city is always ready to slide metaphorically into another of its aspects. Their 'Troubles' city, no matter how immediate, brutal or overwhelming, is not the only Belfast. As Fran Brearton has shown, this version of the city can be mapped as a Great War battleground or as a warground more generally (a point reinforced by *Breaking news*).[36] Another version of 'Troubles'

34 Martin Heidegger, 'Building dwelling thinking', in *Basic writings*, ed. David Farrell Krell (London, 1978), 323–39, 338. 35 Manuel Castells, 'European cities, the information society, and the global economy,' *New Left Review*, 204 (March/April 1994), 18–32, 29–30. 36 Fran Brearton, 'Mapping

Belfast, in Stan Smith's reading of 'The ballad of HMS *Belfast*' (*Fl*, 71–4), renders the city as both mobile and imprisoning.[37] If the activities of the interrogators in 'Question time' and the various renderings of Belfast are all forms of cognitive mapping, we have to allow for the city as potentially also a map of cognition.

The city's byways and side roads seem, at times, as much mindscape as cityscape. 'Question Time' can be read as introspection as much as interrogation ('I am this map' *Bc*, 63). Its prior version, 'Belfast confetti', reinforces this reading by suggesting that the interrogative voices are at best merely implied: 'Why can't I escape? ... / What is my name? / Where am I coming from? / Where am I going?' (*Ifn*, 31) asks a voice in danger of ending in a 'a mental block of dog-leg turns and cul-de-sacs' ('Queen's gambit' *Bc*, 36). Such hints in Carson's recursive writing initiate an intricate chain of inter- and intra-textual connections. The recurrence of various forms of digression and convolution (which can expand from 'the labyrinth of the thumbprint' ('Four sonnets' I *Fl*, 23) to 'thumb-whorl spiral galaxies' ('Cave quid dicis, quando, et cui', *Oec*, 46) in scale recalls Keats's 'Ode to Psyche' with its uncertain state of consciousness ('Surely I dreamt to-day, or did I see') and its possibility that the poet is addressing himself ('thine own soft-conchèd ear'). The 'fane / In some untrodden region of my mind' with its 'branchèd thoughts' becomes the 'wreathed trellis of [his] working brain'.[38] Keats is not the only poet for whom examination of his state of consciousness is figured as 'wander[ing] in a forest'; Carson has inhabited through translation the visionary figures of both Dante ('I came to in a gloomy wood', *Ti*, 1) and Brian Merriman (in his 'neck of the woods', *Tmc*, 19), and such wanderings in 'the forest of the books of Arden' ('The rising sun', *Ttn*, 20) irresistibly recall *Belfast confetti's* epigraph from Benjamin: 'to lose one's way in a city, as one loses one's way in a forest requires practice'. Even more pertinent is an elided passage: 'Street names must speak to the urban wanderer like the snapping of dry twigs, and little streets in the heart of the city must reflect the times of day for him, as clearly as a mountain valley'.[39] The balance of the familiar and the strange, the traditional and

the trenches: gyres, switchbacks and zig-zag circles in W.B. Yeats and Ciaran Carson', in *Irish Studies Review* 9:3 (Dec. 2001), 373–86. **37** Stan Smith, 'Cruising to the podes', in this volume, 107–25. **38** John Keats, 'Ode to Psyche', *The complete poems*, ed. John Barnard, 3rd edn (London, 1988), 340–2. It is probably unnecessary to note that the Borges stories which seem most relevant to a reading of Carson (e.g. 'Tlön, Uqbar, Orbis Tertius', 'Pierre Menard, author of the *Quixote*', 'The library of Babel') were originally collected in a volume called 'The garden of the forking paths' (1941). See Jorge Luis Borges, *Collected fictions*, trans. Andrew Hurley (New York, 1999). **39** Walter Benjamin, *A Berlin childhood around the turn of the century*, 53–4. This recent edition is a convenient reference, but Neal Alexander, "A fount of broken type: representations of Belfast in prose" (PhD

the modern is as applicable to an individual subjectivity as to a cityscape which, as in 'Ode to Psyche', produces uncertainty about the location of the boundary between interiority and the exterior world. Ultimately, the poetry reserves its right to deploy 'that effect where one image warps into the other' ('Jawbox' *Bc*, 93). Interior becomes exterior, the familiar becomes strange, the traditional becomes modern. Such liminality takes us back to Carson's early versions from the Irish such as 'St Ciaran's island' ('Through the holes in the trellis / Falls thin rain. What drizzles / Slowly into my skull is this' *Tne*, 14) or 'Tuaim inbir' ('My little house is lit / By trickeries of sun and moon … / God … lets his changing skies / As thatch to my roof' *Tne*, 62).

The move from *The new estate* to later volumes is not straightforwardly a move from the rural to the urban. As its title indicates, *The new estate* contains a number of urban poems while *The Irish for no* begins with two poems ('Dresden', 'Judgement') with rural settings. More important is the shift from largely domestic interiors to the very public world of the succeeding volumes: the world of the streets. Buildings are comparatively rare compared to the references to streets, but the most frequently referenced buildings (pubs, mills, shops, libraries, churches, schools, taxi depots and even jails) are public places, and more importantly places of connection and communication – libraries, campaniles, pubs and post offices are typical – but the streets themselves are the places to which the poetry resorts. This stress on the public and on communication is reinforced when one considers that 'home' in Carson's work, as already remarked, provides no refuge, but seems instead to be another kind of dead end. Cul-de-sac is, of course, part of the declension of text, textile, material that Carson so often invokes: other kinds of sack – the mail bag, the flour sack – appear as part of the weave, of the fabric of life (and usually either contain forms of text or are written on), so the 'bottom of the bag' becomes a version of that ultimate limit which cannot be transgressed except by death.

QUB, 2004) is right to suggest that Carson's likeliest source for the epigraph is Susan Sontag's 'Introduction' to *One-way street and other writings* (1979) trans. Edmund Jephcott and Kingsley Shorter (London, 1985), 7–28, 10, where she introduces the passage as cited by Carson with the sentence: 'Reminiscences of self are reminiscences of place, and how he positions himself in it, navigates around it.' An even more suggestive version of the passage can be found in 'A Berlin chronicle': 'But to lose oneself in a city – as one loses oneself in a forest – that calls for a different schooling. Then, signboards and street names, passers-by, roofs, kiosks, or bars must speak to the wanderer like a cracking twig under his feet in the forest, like the startling call of a bittern in the distance, like the sudden stillness of a clearing with a lily standing erect at its centre.' *One-way street and other writings*, 293–346, 298.

The city itself is material as is made clear by Carson's associative chain of 'brick, break, brack': 'Yet even this paradigm of honesty [brick] has its verbal swamp. Its root is in *break*, related to the flaw in cloth known as a *brack*' ('Brick', *Bc*, 72). The city itself is a fabric: 'the wrack resolves itself in skeins and hanks … the knitted, knotted streets' ('John Ruskin in Belfast', *Bc*, 96, 97). This material quality makes the city textile and therefore, in Carson's declension, text ('Belfast Confetti', *Ifn*, 31; 'Linear B', *Ifn*, 33; 'Punctuation', *Bc*, 64). The city then is not just written about or written on, it too is a kind of writing: 'this ubiquitous dense graffiti of public houses, churches, urinals, binding stores, graving docks, monuments, Sunday schools and Orange halls – terraces and terraces of kitchen houses' ('Intelligence' *Bc*, 81). The city also writes: 'the sprawled city-wide Armada of tall mill funnels writing diagonals of smoke across the clarity of our vision'.[40] Its components, regardless of scale, share this ability: tea leaves and trees are both 'calligraphic' ('Jawbox', *Bc*, 91; 'The white devil', *Ttn*, 38). The city is structured like a language, its paradigmatic places – pubs, post offices and prisons – strung along the syntax of its streets: 'It's like a sentence crammed with grammar, phrases, ages, hyphens, stops.' ('Two to tango', *Fl*, 20).[41] Reading the writing of the city, like all reading, leads to more writing: 'Now that I can see the city's microscopic bits transfixed by my attention, I wonder how I might assemble them, for there is no instruction leaflet; I must write it' (*Tsf*, 15).

Urban literacy is, must be in Carson's linguistic economy of the city, accompanied by urban orality. Belfast is a writerly but also a clamorous place – 'a world of talk' ('Second language', *Fl*, 12) – in which everything has its voice. While 'Second language' most directly refers to Carson's acquisition of English, the poem is also about the acquisition of the various languages of the city itself: how the 'Wordy whorls and braids and skeins' unfold themselves. Although various languages can be distinguished, the shape-shifting aspect of things ('Things are kinks … That became a hieroglyphic alphabet') means that they can never quite be disentangled. Adults round the cot 'campaniled above me, and twanged their carillons of bronze', but 'mill-stacks' (in 'sheaves' like corn) can also be 'campaniles'. Between times 'Shipyard hymns' in 'Six-County hexametric' and the products of the ropeworks 'Ratlines, S-twists, plaited halyards, Z-twists, catlines; all had their say.' The Church too has its 'dim bronze noise' but 'Its

---

40 Ciaran Carson in John Kindness, *Belfast frescoes*, with an essay by Ciaran Carson, (Belfast, 1995), np. **41** 'Two to tango' as a mock guide to creative writing helpfully explains how to represent place: 'Aromas, sounds, the texture of the roads, the heaviness or lightness of the air – /All these contribute to the sense of place' (18).

ornate pulpit/Spoke to me in fleur-de-lys of Purgatory.' Textile mills 'pirn and
shuttle in Imperial / Typewriterspeak'. In all of this 'The future looms into the
mouth incessantly' bringing with it 'the noise of years'. Carson assures us that 'the
bell in Belfast's civic coat of arms is a feeble pun' ('Farset', *Bc*, 47), but as the
foregoing suggests, campaniles and carillons ring through his writing giving voice
to the city and making of Belfast an Isle Sonante.[42]

While there is still much to be gained by uncovering intertextualities, Carson's
deliberate display of them suggests that it is not just individual allusions to which
we should attend. Going to specific sources (though with an uninnocent
awareness that they are implicated in both Carson's reading and writing and
therefore in our reading of his writing) is still worth while, but it is as important
to recognise not just that so many of his sources thematize precisely those
concerns of his writing that we would want to analyse but also that taken together
his inter-, intra- and para-textual play is itself part of that thematics. For all that
Carson owes a debt to oral traditions, his paratextual play situates his writing (and
its antecedent reading) in the world of commodity and exchange,[43] the world of
the urban. His version of the city both enables and emerges from this intersection
of traditions and the world of material print culture which it both rests upon and
sustains. The city itself can never be represented in its totality, and all of its aspects
– psychological, material, textile, text – are equally necessary for the voices of and
about the city to speak and to write. Neither the city nor any of its representations
can take precedence then since they are as interdependent as strands in a rope
('For every hempen rope is wound of many strands,' 'Mountain dew', *Ttn*, 42),
as warp and weft in a weave ('this apron weft/And warp of life we strut upon a
brief while ...', 'Oscar', *Oec*, 81). Cul-de-sacs and graveyards abound in Carson's
writing as a reminder of the terminus for every journey ('for I have miles to go:
when I deliver all the letters, that's the text,' 'Z', *Oec*, 36), and his recursive style
acts as a form of resurrection allowing the city 'the realm of the Metamorphoses'
to 'burgeon ... with versions of our species' ('Sod of death', *Ttn*, 23). Carson's
work is therefore less an effort to represent Belfast, or the urban more generally,
than a participation in the urban: his work is as much an affirmation of
citizenship as it is writing and it is citizenship in the way that it seeks to examine

42 François Rabelais, *Gargantua and Pantagruel*, trans., ed., intro., & notes M.A. Screech (London,
2006), 891–911.   **43** Neil Corcoran, *Poets of modern Ireland*, 187–8 provides a list of some of the
brand names used in *The Irish for no* noting that they are often nostalgically and evocatively used,
while delineating a commodity culture which encompasses everything from, say, perfume to military
accessories: 'Or maybe it's the name you buy, and not the thing itself.' ('Calvin Klein's *Obsession*', *Ifn*,
25).

the city as 'the space in which … in our time, the perplexity of the living is most acutely experienced'.[44]

The city, we might say, is a metaphor for the city. Like Andrei Bely's St Petersburg, Carson's Belfast can be at its most basic a point, whether a small black dot on a map or a full stop, since that one mark is itself only possible when print exists and print is possible only when the city exists:

> Petersburg not only appears to us, but actually does appear – on maps: in the form of two small circles, one set inside the other, with a black dot in the center; and from precisely this mathematical point, which has no dimension, it proclaims forcefully that it exists: from here, from this very point surges and swarms the printed book.[45]

---

44 Homi Bhabha, *The location of culture* (London, 1994), 169–70.   45 Andrei Bely, 'Prologue', *Petersburg* (1922), trans., annotated & intro. Robert A. Maguire and John E. Malmstad (Bloomington and Indianapolis, 1978), 2.

Cruising to the podes: Ciaran Carson's virtual realities*

STAN SMITH

'Its map is virtual reality' ('Letters from the Alphabet': 'A', *Oec*, 11)

AMBILOCATIONS

Reviewing Richard Murphy's *The kick* in a piece called, with characteristic wordplay, 'Murphy's lore', Ciaran Carson was seized by the fact that Murphy's mother was 'ambidextrous',

> and it was all the same to her whether she wrote backwards or forwards. She used to have to ask someone on which side of a blank page she ought to begin. When asked to state her nationality on forms in Ireland during the Second World War, she used to write 'British and Irish'. The family believed that no one spoke English as well as the Anglo-Irish, and that the Anglo-Irish were the best administrators in the Empire.[1]

Murphy's father was the last British mayor of Colombo, so that, as a boy, travelling repeatedly between Ceylon and Ireland, says Carson, 'He was shuttled back and forth for some years between these two extremes of climate, like a kind of hyphen.' Finally, Carson touches on a third aspect of Murphy's identity, remarking that, 'Sexually ambivalent, he managed to marry happily, at least for a while.' These three discrete elements clearly connect in Carson's imagination, making up a kind of conceptual rhyming triplet. Ambidextrous, sexually ambivalent, and, a usage I want to coin here, in the manner of Carson, 'ambilocated'. Ambilocation, I would propose, is a different condition from mere 'bilocation', the mysterious capacity to be in two places at once. Rather it's a matter of being always in neither place, or of being between places, or of being always in one place which may be Belfast, but also at the same time in many other places, dis-located, relocated, mis-placed, displaced, everywhere and nowhere, evincing what 'All the

---

* This is a version of the concluding chapter of Stan Smith, *Irish poetry and the construction of modern identity* (Dublin, 2005), 203–19, reprinted by permission of the author and publishers. **1** Ciaran Carson, 'Murphy's Lore', *The Guardian*, 3 August 2002.

better to see you with' calls 'just that air / Of neither-here-nor-thereness. Coming in the act of going' (*Bc*, 23).

The theme is ubiquitous in Carson's writings, summed up in the report of the poem 'Alibi' (*Oec*, 56) that everywhere 'murder is done', which prompts the questions, 'Was I there?' and, if not, 'Where was I then?', only to recognize that in the end 'we are accomplices to all assassinations', and have no alibi. It is not always a comfortable place to be, may indeed be a place of intimidation and putative violence. 'Jawbox' (*Bc*, 90), for example, speaks of how, travelling on an Ulsterbus, 'the border passes through him / Like a knife, invisibly', and of being trapped in the 'Small transgressions', 'caught between "Bel*fast*" and "*Bel*fast", as if in the accordion pleats between two lurching carriages [of a train] / Banging, rattling, threatening', with 'terrifying glimpses' of the tracks below.

What links all three of Murphy's doublenesses is indicated by the phrase 'like a kind of hyphen'. This is an original variation on Stephen Gwynn's famous description of Anglo-Irishness as a form of 'spiritual hyphenation'. For whereas the ambidextrous analogy would suggest a poet both British and Irish, 'a kind of hyphen' rules out both, stranding him in the mere moment of transit between the two, neither both at once nor just one thing or the other, but simply a place where one passes over, is translated, between two worlds. History has many cunning passages, but this moment of passage, this place of transit, is one of the darkest and yet most illuminating places to be, a 'disembodied interim' like that spoken of in 'The wind that shakes the barley' (*Ttn, 32*). It's a space that Carson, speaking, as the title of one poem puts it, a 'Second language' (*Fl*, 10) has clearly made his own.

This space of hyphenation, not of hyphenated being but of being a hyphen, is given a specifically Northern Irish inflection in that chilling little poem in *Belfast confetti* (1989), 'Last orders', its very title loitering between the profane world of the bar and the sacred one of holy orders, with an apocalyptic suggestion of 'last things', personal and collective mortality, its resonating ambiguities connecting, too, with that infamous phrase of morally incompetent self-exculpation, 'just obeying orders'. The poem is a discourse of *double entendres*. The buzzer for the fortified bar is like a trigger, the doorman's spyhole is like rifle sights, and the 'click' of the door opening might be that of a killer's trigger. The whole experience, that is, is a kind of semantic Russian roulette, in which you can't be sure whether it will be the loaded cylinder that the next sentence discharges. We hold our breath, fearing that the playful similes may turn deadly literal. If events are this unpredictable, such chance differences can determine wholly different timelines: a bullet or a bomb now would alter many lives. Likewise the unreliability of language can generate innumerable possible meanings, semantic lines. But this works both ways. Those inside the bar, who take the risk of opening the door to a stranger, might be the victims, not the perpetrators of murder. They too are playing Russian roulette. The way in which the 'sudden lull' suggests both anxiety and the sullen lull of hostility, and the half-rhyme that picks this up to make the barman's lolling head, inviting an order, suggest the lolling head of a corpse, is then taken up by the innocuous neutrality of *Harp* lager, putatively Danish, yes, and therefore beyond all this fiddle, but – harping on it – a musical instrument that might be ordered for a performance in that 'Kingdom Come' to which they might all be blown. Looking daggers in a sectarian Bushmills bar mirror emphasizes the identity in difference of these opposed 'orders'. If 'Taig's written on [his] face', this is not something the speaker can control, simply a facticity he is fated to. Everything is being read here, but nothing is said beyond the laconic call to last orders. Inhabiting that realm of the hyphen between opposing loyalties, these faces along the bar meet through a mirror, as if, as in Auden's 'September 1, 1939', they are meeting their own complicit reflections. But this encounter also signals a momentary truce in the looking-glass war. What they all share, as human beings, is that they're dying for a drink.

Carson's most remarkable achievement in this poem lies in his deployment of those modest little pronouns, those humble parts of speech round which the whole poem is structured. The second line is skilfully constructed to follow the 'but' which ends a line where, because of the imperative, no prenomial subject is identified: 'It's someone else who has you in their sights'. 'Someone else' is the real subject of this sentence, but it takes second place to the impersonalizing 'It's', and is then dispersed into plurality by the colloquial use of 'their'– not because the poem wants to be politically correct about gender, but because this 'someone else' is not a person but a faceless representative of a collective other. The 'you' spoken of in the next line takes on a similar generality, since it's not really 'you', the unique and actual person, but 'one', a collective alterity, that is the subject of this knowledge, or this ignorance, a dispersal into anonymous collectivity underlined by 'who's who, or what …' The poem then comes clean about its dissolution of real subjects into figures, instances in an argument, almost algebraic in their representativeness: 'I, for instance, could be anybody.' The point is that, to these others, who don't know him from Adam, he *is* anybody, just as each of the others is to *him*. Everybody is, from another point of view, anybody. It's within such alienating distances that the bombers and the gunmen operate, reducing each unique other to a generalized otherness, a disembodied interim, abstract cipher: 'anybody', or 'any body'.

The pronouns operate with some subtlety: 'I'm told' (passive recipient of advice from an unspecific other who is merely the agent of the telling – 'they say'); 'See me', a colloquial invitation to look which is really just a way of identifying the self as speaker; the italicized, apparently determining '*I*', insisting on his own uniqueness and particularity, at the very centre of the poem. The juxtaposed 'me / I' quietly emphasizes that double dimension in which we exist, the hyphen between subject and object, self for self and self for others, as that buttonholing 'See' invites in the reader as companion, to become part of that threatened, but also threatening, 'us/ we' who order *Harp*. But if *Harp* is safe because unsectarian, 'everybody drinks it', that everybody briefly collectivized as a unity is then at once dispersed by the reappearance of a solitary and hostile 'someone' who looks daggers at 'us', the momentary community of thirst falling into sectarian division again. 'Someone', however, has not yet finished its political business. In the opening sentence it was 'someone else who has you in their sights', and then 'someone' who looks daggers at 'us' – you and I facing a hostile anonymity of faces. The penny drops differently: 'how simple it would be for someone' – a pause on the enjambment holding off the dénouement – 'Like ourselves to walk in and blow the whole place, and ourselves, to Kingdom Come.' There are multiple perspectives here, and that even smaller and even more insignificant word, 'like', is what hits the spot. 'Someone else', yes, but also 'someone / Like ourselves', in Baudelairian, Eliotic terms, 'hypocrite lecteur, mon semblable, mon frère.' Someone like ourselves could blow the whole place, and ourselves, to Kingdom Come. But speaker and addressee, us, might be just some such other, someone like their selves, for the men already in the bar. Carson's masterly deployment of pronouns enacts a whole political history of alienation and mutual hostility, within a gapped culture where all of them, united by the strife which divides them, inhabit the last, secret order of the hyphen.

Carson had used the metaphor of hyphenation – not of being hyphenated, but of being a hyphen – in another more overtly political commentary in the bar-room setting of 'Barfly' in the same volume. The buttonholing barfly invites us to figure why The Crown and Shamrock and the Rose and Crown bars are at opposite ends of town, but dismisses the presumed reply, 'Politics? The odds change. The borders move. / Or they're asked to', by shifting at once to the anecdote of an armed raid on a bar earlier that evening. 'I buzzed off', the barfly tells us, his metaphoric vocation turning suddenly literal, a Lord of the Flies looking for trade: 'So now, I am a hyphen, flitting here and there: between / The First and Last'.

Carson's a fly guy – like Beelzebub. There are plenty of flies on, or, rather in, his poetry. Another fly may indicate what's going on here – that which in 'Graecum est: non legitur' in *Opera et cetera* (1996), in a dive-bombing rendezvous with the page on which the poet is writing, 'made an audible syzygy'. Originally, according to the *OED*, meaning 'conjunction', the word is 'Now extended to include both conjunction and opposition'. Carson's initial sense here would seem to be that of the next definition: 'the conjunction of two organisms without loss of identity', that last word alerting us to a possibly political dimension. But in his poetry, reality regularly enters into a syzygy, 'both conjunction and opposition', with fantasy, literal with metaphoric. This is what I mean by ambilocation.

WHICH BRINGS US TO THE PODES

Carson's virtual HMS *Belfast* is manned, in apparently unsectarian fashion, by 'Both Catestants and Protholics', the playful transposition suggesting the interchangeability of these opposing creeds but also, perhaps, the fatuousness of their antithesis – in other words, that syzygy which is 'both conjunction and opposition'. But the poem, which sails out on imaginary voyages to some of the places where the real HMS *Belfast* saw service, returns at the end to find its speaker waking up, not bound away but 'bound in iron chains', 'on board the prison ship Belfast', still in dock in 'old Belfast'. The real *Belfast* did manage to elude the wreckers' yard, after all its sailings, on the Arctic Convoy to Archangel during the war, and in the Far East after it, acting in 1947 as the relay station for messages to the sloop *Amethyst* beset by Chinese Communist forces a thousand miles up the Yangtse. These elements of the ship's history are obliquely alluded to in the redundancy of taking 'Ice to Archangel, tea to China, coals to Tyne' (the last variant characteristically altering the proverbial cliché, 'coals to Newcastle'), and in the reference to those 'imperceptible horizons, where amethyst / Dims into blue'. HMS *Belfast* survives, however, not as a prison ship in Belfast harbour but as a museum ship in the Pool of London. The conjunction and opposition of museum and prison proposes, as so often in Carson's poetry, that memory can be a prison-house where the subject, fixated on recall as if identity depended on it, is actually thwarted, erased, cancelled by the very proliferation of calls to remember, as the prose poem 'Schoolboys and idlers of Pompeii' spells out:

> At times it seems that every inch of Belfast has been written-on, erased, and written-on again: messages, curses, political imperatives, but mostly names, or nicknames [...] cancelling each other out in their bid to be remembered. *Remember 1690. Remember 1916. Most of all. Remember me. I was here. (Bc, 52)*

That poem ends by asking 'Where does ... memory falter, and imagination take hold?' – the same preoccupation which underlies the syzygy of actual and virtual realities in 'The ballad of HMS *Belfast*'.

If, on board ship, 'Some sang of Zanzibar and Montalban, and others of the lands unascertained / On maps', the former name probably recollects the ship's ceremonial role in Tanganyikan (subsequently Tanzanian) independence. 'Montalban', however, though in the Philippines, and therefore the Antipodes, may refer instead, as part of that interweaving of fantastic and actual voyages, to the actor Ricardo Montalban, who played the eponymous villain in the *Star trek* movie *The wrath of Khan*, who was also the mysterious host on the TV series *Fantasy island*, an intermediary between the ballad's references to contemporary sci-fi, 'boldly go[ing] where none had gone before', Keats's travels in the Homeric 'realms of gold' and Jules Verne's Nemo ('No-one', the alias of Odysseus also), captain of the *Nautilus*. Such an interweaving of canonical poetry, science fiction and historical actuality is signalled near the start of the ballad, which speaks of the ship being 'full-rigged like the *Beagle*, piston-driven like the *Enterprise* / Express; each system was a back-up for the other, auxiliarizing verse with prose', and the train link between Dublin and Belfast with Darwin and Captain Kirk.

A subsequent couplet extends the wordplay:

> We've been immersed, since then, in cruises to the Podes and Antipodes;
> The dolphin and the flying fish would chaperone us like aquatic aunties
> ...

This is an attention-seeking rhyme. If you remove 'pode' from the middle of the first word, it would constitute (in Northern Ireland as in my own North of England, anyway), a *rime riche*: 'Antis / aunties'. The 'pode' we might say, is a hyphen thrusting itself between 'anti' and 'is'. And this reinforces the whimsicality of that neologism, 'podes'. For of course there is – or was – no such word. And yet it's an eminently sensible word to envisage. For if there is an 'Antipodes', there should, surely, be a 'podes' for them to be antithetical to?

The *OED* gives as a primary definition of 'antipodes': 'Places on the surface of the earth directly opposite to each other, or the place which is directly opposite to another (*esp.* to our own region)', and, by transference, 'the exact opposite of a person or thing', with a nice quotation from Bacon, 'He will never be one of the Antipodes, to tread opposite to the present world.' The podes, then, would be the opposite of an opposite. They are an imaginary location, constructed by a process of back formation from the Antipodes. What the 'Ballad' calls 'lands unascertained' are then, like More's Utopia, William Morris's Nowhere, or Samuel Butler's Erewhon, precisely no place at all. And yet, if the 'antipodes' are the geographical opposite of where we are, then where we are should be the podes. A supposedly 'actual' world, that is, is displaced by an imaginary and 'unascertained' one, that linguistically constructed 'virtual reality' spoken of in the first poem of the sequence 'Letters from the Alphabet' (*Oec,* 11–36), an imagined, imaginary, realm, where fantasy, memory and actuality interpenetrate in kaleidoscopic variations.

Back formation is a recurrent practice in Carson's poetry. Think, for example, of how Horse Boyle gets his name, in 'Dresden': 'Horse Boyle was called Horse Boyle because of his brother Mule; / Though why Mule was called Mule is anybody's guess' (*bHMSB,* 13). And this imaginary identity is related to the story-telling fantasies which this, as so many of the poems, articulates, though in this case the story-line is called back as soon as uttered: 'I stayed there once, / Or rather, I nearly stayed there once. But that's another story.' 'Nearly' here is that hyphen between actual and imaginary, the slash that splices either/or, that intervenes between this story and another one. In 'Second language' we're told that, for the young Carson, the Araphahoes 'whooped and hollered in their unforked tongue' (*Fl,* 10). But this last phrase, while it obviously alludes to Heaney's use in *North* of the 'forked tongue' as an image of Northern Irish duplicities, is actually a back-formation, for it infers that the Araphaho can cast the white man as speaking with a forked tongue only by contrast with their own 'unforked' tongue. Carson, born into an Irish-speaking family in Belfast, found his own tongue hyphenated from the start by this English/Gaelic duality.

The poem 'Opus 14' asks:

> Did you know that 'the set of all objects describable in exactly eleven English words' Is called an 'R-Set'? I didn't. It was dreamed up by the people who put the 'surd' in 'absurd'.

> (*Fl,* 31)

Though the phrase in quotation marks would seem to belong to this set (it comprises exactly eleven words) its apparent autoreferentiality falls apart on examination, since it is not the description of an object but the naming of a category. This conceptual absurdity is carried further by the subsequent comment, which has its own sting in the tail. For 'surd', which might appear, like 'podes', to be a word created by back formation from its opposite, 'absurd' ('away from the surd') actually precedes, historically – just – 'absurd' (earliest instances, according to the *OED*, 1551 and 1557 respectively). Nor, in fact, is it its opposite. The *OED* records of 'surd' that, originally meaning 'deaf' and / or 'mute', 'The mathematical sense "irrational" arises from L. *surdus* being used to render Gr. *alogos* … *Math*. Of a number or quantity (esp. a root): That cannot be expressed in finite terms of ordinary numbers or quantities: = irrational.' The *OED* glosses 'absurd' as 'Inharmonious. Out of harmony with reason or propriety; in mod. use, plainly opposed to reason.' In other words, 'absurd' and 'surd', far from being antithetical, the one a departure from the other, come punningly down to the same thing. But this is an illusory concordance, since 'irrational' in mathematics does not have its everyday significance.

There is a moral here for Carson's poetry. Whether you stay on the surd and narrow or depart from it, you are wandering in absurdity. Antitheses turn out not to work like that at all. Binaries dissolve themselves into multiplicity, incompatible overlapping alternatives. Or, as the poem '*Opus operandi*' observes, depicting the antipathetic Paddies and Billies struggling to understand 'the concept "Orange"', and 'the deep grammar of the handshake, the shibboleths of *aitch* and *haitch*' at an empathy class for expectant fathers, 'Everything was neither one thing nor the other' (*Fl*, 60). As Carson says of his blue-black Quink in 'Loaf', 'I liked the in-between-ness of it, neither / One thing nor the other' (*Bc*, 15).

As that 'Cathestans and Protholics' in 'HMS *Belfast*' indicates, Carson is not much enamoured of the simple dualities of identity politics. Antitheses and oppositions figure regularly in his writing only to be deconstructed into plurality. The structuralist binary gets short shrift in the opening poem of the sequence 'Et cetera', 'Auditque vocatus Apollo', in which the observations by his guide on the ascent of Parnassus are immediately subverted by the poet's silly answers and runaway fancy: '*Our mind*, he said, *is split*. Too true. Like he was Quee and I was Queg – // One of those guys. Orpheus. Apollo. Rilke. Ahab, Dick'. The list overflows itself with subversive non-partners, splitting Queequeg into a non-existent couple, substituting Orpheus for Dionysus as the usual antithesis to Apollo, and then dislocating the chain of signification altogether by throwing in

Rilke, the author of *Sonnets to Orpheus*, before undercutting the whole idea by comically curtailing Moby Dick to a supposed surname (a kind of back formation, this) in a ludicrous coupling as a 'guy' with his pursuer Ahab. The poem lurches further into absurdity with the suggestion that 'climbing Mount / Olympia is like that', where not only have we shifted from the mountain of the Muses to that of the gods (poetry versus power), but in the process have got its name wrong, since Olympia, the site of the Olympic games, is on a level plain, while the gods (allegedly) live on Olymp*us*. But this is nothing beside the absurdity of 'enquiring for the whale' on a mountain.

Both whale hunt and ascent conjoin as apparently unending and fruitless quests, for 'You think you've reached the summit when another distant crest / Appears to challenge you. *Quo vadis?* Something like that.' This I take to be the point of the sequence title, 'Et cetera' – 'and the rest' – a potentially endless proliferation of associations on which a restless language puns in 'I asked if we could rest'. If the god appears at the very moment of giving up, announcing, in the last words of the poem '*It's me. Apollo*', this is because, in a slickly autorefer-ential move, the poem about trying to write a poem has somehow been written in the process of lamenting its elusiveness. (Carson glosses the Latin tag, from Virgil's *Georgics*, as 'and Apollo hears when invoked'.) But there remains the rest of the sequence, all those other et ceteras to pursue, mountains to climb, whales to hunt, words to pin down, those 'something[s] like that' which are the very embodiment of difference in their parade of approximate similitude.

As the poem over the page, '*Vox et praeterea nihil*' ('a voice and nothing more'), proposes, 'the notes / Are always different, though the tune remains the same; the "quotes" are really "unquotes."' The Podes, that is, are simultaneously the Antipodes, and yet, as with the campanologists of this poem, they are also '– invariably – [...] out of synch on dangling long / Elastic ropes, though all are trying hard to tell their *Ding an sich* from *dong*.' The elastic ropes of language (a better metaphor than the iron chain of signifiers), permit that dodgy pulling of dong into binary coupling with *Ding*, in a discourse which is always out of synch with the thing itself, which explains, the poem ends, 'why the same refrain is always various', sameness and difference in one *Ding* the very stuff of meaning.

Carson seems as happy amidst the infinite indeterminacies of post-structuralism as a leprechaun in clover, proclaiming in 'Mountain dew' that 'everything can be contained in anything', as 'dragons are implicit in the dragonfly', that 'For every line you write are countless thousands not', and that 'For all the prophets claim, the end is never nigh' (*Ttn*, 42). Language runs away with meaning. It is always, in that recurrent image, 'out of synch' with the real. There can be, in reality, no 'Narrative in black and white', despite the claim implied made by the poem of that title in *Belfast confetti*. It's easy to 'misconstrue' blurred reconstructions, the poem argues, and all one usually encounters in any narrative is 'a faded diagram from which / You'd try to piece together what the action was' (another instance of a kind of back formation). In tale-telling as in telling tales, it continues, 'people don't go shooting off their mouths like that'. However, at times language can dive-bomb shockingly into the thing itself, as metaphor (literally, a carrying across) turns murderously actual, carrying us across that frontier to a place where words are taken literally, and mouths are really shot off. Earlier in the same volume, 'The mouth' had already opened up the idiomatic cliché which concludes 'Narrative in black and white'. 'There was this head had this mouth he kept shooting off', biting off 'more than he could chew.' The poem concludes, chillingly, with the literal application of the metaphor, the indiscreet gossiper's face blown off by (wordplay insinuates) Provisional gunmen. Carson here makes a literal application, too, of his usually playful rhetorical trick, the face of the murdered man reconstructed, by back formation, from the tooth marks in the last apple he ever ate by – the malapropism a final insult to 'what he used to be' – the 'Forscenic lab'.

THE GROVES OF BLARNEY

The question, '*Was it a vision or a waking dream?*', that opens the title poem of *The Irish for no* (1987) calls up Keats as a drugged or drunken companion in hyphenland, and the joky intertexts that pervade the poem place everything within 'the dangling / Quotation marks of a yin-yang mobile'. But though the poem 'slips away to perilous seas as things remain unsolved', confronting the death – murder or suicide? – of the UDR corporal on the headland, or the Belfast businessman with thirteen Black and Decker drill-holes in his head, the one phrase from its Keatsian repertoire that it doesn't open charmed casements on to is 'fairy lands forlorn'.

It's precisely this domain that's addressed by *The twelfth of never*, in 1999. The volume explores a fantasy island which, like the island of Dr Moreau, is 'the realm of the Metamorphoses, / Whose shapes are as innumerable as Chaos / Ever burgeoning with versions of our species'. The labyrinthine intertextuality of this poem finds its guiding thread in calling up Keats, Coleridge, De Quincey and other Romantics as the connoisseurs of a chaos where the dreams and visions of

Romance metamorphose into the Nightmare Life-in-Death and Belle Dame sans
Merci of addictive political traditions. Those twee eighteenth-century personifications, 'Hibernia' and 'Erin', the sentimental repertoire of Irish popular and
patriotic song, and the kitsch pooka, cluricaine, and leprechaun, lead astray
tourists and terrorists alike in pursuit of fairy gold at the end of the rainbow. The
Irish theme-pub called 'The Elfin Grot', where 'Karaoke singers mouth their lip-
synch rhymes' in the Keats-baiting poem 'Hippocrene', is less likely to be located
in Ireland than in that Japan which is one of the sequence's ambilocations. This
simulacrum of Ireland and Irishness can be displaced to an oriental antipodes
because it only ever really existed in discourse, fantasy, drunken delusion. One can
cruise to these Irish podes anywhere. 'Hibernia' can beckon from across the sea if
one drinks too much green tea below the snows of Fujiyama ('Green tea'); one can
enter an Irish Paradise by going with the flow, 'Fuelled by Japanese poteen and
sticks of joss', in a Japanese shebeen ('Sod of death').

What the sequence explores is a karaoke politics lip-synched by nationalist and
unionist alike, addicted to a 'Tape-loop music' for which Kafka's absurdist 'K is
the leader of the empty orchestra of karaoke.' Of the many names the sequence
offers for this fantasy realm, the most comprehensive is 'The groves of Blarney',
for it suggests the extent to which the Ireland of both major traditions, and of
internal and external perception, is a rhetorical and self-deluding construct, a set
of interpenetrating, interactive tall tales and fairy stories on or off the native soil,
where the fetichised icons of allegiance come with authorizing narratives attached,
whether the Stickies' 1916 lily or the Loyalists' 1914–18 poppy. The archetype of
martyred heroism is actually an otherworldly phantasm, 'The Man-from-god-
knows-where'. Humble praties can be retrospectively mythologized, through the
rear-view mirror of the 1840s, into glamorously addictive poppies in the poem
'1798', where Keats's fairy beldam, encountered in 'the garden where the poppies
grow', 'suck[s] the broken English from my Gaelic tongue'. 'Fear' sums up all
these mythical beasts and succubi, 'the gremlins that have colonized my brain', in
terms of Lewis Carroll's comic creation: 'I fear the Jabberwock, whatever it might
be'. As in 'Sunderland and Spencer', the coy periphrases and sentimental
personifications of an eighteenth-century discourse recruit acolytes 'smitten by the
lovely Erin, who'd / Seduced them by her words of faery glamour'. The reality is
that of the hanged man in 'Spraying the potatoes', with 'popping eyes of
apoplectic liberty'.

But the sequence's central concern is with what the title of one sonnet calls
'The legions of the dead', whether their icons of allegiance are 'The hand cut off

and thrown to the Ulster shore' or 'The harp that once resounded in the High King's hall'. Both alike belong to 'The indecipherable babble of days of yore', the schmaltzy archaism of the phrase sufficient commentary:

> Their armies were composed of hieroglyphic men
> Like us, who marched through history, and saw kings fall.
> Opposing soldiers are at one within our regimen.

As 'Banners' puts it, 'dear old Ireland: / Fields of corpses plentiful as dug potatoes'. '1798' allows Carson to make a brilliant and daring leap, via 'The year of the French' (the title of another sonnet), to the 'Galactic battalions of those fallen in war' from a Pharaonic Egypt rediscovered by Napoleon's archaeologists, through his invasion of Russia, to the battlefields of Flanders and on beyond the present to Star Wars of the future. All have died, or will die, 'Envoy' suggests, for nothing, for 'high cockelorum', the imaginary land of Cockaigne where 'everything is slightly out of synch'. The punning allusion to 'cocaine' echoes back to the tramps' Big Rock Candy Mountain of the opening sonnet, and implicates all the other drugs that have created delusory allegiances, addictions and intoxications throughout the sequence (to name a few, poppy, 'the emblem of Peace and the Opium Wars', tobacco, 'Catmint tea', 'Green tea', 'Belladonna', 'Drops of brandy', 'Wallop', 'Mountain dew', 'Saké', 'Digitalis', 'Milk of paradise', 'Crack', 'Doctor ecstasy'):

> With their long ladder propped against the gates of Heaven,
> They've queued up to be rewarded for their grand endeavour,
> And receive their campaign haloes on the Twelfth of Never.

'Tib's eve' speaks of this fantasy Ireland as a realm 'Where everything is metaphor and simile', where the adjective 'green' valorizes all impossibilities, like the linguistic philosopher's hypothetical 'green rose', and Zeno's paradox creates an intercalated space and time that's a paradise for stumbling somnambulists. But as 'Twelfth day' makes clear, this volume is not a sectarian tract. The Shakespearian fairies with which the sonnet opens mutate rapidly into the 'tiny Arcadians' of a lilliputian world such as the ambilocated Swift imagined, 'troops of little fellows marching up and down … as if transistorised', 'the whole field pulsing like an Orange drum'.

The 'glorious twelfth', another fantasy time replete with its baggage of myths, is also a variant on the Twelfth of Never, since it never really existed except in discourse. The Battle of the Boyne actually took place on the First of July 1690, but an adjustment was made when eleven days were lost with the change from Julian to Gregorian calendar in 1752. The absurdity of this iconic achronism compounds the definition offered in the book's epigraph from *Brewer's dictionary of phrase and fable*, a non-time to match the back-formed, utopian no-place of the Podes:

> St Tib's Eve. Never. A corruption of St Ubes. There is no such saint in the calendar as St Ubes, and therefore her eve falls on the 'Greek Calends', neither before Christmas Day nor after it.

This is not as straightforward as it sounds. The 'original' of St Tib is the St Ubes of which it is a corruption. But if St Ubes doesn't exist either, it is in a sense a back formation from St Tib, as the eve – the night before – of St Tib is in turn a back formation from the non-existent saint's day, and the 'Greek Calends' are a non-existent back formation from the actual Roman Calends. Similarly, Brewer's apparently paradoxical last sentence is skewed into a kind of commonsense by verbal slackness. For if St Tib's Eve is neither before nor after Christmas day, the unintended implication is that it could be Christmas Day itself, that Saturnalian time of intercalated merriment when the world is turned upside down and another mythic saint, Santa Claus, briefly (mis)rules. The Twelfth of Never also, of course, suggests Twelfth Night, another eve of transition and reversal that connects, in the sonnet 'Twelfth day', with the syzygial 'Glorious Twelfth' of Unionist celebration.

The twelfth of never opens with a recollection of that Victorian pseudo-archaism which bedevilled generations of schoolchildren: 'There is a green hill far away, without a city wall' ('Tib's eve'). Why on earth would anyone expect a green hill to *have* a city wall in the first place? The double meaning of 'without' – outside, as well as lacking – confirms Carson's vision of the world as a nexus of hermeneutic cruces. But it's interesting that this schoolboy puzzle finds an echo of sorts in another problematic inversion in the sequence's final sonnet, its title, following on from 'The ambassadors', suggesting it's about a diplomatic 'Envoy', when it turns out to be a parting *Envoi*: 'These words the ink is written in is not indelible'. The word order is clearly out of synch here, as the lack of agreement in the verb confirms, and this leads to a confusion of ends and means (words / ink). In scholarly fashion one should perhaps note: '*scilicet*. The ink these words are written in is not indelible'.

Is this a misprint, or a breaking theme? If, as the next line tells us, 'every fairy story has its variorum', every sentence can be re-phrased, even though some rephrasings are just plain wrong. What Carson is doing here is underlining the textuality of the whole bundle of ideological narratives he's been negotiating, by reminding us of the textuality of the sequence itself, as prone to misprints and misprisions as are the conflicting 'histories' it deconstructs. For, as the octet concludes, 'the printed news is always unreliable.'

THE TWILIGHT ZONE

A bundle of aphorisms:

(1) 'The world', said Wittgenstein, 'is everything that is the case.'
(2) 'The limits of my language mean the limits of my world.'
(3) 'Philosophy is a battle against the bewitchment of our intelligence by means of language.'
(4) 'What is your aim in philosophy? – To show the fly the way out of the fly-bottle.'
(5) 'What can be said at all can be said clearly; and whereof one cannot speak thereof one must be silent.'

This isn't particularly erudite. These five magical and familiar one-liners are the philosopher's total *oeuvre*, as collected in *The Concise Oxford dictionary of quotations* (1993). Carson's poetry enters into complex negotiations with all of them, seeking to show all those Irish flies that buzz around his poetry the way out of their fly bottle. And he does this by speaking clearly about the host of confused sayings that constitute the dark passages of a culture, and by refusing to remain silent about that of which, one might be warned, it would be better not to shoot off one's mouth. Carson's natural element, that is, is that Pynchonesque 'interface' he writes of in the prose poem 'Intelligence', where

> We track shadows, echoes, scents, prints; and in the interface the information is decoded, coded back again and stored in bits and bytes and indirect addressing; but the glitches and gremlins and bugs keep fouling-up, seething out from the hardware, the dense entangled circuitry of back streets, backplanes, while the tape is spooling and drooling over alphanumeric strings and random-riot situations […] (*Bc*, 78–9)

'The world is everything that is the case'. 'Everything' is a favourite word of Carson's. Paradoxically, its very inclusiveness may reduce all specific things to one thing, their mere totality. Yet regularly, his deployment of the word is in contexts which emphasize evanescence, indeterminacy, volatility, displacement, the deconstruction of the totality 'everything' would appear to posit: 'Like a fishnet stocking, everything is full of holes' ('Snowball', *Ifn*); 'everything as full of holes as a Swiss cheese' ('Whatever sleep it is', *Ifn*); 'Everything dissolves' ('All the better to see you with', *Bc*); 'everything's chalked up, and every now and then, wiped clean' ('Barfly', *Bc*); 'Difficult to keep track: / Everything's a bit askew' ('Gate', *Bc*); 'Everything was neither one thing nor the other' ('*Opus Operandi*', *Fl*); 'everything can be contained in anything' ('Mountain dew', *Ttn*); 'Everything reverses south' ('Yes', *Bc*); 'For the moment, everything is *X*, a blank not yet filled in'('Punctuation', *Bc*); and so on.

And this is repeatedly the condition of the city, which, as the title of one of those remarkable prose poems in *Belfast confetti* puts it, is perpetually a 'Revised version': 'For everything is contingent and provisional; and the subjunctive mood of these images is tensed to the ifs and buts, the yeas and nays of Belfast's history'. Or again, in 'Question time', a place of shifting sands and shifting meanings,

> The junk is sinking back into the sleech and muck. Pizza parlours, massage parlours, night-clubs, drinking-clubs, antique shops, designer studios momentarily populate the wilderness and the blitz sites; they too will vanish in the morning. Everything will be revised [...] sliding back into the rubble and erasure. (*Bc*, 57–8)

This is where Carson renegotiates Wittgenstein, for 'everything that is the case' also includes everything which is not, those mere possibilities of the actual as possible which pervade his poems, the subjunctives of Belfast's history, the 'plan of might-have-beens, legislating for all the possibilities' we each carry in our heads:

> For maps cannot describe everything, or they describe states of mind, like Dubourdieu's 'very incorrect' plan of 1811, which shows *streets and blocks of buildings which have never existed [...] a bridge [...] proposed but not carried out* ... the intoxicating draught of futures swallowed at one gulp, as someone sets another up. ('Revised version', *Bc*, 67)

If the limits of our language are the limits of our world, that world, as *The twelfth of never* demonstrates, includes all those negatives and subjunctives that not only crowd around the actual but pervade it, shape it, force revisions upon it, in an endless interaction of the imaginary and virtual with the actual and factual. In 'Dresden' the young Flynn, gaoled for seven years, learns in prison 'to speak / The best of Irish', which includes the not exactly useful 'thirteen words for a cow in heat; / A word for the third thwart in a boat' and 'the extinct names of insects'. But he also learns to redefine himself within the quotation marks of a nationalist fantasy. 'F', in the sequence 'Letters from the alphabet', registers the unreality of a world constructed by discourse, in which it seems 'everything was dubbed: / The *mise en scène*, the plot, the lines'. 'H' affirms that 'Everything is in the way / You say them', for whether the *H* in H-Block is pronounced as 'aitch' or 'haitch' sorts out which tribe you belong to, and can mean the difference between life and death. On this fantasy island language is so important that its speakers may have to be subjected to a form of institutionalized karaoke, so that when prisoners complain,

> We cannot reproduce his actual
> words here, since their spokesman is alleged
> To be a sub-commander of a movement deemed to be illegal.
>
> ('H', *Oec*, 18)

The 'shibboleth' is an important motif in Carson's poetry, but it needs to be read in tandem with the idea of the karaoke. Nuances of pronunciation can assume such ideological importance for his characters that when 'H' says, of the dubbed Republican spokesman, 'An actor spoke for him in almost-perfect lip-synch', purists complained that the Belfast accent 'wasn't West enough', while apparently accepting the whole absurdity of this Thatcher-years embargo on the voice of the man himself. 'Opus 14' repeats the topos:

> Spokesman for censored political party spoke in someone else's lip-synch
> So perfectly, you'd think it was the man himself, though much of this is
> double-think.

'You'd think' is picked up by 'double-think', in a way which destabilizes the whole communicative process by not clarifying what 'this' refers to. The implication remains that the phrase 'the man himself' may well be the deepest double-think, presupposing a free, self-articulating subject, when the speaker is merely repeating the mantras of a discourse that has become depersonalized, self-sufficient, so emptied of authentic meaning that an actor can mouth them, karaoke style, with as much conviction and authenticity as a supposed true believer. Wittgenstein's 'bewitchment of our intelligence by language' is Carson's central theme, but living in the hyphen, in the slash of the either/or, he responds to all the ambiguity and ambilocatedness (another back formation there) of that 'bewitchment'. What is almost but not quite a malapropism sums this up when the prose poem 'Brick' observes that 'Belfast has again swallowed up the miniature versions of itself in its intestine war' (*Bc*, 75) (*scilicet*, 'internecine', but playing on the Latin *bella intestina*, civil wars).

The prose poem 'Farset' starts in the realm of language, attempting to understand Belfast by pursuing the multiple possible etymologies of its name – a kind of back formation in which the imagining of origins is slowly transformed into an elaborate fantasy spun out of their interactions, after the fashion of Borges' story 'The garden of forked paths'. The idea that that 'which gives Belfast its name' can somehow explain its present reality soon succumbs to a sense, like that attributed to George Benn in the 1820s, of 'The utmost obscurity and perplexity [which] attend the derivation of the name [...] of *Bealafarsad*', 'a matter of complete hypothesis', with 'further room for further speculation' – what Carson dubs 'all this watery confusion' (*Bc*, 47–8). This quest for origins, however, turns into a different kind of project in 'The exiles' club' (*Ifn*) and 'Schoolboys and idlers of Pompeii', both of which report the regular meetings of the Falls Road Club in Adelaide's Woolongong Bar, its members, according to the latter, products of the emigrations of the 1950s and 60s, 'immersed in history, reconstructing a city on the other side of the world, detailing streets and shops and houses which for the most part only exist now in the memory' (*Bc*, 53). Carson's interpenetrating, plural histories, the stories, memories, mental maps of many generations sliding in and out of each other in discourse, as in the multiple parallel universes of science fiction, *Star trek* and *Sliders*, then take on a more tangible form, as 'Schoolboys and idlers' imagines a city which is a physical palimpsest of centuries of real estate, of all the building and streets that ever existed on the site, recreated simultaneously in the one packed, multidimensional space:

> Running back the film of the mind's eye, the alphabet soup of demolition
> sorts itself into phrases, names, buildings, as if, on the last day, not only

> bodies are resurrected whole and perfect, but each brick, each stone, finds its
> proper place again [...] bridges within bridges [...] who will sort out the
> chaos?   (*Bc,* 54)

It's a remarkable postmodern parable of the way in which language can accommodate, in its very insubstantiality, the dense competing clutter of the real which appears to crowd it out, but which is itself as evanescent as smoke, as 'the very city recycled itself and disassembled buildings – churches, air-raid shelters, haberdashers, pawnshops' ('Brick', *Bc,* 73). If I had space I'd want to relate this to that other astonishing poem, 'Queen's gambit' (*bHMSB*), in which diverse narratives intersect and disrupt each other, not only in the levels and layers of their telling, but in the actual, on-the-ground unfolding of events, as a series of narratival interference patterns that leak into and disrupt each other, 'Like the names on a school desk, carved into one another till they're indecipherable' (*bHMSB,* 67), or 'the sketch that's taking shape on the Army HQ blackboard, chalky ghosts / Behind the present, showing what was contemplated, Plan A / Becoming X or Y; interlocked, curved arrows of the mortgaged future' (*bHMSB,* 69); or, most evocatively, like the tea spilt on a discarded *Irish news*, so that 'A minor item bleeds through from another page, blurring the main story. / It's difficult to pick up without the whole thing coming apart in your hands' (*bHMSB,* 69).

But I want to end back in the Twilight Zone of the Podes, by focusing on the poem 'The words', which opens the sequence 'Alibi: after Stefan Augustin Doinas' in *Opera et cetera*, precisely because this sequence is crucially ambilocated, neither one thing nor the other – neither translations nor original poems but creations 'after' (but for us standing *before,* in front of) a completely different text. In other words these poems inhabit the space of the hyphen between Ciaran Carson and Stefan Doinas. They are literally an elsewhere from which both Carson and Doinas are absent, yet in which they are also presences. 'The words' declares as much in *its* opening words, conceding 'Yes – someone lived here once.' The poem could be speaking about itself, but it is also talking about the words that constitute it, and about the nature of all language. It is 'like the hieroglyph / Of where we are'. Where we are, however, is not here. Being 'like' is not the same as being identical with. 'Like', similitude rather than identity, is the hyphenic space where all language operates, and 'where we are' becomes simply the sign or written trace of a departed presence, a hieroglyph. The very crudity of Carson's similitudes reinforce the idea of the discrepancy between 'real presence' and presence in language, between 'the pungent dragon-whiff' and the ghostly music of the sea blown from conches, between 'The dog-rough breath that slabbered here' and the 'mere miasma' it is 'now'. The limestone sea of the geological metaphor is now imaginable only in back formation from the limestone deposits of its once living denizens. In this liminal place, 'the guardian angels of its threshold are connected to us by an ampersand / When we talk in our sleep'. All discourse is in a sense sleep-talking, since it stumbles on things we don't know, don't intend, which come as 'revenants' from elsewhere, from that 'reservoir of silence, or a Twilight Zone' – the capitalized phrase poised between 1960s TV sci-fi and an apocalyptic *Untergang des Abendlandes*, in, that is, an ambilocated space, the place of the hyphen.

The word as object: commodification in the poetry of Ciaran Carson

MICHAEL McATEER

Ciaran Carson's 2003 collection, *Breaking news,* is a recent instance of the versality that is a hallmark of his literary achievement to date. Since his 1987 collection, *The Irish for no,* Carson has maintained an astonishingly prolific and various output, ranging from verse translations from French, Irish and Latin (culminating in *The inferno)* to the imaginatively copious prose works *The star factory, Shamrock tea* and *Fishing for amber.* Through the course of this chameleon industry, a distinctive voice emerges that is marked by verbal dexterity and nervous excitement ducking and weaving the swings and arrows of outrageous Ulster fortune. Carson's style to date appears the poetic embodiment of Bakhtin's idea of polyphony; dexterous, risky, generative, tight yet capable of ecstasy, a language constantly attending to itself. *Breaking news* strikes a new note in this context, moving as it does towards contraction rather than expansion. This essay aims to explore Carson's earlier work in order to illustrate how, for all the significance of the move towards minimalism in its opening sequence, *Breaking news* can yet be considered a culmination of certain thematic preoccupations. In particular, attention will be drawn to Carson's treatment of the nature and function of the commodity as well as its relation to language in collections such as *Belfast confetti* and *The twelfth of never* in order to lay out a context within which this more recent collection can be set. The value of this consideration lies not simply in the way commodities bring into view sequences of codes and processes of exchange through which Carson addresses questions of urban social experience and political violence. Beyond this, it illuminates the extent to which the psychic flux of Carson's *timbre* registers the ways in which global patterns of production and exchange congeal or split open in the particular climate of Belfast. Through this focus on commodities, the dichotomies of urban/rural and realist/romantic within which critical discourse of contemporary Irish poetry still tends to be framed are not so much subverted as reconfigured.

Perhaps the rhythm of Carson's poetry might best be described as that of the cultivated stammer. Indeed, it may be that Carson's *ouevre* calls for a cultural

politics of the stammer through which it might receive adequate interpretation.
It is not so much the case that readers come to sense the prospect of the poetic
voice failing to go on, though it must; it is more that we never know what's
around the corner, what utterance might spring from the mouth, what might spill
onto the page. At times it seems as if the body has vacated the room and all that
remains is a talking head, out of control, capable of saying anything. And Carson
makes the danger of an unheld tongue in a tight-lipped city only too apparent:

> There was this head had this mouth he kept shooting off.
>   Unfortunately.
> It could have been worse for us than it was for him.
>   Provisionally.
> But since nothing in this world is certain and you don't know
>   who hears what
> We thought it was time he bit off more than he could chew.
>   Literally.
> By the time he is found there"ll be nothing much left to tell
>   who he was.
>
> ('The mouth', *Bc,* 70)

The precedent that springs to mind most immediately is the disembodied Mouth
from Beckett's 1972 play *Not I*, a monologue in which language is like a 'buzzing'
in the head, incapable of ceasing or making sense.[1] Drawing on poststructuralist
theory, Elin Diamond argues that rather than generating language, the 'I' of this
play is generated by it: 'Mouth is a pulsing muscle that spews out words like
excrement, pouring it out in gasping, spittling, hysterical somatic mimicry of
lexical and syntactic norms'.[2] The structure of Beckett's play also anticipates
Carson in the function of the persistent pauses punctuating the monologue,
lending it a staccato quality creating the effect upon the audience that what they
are hearing is a stammer. In this sense Diamond's image of 'pouring' is not
appropriate, since the effect that Beckett achieves is one of constant interruption
and constant digression. The voice doesn't so much pour out as shoot off in
different directions, while always trying to draw itself in. Pulsing, spewing and
pouring suggest a bursting forth of language liberated from a controlling 'I';

1 Samuel Beckett, *The complete dramatic works* (London, 1986), 371–83. 2 Elin Diamond, 'Feminist
readings of Beckett', in Louis Oppenheim (ed.), *Palgrave advances in Samuel Beckett studies* (London,
2004), 49.

Carson's image of 'shooting off' is much closer to the tenor of *Not I*, indicating as it does not liberation but loss of control.

The spontaneous sequencing of correspondences within *Not I* is reflected in the movement of 'The mouth', a poem in which the precariousness of this mode of articulation is invested with a sinister political dimension. It is a poem obsessed with codes, structured according to a sequence of codes, but a sequence that threatens to elude semantic control. The poem commences in a narrative enunciative voice but already causal sequence leads into dark alleyways. The 'head' of the opening line is Belfast slang for a person that at once manages to convey a sense of the nonedescript and the peculiar. At the same time, the phrase carries the shadow of its articulator, 'this head' who speaks this story, 'this mouth' that may already be out of control in speaking it. The precariousness of the voice articulating the poem is intertwined with the trauma it both signals and deflects. The mouth 'kept / 'shooting off', an image that expresses the proximity of violence to spontaneous articulation and conjures the sense of a situation psychically and politically out of control. In these circumstances, sequences of semantic codes are deflected hither and thither, words becoming overladen with dark connotation. Thus, Carson gives us 'Unfortunately', 'Provisionally' and 'Literally', euphemisms of official discourse sitting curiously alongside the streetwise lingo of 'this head', 'shooting off', who 'bit off more than he could chew'. The poem steps beyond even the relative stability offered by this juxtaposition, however, to recast these euphemisms as the signifiers of the pseudo-official jargon of paramilitaries. This language is appropriated to lend them a sententious air they half believe in, while at the same time offering a cruel parody of the way such language conceals the brutality to which it ostensibly refers. Thus, 'Unfortunately' carries a piteous tone directed at the mouth incapable of self-discipline while simultaneously mocking such pity in the resignation it signals to the 'necessary duty' of violently imposing such discipline. 'Provisionally' quite obviously refers to the provisional IRA while 'Literally' brings into the most intimate contact possible the euphemistic and the vicious even as it retains an ironic distance between the two. The mouth becomes obliged 'literally' to 'bite off more than he could chew', a phrase in which street-wise idiom is rendered vicious by formal euphemism, an ironic inversion of the function normally attributed to official language.

The poem does more than address a crisis of articulation in a situation of violence; it is itself an instance of that crisis. In its subversions, displacements and innuendoes, it constantly extends a sequence it seeks to conclude, a Beckettian mouth that cannot stop itself. Roman Jakobson's observations on aphasia offer an outline for understanding the arrest of communication that this communicates:

> Every form of aphasic disturbance consists in some impairment, more or less severe, either of the faculty for selection and substitution or for combination and contexture. The former affliction involves a deterioration of metalinguistic operations, while the latter damages the capacity for maintaining a hierarchy of linguistic units. The relation of similarity is suppressed in the former, the relation of contiguity in the latter type of aphasia. Metaphor is alien to the similarity disorder, and metonymy to the contiguity disorder.[3]

Aphasic disturbance of the first type described here characterizes some of Carson's most compelling poems. The possibility of metaphoric unity that might lift poetic vision beyond the immediacy of the situation it encounters is denied. Instead, the reader is confronted with sequential associations that constantly deflect individual images from the throne of symbolic meaning, leaving us instead with an entirely situational poetics. One of the finest examples of this is 'Belfast confetti'. Like much of Carson's work, this is a poem obsessed with language as the end rather than the means of communication. His handling of this issue, however, is distinguished here by two aspects. First, the poet denies any gap between himself and his subject-matter that might enable him to render linguistic autonomy mystical, as in Heaney's 'Anahorish', for example, where the name becomes metaphoric, drawing the entire landscape of the poem into its texture. Second, the poem interweaves the question of language with the suspension of communication; the moment in which linguistic autonomy is realized is also the moment in which communication fails, a moment of linguistic collapse rather than linguistic power:

> I was trying to complete a sentence in my head, but it kept stuttering,
> All the alleyways and side-streets blocked with stops and colons.
>
> ('Belfast confetti', *bHMSB*, 23)

Here Carson foregrounds the process of poetic creation and the frustration of that process as the subject of the poem itself. The stutter here involves a subtle play of

---

3 Roman Jakobson, 'Two aspects of language', in Julie Rivkin and Michael Ryan (eds), *Literary theory: an anthology* (Oxford, 1998), 91.

flow and stasis. The poet searches for a full stop, an 'arresting' of speech that might lend it communicative efficacy. Yet he cannot find such a stop because all the possible avenues to it are blocked – flow is desired in the pursuit of a final stasis, but frustrated by intermediary diversions. The process of selection and substitution through which relations of similarity are established in the constitution of metaphoric unity is disrupted here. Instead we are presented with metonymic dispersal, in which images cannot escape the context within which they emerge and are thereby incapable of offering metaphorical unity for the poem as a whole. The language is one of contiguity; a series of scattered alleyways and side-streets rather than a central thoroughfare that might absorb them, enabling passage to a final terminus, a linguistic home where word and object coincide.

It would seem obvious that Carson attributes this mode of aphasic disruption to the circumstances of political violence within which the poem is situated. There is a critical tendency to take this attribution for granted. Neil Corcoran, for example, sees in Carson's strategies of parodic imitation (again deflecting direct communication) 'one of the most accurate poetic witnesses to the pressure and texture of Belfast street life as it has been lived, or endured, since 1969'.[4] A poem like 'Belfast confetti' in which '[e]very move is punctuated' seems a perfect case in point. However, it is questionable even whether this poem is to be conceived as a sundering of signifier from signified, let alone a depiction of violence as the condition for such a sundering. In one sense, language is entirely adequate here to that which it denotes; it's just that the content of the denotation is the act of writing itself. Carson conveys the semantic uncertainty generated by syntactic diversions with admirable transparency and poetic self-confidence. In any case the terms upon which the critic derives a political interpretation from this uncertainty need to be addressed; to move from aphasic to political disturbance without attending to the complexity of such a relationship is to grant the poem a hermeneutic stability its very theme denies.

This relation of arrested linguistic process and a situation of political danger is best explored through the role of commodities in Carson's poetry. The commodity functions not simply as analogy for the linguistic unit in his poetry; it constitutes the linguistic procedures by which many of the poems are structured. The opening of 'Belfast confetti' appears to convey a breakdown in linguistic denotation of a violent situation as a condition of that situation. However, this presumes a perspective beyond the semantic field of the poem itself,

---

4 Neil Corcoran, *After Yeats and Joyce: reading modern Irish literature* (Oxford, 1997), 151–2.

a perspective the absence of which is integral to the particular vision the poem achieves. Carson continually insists on bringing the reader into the situation without the distancing effect of framing devices. The opening lines of many poems are dominated by verbs and adverbs: 'suddenly as the riot squad moved in' opens 'Belfast confetti'; 'Jerking his head spasmodically as he is penetrated by invisible gunfire' opens 'Night patrol' and 'Army' opens with '[t]he duck patrol is waddling down the odd-numbers side of Raglan Street'. This movement, however, is jarring. Hard consonant sounds dominate – 'suddenly', 'riot squad', 'Jerking', 'penetrated', 'duck patrol' and 'waddling down'. In fact, something more than a failure to achieve reflective distance is at work in Carson's poetry; words themselves are becoming things, bearing the hallmarks of the process of commodification to which they allude. In this constitution of words as things, words are divested of expressive potency and acquire both an autonomy from and a power over the voice delivering them. While it is tempting to take 'the exclamation marks' that rain down in the opening lines of 'Belfast confetti' as metaphorical of the actual 'Nuts, bolts, nails, car-keys', they are every bit as much objects as these, as the line, '[a] fount of broken type' indicates. Indeed, all of these objects, in their aspect as commodities, bear the characteristics of aphasic disturbance outlined already. Their design function is to secure, tighten, block, yet in this context they are instruments of disorder. This corresponds to the loss of metaphoric function in the first type of aphasia described by Jakobson. Individual linguistic elements are coherent but because they are not linked to one another through metaphor, a final semantic closure remains unrealized.

The status of these objects as commodities suggests why such aphasic disturbance might arise. Removed from their functional context, they throw into relief the fetishism of commodities as originally outlined by Marx. In their conventional function of providing security and solidity, they necessarily conceal the vast, unstable labour-intensive process of their production, exchange and circulation. In the riotous situation, the congealment of labour-process in the form of the commodity is suddenly reversed, allowing a sense of this process to come momentarily into view. This is not to conceive the riot as a reappropriation of the object by its producer, though it certainly reconfigures the relation of human beings to the objects they produce. On the contrary, the poem brings the power exercised by these objects over their producers all the more sharply into focus by the shift in their instrumental function from security to danger. The loss of agency that poems like 'Belfast confetti' address exist neither solely nor even primarily at the linguistic level; it is rather in the power instruments acquire over their creators – including the instrument of language – in the process of objectification that this loss is felt most deeply. In *The economic and philosophical manuscripts* Marx, drawing on Hegel's notion of 'thingification', identifies this as the basis of alienation in capitalism:

> The externalization of the worker in his product implies not only that his labour becomes an object, an exterior existence but also that it exists outside him, independent and alien, and becomes a self-sufficient power opposite him, that the life he has lent to the object affronts him, hostile and alien.[5]

This power objects exercise in Carson's poetry, particularly objects of functional security, is sometimes overlooked in the haste to read them as emblems of the Troubles. At the opening of 'Queen's gambit' for example, the robot exercises a farcical control over soldiers and citizens alike:

> A Remote Handling Equipment (Tracked) Explosive
> Ordnance Disposal unit – *Wheelbarrow*,
> For short – is whirring and ticking towards the Ford Sierra
> parked in Tomb Street. (*Bc*, 33)

Crucial here is the object's remoteness; its strange, artificial movement captures the awkwardness in naming the object itself; it is as if the voice simply gives up attempting to denote it, calling it a wheelbarrow out of comic exasperation. This remoteness indicates not only the separation of product from producer, it marks the object out as the point of proxy communication between the army and the community it polices. The robot is the only point of conversation between state and citizen in this instance. One soldier is dressed in '[a]n M69 flak jacket, Dr Marten boots and non- regulation skiing gloves', imitating the stilted strangeness of the robot, while another is 'armed with Self-loading Rifle', another image of the autonomous object. The IRA is almost entirely an absent presence, reduced to a 'Ford Sierra', a 'Flourish of graffiti', 'a glittering, tilted view of mercury'. The only one named is '"Mad Dog" Reilly', a parodic echo of 'Mickey Mouse' and a name that quickly becomes a strategy called 'Operation "Mad Dog"', while the only voice is that of 'the recorded message'. Indeed, the entire poem might be a

5 Karl Marx, *Economic and philosophical manuscripts*, in *Karl Marx: selected writings*, ed. David McLellan (Oxford, 1977), 79.

series of televisual or photographic images as the 'close-up of a soldier', the streets in 'bad photostat grey' and 'the missing reel in the film' suggest. Thus 'Queen's gambit' is more than a reflection on how Irish history has reached its present impasse. It presents us with that 'externalization of the worker in his product' Marx described one hundred and sixty years ago, the soldiers in the thrall of the objects they operate, the terrorists in the thrall of the media reporting them; 'the life that he [the worker] has lent to the object affronts him, hostile and alien'. Thus objects often acquire anthropomorphic features even as they act upon their progenitors. The opening of 'Jump leads' sees the helicopter overhead as 'the eggbeater spy in the sky' causing the television to 'develop a facial tic'. This hints at the 'repeated tic' at the opening of 'Asylum', ambivalently suggesting 'the latch jigging and clicking' or 'Uncle John' who 'was not all there'.

The question remains as to how we evaluate this process of commodification, in terms of Carson as a poet of the city writing at a time of political conflict. Baudrillard's development of Marx's understanding of the object allows us to understand this process both in terms of urban social experience and political violence. Baudrillard's advance on Marx lies in his understanding of the effect of alienation upon the category of the human itself. Baudrillard does not identify contemporary social disequilibrium in the servitude of the labourer to the objects of his/her production but argues that the notion of a self-contained humanity debased by commodification is itself an abstraction consequent upon the process of reification originally outlined by Marx. In a story curiously parallel to the image of soldiers imitating the bomb-disposal robot in 'Queen's gambit', Baudrillard recalls the story of an illusionist who created an automaton so effective he was obliged to make his own movements more mechanical in imitation of it before his audience. He offers the story as a parable for the way objects act upon human beings in their interaction with them once a threshold of objectification has been crossed. Imagining the prospect of human society entirely saturated with technical objects, Baudrillard proposes that the category of man would at that point become an abstraction: 'If the simulacrum is so well designed that it becomes an effective organizer of reality, then surely it is man, not the simulacrum, who is turned into an abstraction'.[6]

Carson's poetry is saturated with figures blurring into the objects they produce, consume or operate. The soldiers of 'Queen's gambit' are one instance. We might also think of that parody of Heaney's 'Digging', 'Bloody hand' in which '[m]y

---

6 Jean Baudrillard, *The system of objects*, trans. James Benedict (London, 1996), 57.

thumb is the hammer of a gun. The thumb goes up. The thumb goes down'. In 'Jump leads', '[t]he victim is his wedding photograph' on the news while the voice is 'drinking in the 7-Up bottle-green eyes of the barmaid' at the opening of 'Yes'. Another instance of communication diverted, 'someone looks / daggers at us / From the *Bushmills* mirror' in 'Last orders' while the sumptuous texture of MacNeice's 'snow' becomes not even the hard tapping of table-tennis but the more remote simulated tap of computer ping-pong. In 'The Irish exile Michael Hinds' the poet imagines being driven in Tokyo in 'your toy Toyota car' while in 'Fuji film' he becomes the commodified image of the commodity-saturated Japanese tourist as he worries about the value of the yen and photographs 'the crowd that swarmed beneath the acid rain':

> I snapped them slashing floating dollar bills in half
> Beneath the signs for Coke, the giant neon roulette wheel,
> The money index pulsing like a cardiograph. (*Ttn*, 66)

In each of these instances Carson places the semblance of an unmediated humanity at a further remove. The pulse of the money index reminds him not of a human pulse but the technical imitation of one. He imagines the car as an imitation of a car, the dot in the computer game as the image not of a snowflake but of the table-tennis ball as the semblance of a snowflake. Aphasic disturbance is again in evidence here; no single image is capable of providing metaphoric unity closing the extended string of associations. Instead, the significance attributed to each single image is purely contextual, their meaning derived entirely from their function within a provisionally delimited game.

Because of this, it comes as no surprise that the dominance of objects in Carson's poetry stimulates an obsession with games. 'Queen's gambit' is the most obvious example of this but games are constantly being played throughout his poetry. 'Belfast confetti' is, among other things, a set-piece, a game of cat-and-mouse, and while much attention has been directed at the cartographic significance of 'The exiles' club', mentally reconstructing the streets of Belfast is also a game these men play out each Thursday night, a test of their belonging. In 'Letters from the alphabet' from *Opera et cetera* the poet writes, '[w]e have this plan, because if all else fails, we will / rehearse its contemplated moves', and 'Coded neon glimmered in a game of rouge et noir' in 'The tobacco and salt museum' of Toyko in *The twelfth of never*. It is also significant that Carson's take on MacNeice's 'snow' moves its imagery into the context of games, table-tennis and computer ping-pong, while so many poems attending to political violence present all as a sequence of roles played out. The recurrent motif of the game is hardly coincidental, nor is it accounted for simply with reference to the formulaic pattern of atrocity and response into which the Troubles had 'settled' by the 1980s. Baudrillard argues that the process by which objects come to exercise control over their producers and consumers is a functional process, but functional in the systematic rather than the instrumental sense. It is not the capacity of technologies to realize objectives that is important here, but their effectiveness in integrating into an overall system:

> '[F]unctional' in no way qualifies what is adapted to a goal, merely what is adapted to an order or system: functionality is the ability to become integrated into an overall scheme. An object's functionality is the very thing that enables it to transcend its main 'function' in the direction of a secondary one, to play a part, to become a combining element, an adjustable item, within a universal system of signs.[7]

Indeed, Baudrillard makes the point that an increased efficiency of objects in relation to their specific function can unbalance their structural function within a given system producing an overall decrease in efficiency.[8] The burden of gadgets and the cumbersome naming of the robot in 'Queen's gambit' seem to bear this out, as might the helicopter's interference with the television signal in 'Jump leads'. It is important to observe, however, that this does not correspond neatly to a Saussurean structural linguistic model. Baudrillard points out that the systematic integration of technologies is continually modified by the emergence of practical objects, in contrast to the relative immunity of *la langue* from the contingencies of individual speech acts. The technological system is in a state of 'permanent revolution' because it is continually modified by the alteration in its network of relations generated.[9] Consequently, the virtuality of games paradigmatic for the system of objects Baudrillard describes is firmly grounded in a material process of objectification that, for all its disagreement with the humanism of the early Marx, bears the hallmarks of commodification. Considered from this perspective, the games played in Carson's poetry, even the language games of *First language* and *Opera et cetera,* witness not to the autonomy of signifiers but to that of material objects, including speech and writing. The power they exercise through this autonomy is that of systematization itself, in

7 Ibid., 63. 8 Ibid., 8. 9 Ibid., 10.

which words – as objects – hold open the prospect of the object reappropriated by its creator while constantly frustrating this.

The relation of games to commodification in Carson's poetry is most transparent in the game of collecting. Carson's passion for collecting is strongest in his prose works *Shamrock tea* and *Fishing for amber* but it pulses through much of his poetry also, in the concern for meticulous detail of the object and repeating images like those of the severed head, salt, the severed hand. Benjamin remarks that the 'collector proves to be the true resident of the interior. He makes his concern the idealization of objects. To him falls the Sisyphean task of divesting things of their commodity character by taking possession of them'.[10] Conceiving collecting as 'a marginal system', Baudrillard sees the key to collecting not in the objects but in the 'fanaticism' of the collector. Because he believes that everything that cannot be invested in human relationships is invested in objects, he regards collecting as 'regression' and the passion to collect as 'a passion for flight'.[11] In 'Berenice' from *Fishing for amber* this passion is lent a magical air:

> Having read this account of Hermes, I remember how I used to dream recurrently of finding coins – usually, the old king's or young queen's shillings – lying in the gutter, shimmering in the black silt after rain. I see one in the corner of my eye; I stoop, and pick it up; another one appears. One thing leads to another, until pounds of shillings jingle in my pockets. (*Ffa*, 14)

Like *Opera et cetera*, *Fishing for amber* expresses Carson's passion for collecting letters and words. Whether we see this from Benjamin's perspective as the noble attempt to redeem the object from commodification or as regression depends in large measure on the residue of the human that remains within the collection itself. Edna Longley comments that Carson's 'litanies of city-names which have lost their referents (due to development as well as the Troubles) not only make a point about signifier and signified. They mark a break with older forms of cohesion which the Falls Road long maintained after its rite of passage from rural Ulster'.[12] The list of Belfast street names Carson gives in 'Belfast confetti', 'Hamlet' and elsewhere are also collectors items, names invested with a resonance intended to release these streets from their innocuous status while yet enabling them to move beyond themselves in the nature of their reference:

10 Walter Benjamin, *The Arcades project*, ed. Rolf Tiedemann, trans. Howard Eiland and Kevin McLaughlin (Cambridge, MA, 1999), 19. **11** Jean Baudrillard, *The system of objects*, 90. **12** Edna Longley, *The Living stream* (Newcastle-upon-Tyne, 1994), 59.

I know this labyrinth so well – Balaclava, Raglan, Inkerman, Odessa
Street –

('Belfast confetti', *bHMSB*, 23)

In this instance and elsewhere, the compulsion to collect arises from a desire to
escape what is described, as if by naming the object its mastery could be
contained. Benjamin suggests that 'there is a peculiar voluptuousness in the
naming of streets', testament to a subtle eroticism at play even in the darkest of
Carson's poems.[13] The line also points to a failure in communication again, not
simply in words turning in on themselves, but in objects standing in for the
failure of human relationships, a failure witnessed most brutally in the wars to
which the street names allude. Carson appears seduced as Benjamin was by the
Parisian *flâneur*'s inebriation upon the names of city streets:

> They spoke of Paris as *la ville qui remue* – the city that never stops
> moving. But no less important than the life of this city's layout is here the
> unconquerable power in the names of streets, squares, and theaters, a
> power which persists in the face of all topgraphic displacement.[14]

In spite of this evident seduction in the aura Belfast carries through his poetry, the
voice in 'Belfast confetti' appears as a kind of reverse *flâneur*. The labyrinth is a
trap and, in any case, the names conjure moments of collapse and destruction
rather than durability. Longley's take on this is sharp, not because it localizes
Carson, but because it tempers this seduction with observance of anxiety:

> The 'Exiles Club', who meet in the 'Wollongong Bar' to reconstruct an
> obsolete map of a collapsing Belfast, are viewed with sympathy as well as
> irony. Carson's 'post-modernism' may really be a post-traditionalism; his
> return to poetry, like Edward Thomas's arrival there, triggered by
> memory and the dislocation of familiar landscapes.[15]

Baudrillard's view of the collector's impulse as regression is given a local flavour in
this reading if indeed we regard those street-name lists as a collection of sorts.
'Belfast confetti' is a stark example that certainly strengthens Baudrillard's
argument; in poems such as 'Loaf' the case is less certain because the human
element is more directly evident in the texture of the objects themselves. The

---

13 Walter Benjamin, *The Arcades project*, 516.   **14** Ibid., 516.   **15** Edna Longley, *The living stream*, 60.

poem revels in the sumptuousness of objects, from the aroma of baked bread to the texture of its wrapping, capturing the residual uniqueness of objects in the names attaching to them – '*Conway Stewart* fountain-pen', 'McWatters' pan loaf', 'Jamesons' *Three Swallows*', 'Gallahers' *Greens*'. The poem is not without the anxiety fuelling 'Belfast confetti', 'Campaign' or 'Hamlet', but these items collected in the head of the poet conjure the intimacy of a short friendship and the passing of youth in all its transitory allure. The experience can finally be no more appropriated than the aroma of bread be pinned down, but it is more difficult to conceive collecting here as regressive, not simply because of the effect objects have in conjuring the memory of a frail human intimacy but also because the passing of objects themselves is part of the poem's concern. This is not always the case with Carson; the hagiographic project of *Shamrock tea,* for example, can be criticized for investing collection with redemptive potential and thereby deflecting the anxiety generated by the object. In much of his poetry, however, Carson attends to this anxiety even as he articulates the fractured traces of human intimacy discreetly shadowing the gesture of collecting.

Having considered Carson's poetry in terms of aphasic disturbance consequent upon commodification, the minimalism of the first part of *Breaking news* is less surprising. As with William Carlos Williams, the obvious precedent for this stylistic departure, the effect is not so much preciocity as objectification. The concentrated exactitude of language lends the poems a quality of hardness traceable back to Hulme, H.D. and Pound, but its most immediate effect is to convey the sense of the poem itself as a concrete object, a thing in a world of things. This is not to discount the degree to which the sequence nods towards *Japonisme* when considered against *The twelfth of never.* As with Imagism and Vorticism, however, such predilection for minimal forms reminiscent of haiku displays a sense of the poem as a material object arising from a more underlying attentiveness to objectification within the immediate society, a sense that Carson makes quite explicit in *Breaking news.* Take 'Horse at Balaklava, 1854' and 'Some uses of a dead horse' for example. The first captures the immediacy of horror in war, acting as a kind of freeze-frame of a moment in which a horse, 'the picture of life' is, in one moment,

> Ripped open by
> a shell
>
> from chest
> to loin

('Horse at Balaklava, 1854', Bn, 18)

The effect is to render the horse, just now a vital creature, no more than a pile of objects, a 'glaring eyeball', 'distended nostril', 'gnashed teeth', 'a debris of skin'. While certainly conveying the horror of war, the poem can hardly be called tragic, nor even elegaic. The poignancy of the subject is offset by Carson's movement between Romantic and scientific forms of perception competing with one another at the time in which the poem is set. Thus, a note of irony colours the rhyme of 'the picture of life', with its Carlylean undertone, and 'surgeon's knife', while the eye itself is drawn from that picture to 'the glaring eyeball' that the voice, in the manner of a surgeon, instructs us to 'remark'. The resistance this puts up to tragedy and elegy is tougher in 'Some uses of a dead horse' where latent commodification is made explicit:

> the bones give
> buttons
>
> snuff-boxes
> and knife-handles
>
> the hooves
> yield
> a beautiful
> Prussian blue
>
> the shoes
> shot   (*Bn*, 32)

Any sentimental nostalgia for the horse in the first poem is wiped away by the note of farce here. The metonymic tendency of Carson's poetry is again in evidence and again it is aligned with objectification. Viewed as a companion piece to 'Horse at Balaklava, 1854' we can see how commodities return to invade the 'the picture of life' in that here we are given the constituents of such a picture, the buttons, snuff-boxes, knife-handles and Prussian blue uniform of a Crimean war scene. This reminds us not only of the poet's reverence for the collected object and his awareness of the violence gone into its making. It also draws attention to the self-referentiality of the game as consequent upon commodification; the shoes are for the game of shot-put, and in a Beckettian begin-again, this last word 'shot' is taken up as the first word of 'Campaign' in which the shot horse directs us back to 'Horse at Balaclava, 1854'. But most of all, the poem presents itself to us as an object, a thing itself of precise detail caught in the circulating sequence of commodity exchange it attempts to forestall in that very precision. Constantly attending to sequence, Carson avoids all sense of preciocity not simply in the roughness of subject matter but also in repeating poems as if their aspiration to articulate has once again been frustrated. These 'Horse' poems, themselves echoes of a persistent 'horse' motif coursing through Carson's poetry that, significantly, he lends anthropomorphic effect on occasion (as in 'Dresden'), are one example of sequentiality.

Even more obvious are 'Spin cycle' and 'Spin cycle 2', a pair of poems that move together like table-tennis bats or, as Carson might prefer, the simulation of such a pair. In imagining the sound of a helicopter as the spin of a washing machine, the poem recalls the connection drawn between helicopter and television in 'Jump leads'. As with that poem, all relationships exist purely in terms of objects; washing machine, helicopter, ear-plugs. The poem carries an echo of Vorticism, drawing spinning images into a centre that springs open in the word 'centrifugal'. Like 'The mouth', the poet's voice is not his own, but the attempt to retrieve it requires a technology that places it at an even further distance. This is in large measure the meaning of 'Spin cycle 2', a poem that relates to 'Spin cycle' as 'Horse at Balaklava, 1854' relates to 'Some uses of a dead horse':

> gun-gun
>
> ear-plugs in
>
> blank-blank
>
> ('Spin cycle 2', *Bn*, 40)

Here we are confronted with writing degree-zero, in which the poet takes the commodification of language to its furthest point. There is no longer a desire to retrieve the object. The autonomy of the signifier is made stark in 'blank-blank', a line that simultaneously muffles gun-shots and alludes to nothing – blanks that are filled in by blanks. But this is already present in 'gun-gun' replacing a conventional bang-bang in order to draw attention to the words themselves as objects, like guns. Evident once more is an ever-growing distance from any realm beyond objectification in which word and object might coalesce. Everything about the poem is muffled, incubated from immediate human engagement. What is striking, however, is that Carson has reached a coalescence of sorts here in the phrase 'blank-blank', a line in which the words are complete objects signifying nothing beyond themselves. It is as if he has reached the furthest distance possible from Romanticism and, in so doing, arrived at the goal to which Romanticism aspires. Something similar occurs in 'Trap' in which the final word 'over' is the soldier's conventional mode of communicating the end of a statement on walkie-talkie, the end of the soldier's life and the end of the poem. In all three instances, its 'over' and so the word, like 'blank-blank', is immediately returned to itself.

Indeed, there is a sense in which objectification has so deeply invaded form itself in *Breaking news* that the poems almost move into the Heideggerian realm, as in 'Breath' for example, where the clarity of the space vacated by a helicopter leaves the poet feeling 'rinsed' like the silence after the washing-machine has completed its spin. In 'The origin of the work of art' Heidegger writes:

> In the midst of beings as a whole an open place occurs. There is a clearing. Thought of in reference to beings, this clearing is more in being than are beings. This open center is therefore not surrounded by beings; rather, the clearing center itself encircles all that is, as does the nothing, which we scarcely know.[16]

The imagery of 'Breath' captures this sense of an open centre quite precisely in the 'clear blue space' after the helicopter is 'gone' and 'that quiet' after the washing-machine 'stops shuddering'. This sense of a clearing also calls to attention the space around the poem itself and the space between the words. This might suggest that the minimalism of the opening sequence in *Breaking news* approximates to a meditation on Being that is Heaneyesque without the Heaneyspeak. However, if 'Breath' momentarily achieves release from objectification here, from the whirrings of helicopter and washing-machine, nothing remains except the words themselves, words that, in the staggering of their articulation, are still 'shuddering'. Furthermore, because the poem, through its images of these machines, is so caught up in the sequence as a whole, its composure is purely transitory, its clarity and silence a certain sign that the noise will start again. In any case, the sequence reminds us that silence is both release and foreboding. 'Breaking' is a perfect illustration, playing out the typical Carson game of cat-and-mouse but lengthening the suspense to a point in which it shifts into a different order of temporality. The opening 'red alert' clears the area for an expected

---

16 Martin Heidegger, 'The origin of the work of art', in *Basic writings*, 2nd edn edited David Farrell Krell (London, 1993), 178.

detonation but the space becomes so eerily quiet as to allow the slow, silent degeneration of the object, the car, become audible. Considered against 'Breaking', then, the airy quality of 'Breath' ought to be read with a degree of scepticism; while it comes close to a resolution of aphasic disturbance, final closure is never achieved. Such scepticism is confirmed by 'Minus', a fragment that nods to Leonard Cohen's 'Last year's man' with 'this hour / gone by' and to Carlos Williams's 'This is just to say' with 'and oh / so cold'. Here, silence is frozen; absence is, as the title indicates, something hard, jarring. There is the slightest hint of longing for the familiar disgruntlement of the helicopter and impatience with the poetic predictability of a bright moon. All appears caught here in the moment of the poem itself, a moment of negative capability so doubled in on itself as to produce a curiously satisfying paralysis. It seems as if in poems like 'Minus', 'Spin cycle 2' and 'Breath' Carson has reached into the mysterious heart of the moment of the stammer itself, the moment of primary metonymic suspension, and therein unlocked the secret of objectification, what Hegel describes as the 'thinghood' of things. Of significance to the minimalist mode of these poems, Hegel considers this 'thinghood' as negative in its essence. The properties of the object, its colour, shape and odour are determined by their relations of opposition to one another but the object remains simply what it is and in this simplicity, stands apart from these relations of opposition: 'The One is the moment of negation; it is itself quite simply a relation of self to self and it excludes an other; and it is that by which "thinghood" is determined as a Thing'.[17] The achievement of the opening sequence in *Breaking news* is to bring out this negativity upon which the uniqueness of the object rests, thereby resisting the seduction of preciosity. These poems are objects in the moment of their immediacy, a moment that, because essentially negative, is also the moment of arrested voice, the moment of the stammer. In their essential estrangement, word and object coalesce.

---

17 G.W.F. Hegel, *Phenomenology of spirit*, trans. A.V. Miller (Oxford, 1977), 69.

Ciaran Carson: the spy in the superior turret

TIM HANCOCK

In his recent exploration of the close and problematic relationship between poetry and academia since the mid-eighteenth century, Robert Crawford diagnosed a certain kind of cultural schizophrenia as an identifying characteristic of the modern poet. According to Crawford, the loyalties of the creative writer are almost invariably divided between the sophisticated and the primitive:

> Whatever culture they come from, poets may incline towards the scholarly: it is Russian 'maker' Joseph Brodsky who produces the Alexandrian statement that 'a footnote is where civilization survives'. Yet for every such inclination, a countering gesture can be cited: it is the Alexandrian poet Cavafy who longs for the uncivilized primitives, presenting them in his famous Greek poem 'Waiting for the Barbarians' (with an amount of irony which may be minimal) as 'a kind of solution' attractive to the poet of a sophisticated society [...] Twentieth century poets such as Deguy, Brodsky or Cavafy, who may veer at times between attraction to barbarism and to sophistication, and who may even wish to combine the two, are not being straightforwardly inconsistent. Rather, they are enacting a variation on a centuries-old pattern [...] It might be that some readers feel poetry over the last hundred years has become immured in classrooms. There is a popular perception of much twentieth-century poetry as rebarbatively obscure, demanding the kind of study possible only under seminar conditions. This attitude may have been developed by some of the last century's most academically-nurtured poets, particularly T.S. Eliot who wrote in 1921 that 'it appears likely that poets in our civilization, as it exists at present, must be *difficult*'. Yet even Eliot a dozen years later told the students and professors of a Harvard University lecture hall that he would 'like an audience which could neither read nor write', and linked the poet with the most primitive as well as the most educated mentality.[1]

1 Robert Crawford, *The modern poet: poetry, academia and knowledge since the 1750s* (Oxford, 2001), 7–8.

Searching for contemporary authors to illustrate his thesis, Crawford finds two who hale from Northern Ireland: Seamus Heaney, whom he describes as 'both professorial and primitive',[2] and Paul Muldoon, who similarly 'inhabits the academic machine, yet delights in spoofing its procedures'.[3] These two certainly fit the bill, but perhaps it is the work of another Ulster poet – Ciaran Carson – that is most interestingly illuminated by Crawford's ideas; this chapter will be devoted to seeing what light the diagnosis of 'primitive-sophisticate' can shed on Carson's distinctive poetic persona. In order to describe this persona, I want to range fairly widely across Carson's writing, paying special attention to the margins of his art – footnotes, appendices, acknowledgements, interviews, prose works and so on – for these areas prove to be full of revealing indicators. However, having temporarily abandoned the more familiar passages in order to explore some less well-surveyed byways of Carson's work, I want finally to return to his poetry, and to what may initially seem a rebarbatively obscure, scholarly poem, in order to reveal that the tension between sophistication and primitivism is more than just incidental in his writing, and to show this author's growing self-awareness regarding his own divided artistic identity.

First impressions might appear to indicate that Carson's loyalties are somewhat less divided than those of his celebrated Ulster contemporaries. We could, for example, contrast his take on schoolboyhood in 'Slate Street school' to that of Heaney in 'Alphabets', both of which appeared in volumes published in 1987.[4] Heaney's poem can be read as a reluctant sophisticate's elegy for the death of his primitive self, one whose innocent perceptions are already compromised in the poem's first stanzas as his link to reality begins to be mediated by signifiers. After his schooling, the figure that emerges in the final part of the poem looks and sounds more *doctus* than *poeta*: an authoritative lecturer who stands in the 'wooden O' of a theatre alluding to Shakespeare and Robert Graves. However, these new surroundings also figure him as a little isolated, and the lecturer hardly revels in his hard-earned sophistication, giving us cause to question Helen Vendler's ecstatic appreciation of this poem as a 'series of joyous scenes' wherein 'Heaney implies that whatever infant alphabet we may start from, we will go onto others, by which we hope to encompass the world'.[5] It is worth drawing attention to the potential for disappointment implicit in that word 'hope': might this not indicate that we move from one alphabet to the next because *all* alphabets eventually seem unsatisfactory as means to 'encompass the world'? For Heaney, in

2 Ibid., 277.   **3** Ibid., 278.   **4** *The Irish for no*, 46; Heaney, *The haw lantern* (London, 1987), 1–3.
5 Helen Vendler, 'Second thoughts', *New York review of books*, 28 April 1988, 41–5, 44.

this poem at least, there is surprisingly little joy to be found in the acquisition of book-learning: in part one the child senses a bewildering and intimidating plethora of new rules and regulations to be obeyed; the second section of the poem leaves as much of an impression of the constrictions of writing as it does of the new freedoms that it grants us access to; and the third part commences not with any 'joyous scene', but with melancholic reflections on a past world that is (Heaney borrows Vaughan's plangent phrase) 'all gone'. This world is now twice removed from the poet: once in reality, as the bulldozers have demolished all traces of his school, but more significantly a second time as immediate sensory experience has also retreated behind a fence of letters and numerals: where the child once saw signs as resembling things (a 'Y' like a 'forked stick', the '2' like 'swan's neck and a swan's back'), the adult finds that this relationship has been inverted ('bales like printouts', 'stooked sheaves' like 'lambdas', 'the delta face of each potato pit'). The fact that reality is now concealed by Greek letters turns what had appeared to be a merely dutiful Harvard 'Phi Beta Kappa' poem into something a little more subversive: less celebration of academic achievement than commemoration of a pre-reflective age of unmediated sensuous pleasures. The impression Heaney leaves is that, where education may open up a new dimension of words, it also cuts one off from the innocent apprehension of an old dimension of things. The imagery of his penultimate stanza is deliberately equivocal:

> As from his small window
> The astronaut sees all he has sprung from,
> The risen, aqueous, singular, lucent O
> Like a magnified and buoyant ovum.

On the one hand, the astronaut represents the apogee of sophisticated achievement, but on the other, he also experiences ultimate solitude; he looks backwards, not forwards, and is literally cut off from the Earth just as the poem's speaker is cut off from the earth of his childhood.

Primitivism and sophistication may seem utterly irreconcilable here, although Heaney (characteristically) attempts to find some form of compromise in his final stanza, where both 'pre-reflective' and post-lapsarian identities are fused in an image of strange letters trowelled on in plaster – the trowel another variation on the pen once dug with in *Death of a naturalist*. Carson offers no such compromise in 'Slate Street school'. Where Heaney loses himself in the seductive coils of writing, Carson struggles to escape from his bleak educational surroundings, which are itemized through the clenched teeth of an oppressed schoolboy:

> Back again. Day one. Fingers blue with cold. I joined the lengthening
> queue.
> Roll-call. Then inside: chalk-dust and iced milk, the smell of watered ink.

The student of 'Alphabets' is a dutiful one who is rewarded by the discovery of a
writing, a 'new calligraphy', that feels like 'home'; the student of 'Slate Street
school' is a sullen rebel, a primitive trapped in the purgatorial classroom and
longing to escape, to abandon the dry 'chalky numerals' of education for the
flurry of snowflakes that he moves to the window to see. Where Heaney mourns
the destruction of his school, the birthplace of his 'poet's dream', Carson's aversion
to rote-learning prompts him to turn iconoclastic destroyer in a radically cleansing
poetic vision:

> And I am the avenging Archangel, stooping over mills and
>   factories and barracks.
> I will bury the dark city of Belfast forever under snow: inches,
>   feet, yards, chains, miles.

This image of poet as 'avenging Archangel' forms a marked contrast to that of the
allusive (albeit clandestinely subversive) poet-lecturer in 'Alphabets': the latter is
now irrevocably sophisticated, a citizen of the educated world looking back on a
genre scene of rural innocence; the former figures himself as defiantly primitive,
a Blakeian visionary looking out towards the elemental forces of nature and the
dark matter of the city.

Carson associates this city with a certain kind of artistic motivation and
expression. The emigrants from the Lower Falls who roll back the years in his
prose poem 'Schoolboys and Idlers of Pompeii' also recall 'the taste of school milk
in winter' and 'the names carved on the desks of Slate Street school'; the poet links
such memories to a graffito that he saw in New York's 'Alphabet City', one made
up of 'three-foot-high black letters, saying BELFAST, with the cross-stroke of the
T extended into an arrow pointing east' (*Bc*, 52). Where the narrator of
'Alphabets' absorbs script in a hushed classroom, the wanderer of 'Alphabet City'
celebrates the fugitive street 'scrawl' of outsiders, responding sympathetically to
their instinctive 'bid to be remembered' (*Bc*, 52). Graffiti is, however, conceived
as more than just the instinctive expression of the untutored in this piece. The
'scrawl' is actually a 'careful scrawl', and the terms in which Carson describes one
mural belong more to the discourse of literary criticism that the language of the

street: he sees it as a 'coded, articulated, multi-coloured spray-gunned alphabet – pointing west by style and implication'(*Bc,* 52). If this indicates that there is more to graffiti than mere primitivism, it also indicates that there is more to Carson than recalcitrant schoolboy or avenging Archangel, that his allegiances are more equivocal than one might at first suspect, as we discover when we explore this writer's work further.

It is easy to be seduced by the image of Carson as spokesperson for the 'uncivilized primitives' (as Crawford calls them), partly because this is the image that the writer has presented of himself. Interviews have established a narrative whereby Carson attributes the discovery of his own true poetic voice (the one that emerges in *The Irish for no* and *Belfast confetti*) to lessons learned while playing and listening to traditional music:

> I got a job in the Arts Council about 1975, shortly after I'd written *The New Estate*: the job was concerned with traditional music, song and dance, so I started to get absorbed into that whole area of experience. After a year or two it struck me that poetry, or poems, were so remote by comparison. Removed, academic. Whereas with the music – you're right up against the stuff, it's hitting you from all sides, it's alive, here in front of your very eyes and ears, right now. That's a very attractive immediacy. It's not about withdrawing into your cell to compose these careful utterances about life [...] poetry seemed by comparison to be a self-centred, precious kind of business [...] Maybe around 1985 or so it occurred to me that maybe poetry could borrow something from the whole musical experience, which involves talk and chat and stories as well as the actual music ... everything constantly digressing.[6]

The allegiances are clear for all to see here: poetry is envisaged as a 'precious', cloistered activity, 'removed' from reality and occupying some 'academic' ivory tower; music, by contrast, is imbued with an 'immediacy' and a social authenticity by dint of its association with the street (or to be more precise, the bar).[7] The foundations of Carson's mature art – the art which established his reputation, and that which to date has garnered the most critical attention – would therefore

6 'Ciaran Carson', Interview with Rand Brandes, *Irish Review* 8 (Spring 1990), 77–90, 81–2.
7 Carson made the connection between music and poetry explicit when he talked about this to Frank Ormsby. 'I often think that people don't listen enough, or that their education has made them incapable of listening ... and the same thing can apply to poetry' (Interview with Frank Ormsby, *Linen Hall Review*, April 1991, 5–8, 7).

appear to lie in an energized centrifugal movement away from sterile sophistication: the 'withdrawing' and 'self-centred' attitude is sacrificed for the communal and sociable; the 'careful utterance' opens out to constant digression, what Carson describes as the 'onward rush of pub speech'; the private ivory tower at the symbolic heart of Academe is abandoned for the bars scattered through the backstreets of Belfast.

According to Crawford's diagnosis, however, the schizophrenic condition of the modern poet is a chronic one, and it may be that the compelling centrifugal energy of Carson's argument distracts us from a less obvious, but no less significant, centripetal force that is pulling him in the opposite direction. It is tempting to discern these opposing forces at play in this poet's wildly varying line lengths: on the one hand, we have the long, discursive line of the Belfast poems, culminating in the digressive, tangential narratives of prose works such as *The star factory* and *Shamrock tea*; on the other, we have the translated haiku that punctuate *Belfast confetti*, the suggestive concision of which was to be fully naturalized in *Breaking news*. Both seem necessary components to Carson's art. More clearly, though, there is a sense that even in his most belligerent writing, the sophisticated always remains at least implicitly present. Sometimes it is only there as a necessary evil or goad against which the primitive can define itself, and nowhere is this more evident than in Carson's writing on music – a subject very close to his heart – whereby the attributes of Irish traditional are often delineated against the perceived inadequacies of the classical. Carson's *Pocket guide to Irish traditional music* contains some wickedly funny parodies of academic discourse – this section on the etiquette of 'the yelp', for example:

> The inexperienced punter may be somewhat disconcerted by the custom whereby little whoops and screams are uttered while the music is in progress. These expressions of appreciation may not be as random as they seem. An attentive punter may, for example, make a little yelp at that point where the tune has been played once and is now about to be played again (tunes are played at least twice round), indicating (a) that he knows where a tune ends and (b) that he would like to hear it again, which he will anyway. On the other hand, the yelp may come at a point in the tune which is determined by the punter's perception of a particularly fine melodic variation; to the musician who just played it, it may have been a mistake. Or it may not. (*Itm*, 56–7)

This is light-hearted enough, but when it comes to pitting the traditional against the classical, Carson starts to get serious, adopting a more polemical and occasionally defensive tone: 'People who complain that traditional music is out of tune usually turn out to be brainwashed by conventional music education' (*Itm*, 60); 'Any classical training is disastrous to the traditional singer' (*Itm*, 61); 'The traditional singer or musician learns by ear, not by theory' (*Itm*, , 62). The debate is, once again, between book-learning and life-learning, and it's pretty clear which side the writer is on. Carson further defends traditional territory from classical encroachment in *Last night's fun*, where he derides the attempts of concert musicians to capture the spirit of popular tunes:

> While there is no ultimate correctness in traditional music, there is wrong: the attempts of such as Yehudi Menuhin or James Galway to play 'simple' Irish hornpipes, for example. Such interpretations are simplistic and one-dimensional – they ignore the possibilities. They take the tune as read whilst a traditional musician plays the tune as heard.
>
> (*Lnf*, 11)

This aversion to the arrogance of classical music turns out to be just one aspect of a broader primitivist attack on the soulless nature of technical sophistication: *Last night's fun* opens with a critique of the Compact Disc – 'I remember reading a pronouncement of the maestro Karajan, heralding the new technology in whatever year it was, that before CD, "everything was gaslight"; well, what's wrong with gaslight?' (*Lnf*, 2) – and it ends with a paean to vinyl:

> The ghosts of voices circulate in grooves of dust. Everything is a black gloss: corrigenda and addenda, a thousand couples reeling in a palimpsest of dance-step patterns, as their feet step past the foot-notes.
>
> (*Lnf*, 198)

Note that CD is associated with the concert hall, and vinyl with the dance hall. This could hardly be described as Luddite prose, however, as the vinyl takes on qualities more often found in the realms of textual scholarship, and the primitive 'dance-step patterns' of popular culture metamorphose into the sophisticated 'foot-notes' of academia. Similarly, Carson supports his case for the traditional and against classical 'correctness' in *Last night's fun* by referring to Gerard Manley Hopkins, Marianne Moore, Aristotle's *De memoria et reminiscentia*, and the

Preface to the *Lyrical ballads* (although he thinks that Wordsworth is to the ballad what Menuhin and Galway are to Irish hornpipes). All of which suggests that the academic-sophisticate is not only a goad against which Carson establishes his primitive credentials, but also a part of his own make up – a fact that, as we shall see, this writer knows only too well.

Irish traditional music, and the attitudes associated with it, has wielded a lasting influence over Carson's poetry: it was there in 1985 when the poet realized he could draw on his musical experience in order to forge his own poetic style; it was shaping his verse just as clearly in 1998 when he published *The twelfth of never*, a title borrowed from a popular song.[8] Scratch the vinyl surface of the sonnets in this volume and you often find a traditional lyric underneath, as the poet acknowledges at the end of the book:

> It would be tedious to give a full account of the folk-song influences on the poems, but Colm O Lochlainn's *Irish Street Ballads* and *More Irish Street Ballads* (Three Candles Ltd., Dublin, 1939 and 1965, published in one volume as Irish Street Ballads by Pan Books, London, 1984) were constantly referred to in the writing of this book. (*Ttn*, 91)

The performer in Carson wishes to avoid subjecting his audience to tedium at all costs, but we notice also that the scholar in him is scrupulous in his acknowledgement of a debt. Like the final sentence in *Last night's fun*, this acknowledgement reveals how the appealingly immediate qualities of music are inevitably compromised by the more studied sophistication of research and writing: it turns out that the poetry of *The twelfth of never*, which seeks to capture something of the fluency, serendipity and impact of traditional music, springs not only directly from musical experience but also from scholarly research into transcripts of folk songs. One more glance at the list of acknowledgments at the end of this book reveals another entry showing how the academic and the *craic* exist in an uneasy relationship for this writer:

> I am grateful to Junko Matoba and her colleagues in the International Association for the Study of Irish Literature, who made it possible for me to visit Tokyo; also Michael and Christine Hinds, who showed me some good bars there. (*Ttn*, 91)

---

8 The song contains an appropriate lyric: 'I'll love you till the poets run out of rhyme'.

Here we can see Carson as – metaphorically speaking – part of an awkward *ménage a trois*, conscientiously attempting to do justice to two mutually antagonistic partners: in this case, the organization and the impromptu gathering, the educational and the hedonistic, the colleague and the friend.

All of which locates Ciaran Carson's writing persona more on the nexus between sophisticated and primitive rather than simply with both feet firmly planted on the side of the barbarians, providing a little more evidence to support Crawford's assertion that 'modern poets' almost invariably develop their own 'aesthetic of the primitive-sophisticated'. That Carson's own particular aesthetic has something of the postmodern about it is evident in, for example, the humorous blurring of boundaries between the highbrow and the lowbrow in his work, a range of cultural reference that can encompass the following eclectic mix of books:

> A benefactor had given me £60 worth of Waterstone's book-tokens, so I went to their shop in Royal Avenue and exchanged my tokens for these books:
> *Roland Barthes* by Roland Barthes:
> *Selected Writings, Vol. 1: 1913–1926* by Walter Benjamin
> *Encyclopaedia Acephalia* by Georges Bataille, Michel Leris, Marcel Griaule, Carl Einstein, Robert Desnos, and writers associated with the Acéphale and Surrealist groups, and
> *A Nostalgic Look at Belfast Trams since 1945* by Mike Maybin. (*Tsf,* 26)

Perhaps the benefactor influenced the selection here, as this list is clearly going to keep the sophisticate happier than the primitive; yet by placing Maybin's *Nostalgic look at Belfast trams* at the end of the list Carson gives primitivism the final, subversive word in the argument – this is the performer's reassuringly wry grin directed at friends in the audience. It is worth dwelling for a moment on the other three choices here also. They could obviously be seen as indicating the preferences of a reader abreast with trends and developments in literary theory, that most extreme manifestation of sophistication in English studies; but perhaps the selection is better regarded as focusing on figures who have – in their own ways – all occupied the hinterland between exploratory, creative writing and academia, writers who have all in their time been deemed somehow unacceptable or inappropriate for a university undergraduate education. Certainly, it seems unlikely that any of these authors featured significantly on the English Literature reading lists from Carson's own time at Queen's University. It is no coincidence that John Keats – consistent favourite of literary educators since the days of Matthew Arnold – has been the butt of Carson's poetic jokes on more than one occasion, his transforming glance being turned onto that old standby for New Critics and English examiners alike, the 'Ode to a nightingale':

> We were debating,
> Bacchus and the pards and me, how to render *The Ulster Bank – the Bank That Likes to Say Yes* into Irish, and whether eglantine was alien to Ireland.
> *I cannot see what flowers are at my feet* (*Ifn*, 49)

On one level, this is a fairly playful passage about cultural colonialism, about the incongruities between the foreign and the native. But it is as much about two discourses as it is about two tribes, reflecting tensions between the language of higher education and that of the street, tensions that Carson is acutely sensitive to. Keats puts in at least two more fleeting appearances in his writing, and on both occasions he seems more like a representative of the high-falutin than of an invasive foreign power: in *The star factory* we glimpse 'beaded bubbles' winking at the brim of a bottle of lucozade (rather than 'the blushful Hippocrene') (*Tsf*, 256); in *Shamrock tea* the narrator and his friend Maeterlinck ape the men of 'stout Cortez' when they look 'at each other with a wild surmise' (*St*,199). By such means does Carson assert his primary allegiances. Keats is an alien presence in Carson's literary consciousness – irrevocably associated with 'all that English Lit. debris lying around at the back of my mind'[9]– but I think it is less the 'English' than the 'Lit' (with a capital L) that Carson flinches from. And yet Keats is a presence none the less, reflecting the extent to which this writer has absorbed such 'sophisticated' discourse. The fact that Carson would rather not rummage around in the 'English Lit. debris' is suggested by his dismissive response to an enquiry about the 'Keats quotation' in 'The Irish for no':

> It's just there for a laugh. I don't really know why. Maybe it's putting the romantic agony in a more brutal context. But I don't think explanations are necessary.[10]

'Explanations' are the merchandise of higher education, the alien flowers cultivated within the groves of Academe; by implication, simple communal *experiences*

9 Ormsby, 6.   **10** Brandes, 83

like a shared joke are the native species that thrive in the 'real world' outside of these walls.

This spatial metaphor is one that Carson has himself used elsewhere in a particularly revealing way, a way that further clarifies his own identity as 'sophisticated primitive' rather than simply as champion of the barbarians. One can't miss the pleasure that this writer takes in detailing the topography of his native city: Carson not only encourages us to get to know Belfast as it is, we also get to know it as it was at various stages of its development, and feel the ghosts of its demolished buildings and lost streets. One Belfast landmark that is still very much in existence, and which puts in an appearance in *The star factory*, is the Lanyon Building at Queen's University. A 'badly blurred' photograph on a calendar reminds the writer of his time there:

> JUNE. *Queen's University.* [...] I was an ostensible student at Queen's, between 1967 and 1971; looking at its central tower, I remember the winding stair within it, which led to a superior turret from which you could spy on aspects of a darkened Belfast; having discovered the hidden entrance to this eyrie, I used to bring girl-friends up here on nocturnal expeditions. Similarly, we used to scale the fence to wander the grounds of the Vice-Chancellor's gardens, a mysterious moonlit space of lakes and arbours between Stranmillis and Malone. Above its dark remove, the stars were swayed by moving clouds and branches. (*Tsf,* 92)

Carson is clearly another in that great tradition of poets who were once 'ostensible students' at university, another who courted more than he studied, following his natural creative instincts rather more assiduously than the prescribed curriculum. But before we take this as a simple oath of allegiance to the anti-establishment forces, we should note where he situates himself in this extract: not only within the central tower of the building at the heart of the University, but in a superior turret of the central tower;[11] not just roaming the University grounds, but trespassing on the holy of holies, the Vice-Chancellor's gardens. Hence the transgression against authority is no longer figured as an escape from the confines of educational space, as it is in 'Slate Street school', but as a penetration and occupation of its heart, an annexation of the seat of power. We might apply to Ciaran Carson Crawford's description of Ezra Pound as 'a kind of 'double agent' towards both poetry and academia';[12] Carson's self-image in this episode from *The*

11 The single superior turret is located at the rear left corner of this tower.   12 Crawford, 184.

star factory is that of a fifth-columnist bent on usurping authority in the citadel of
education. More than this, the image leaves a sense that – in a way – he believes
himself to be the rightful occupant of the 'superior turret' and the Vice-
Chancellor's garden: he is the wild eagle that belongs to the 'eyrie', highest of high
points and his natural home. When he gains occupancy of this place, he
transforms it: the ivory tower in the bastion of educational erudition becomes a
Yeatsian symbol (complete with 'winding stair') of creativity and imaginative
independence; the scholarly inward look towards recondite secrets is replaced by
an outward look towards darkened Belfast (the 'real world'). Similarly, by lifting
his eyes towards stars, moon, clouds and branches, Carson romantically transcends
the petty demarcations of academia represented by the fence surrounding the
Vice-Chancellor's gardens. He earns the right to his occupancy of both places by
his responsiveness to the forces that move the creative imagination.

The association between the primitive and the creative imagination is touched
on briefly by Crawford, but it seems to be of central importance in Carson's work.
This becomes clear in *Shamrock tea*, a book set for the most part in an imaginary
seat of learning whose own curriculum is itself dedicated to the powers of the
imagination. That memory of 'nocturnal expeditions' around Queen's probably
lies behind the character Maeterlinck's recollection of ascending the Belfry of
Ghent:

> 'I would gaze down like a god, naming the constituents of my city [...] I
> imagined myself a pilot, or a sailor on the topmast' (*St*, 110)

This is not the only link between the autobiographical *The star factory* and the
novel *Shamrock tea*. In the former, Carson recalls 'dreaming below the dome of
the Belfast Central Library, imagining its radii of knowledge streaming out to the
smaller branch libraries – Falls, Ormeau, Shankill, Donegall Road, Tullycarnet –
the dome like the focus of a pulsar, or a flying saucer, emitting radio-beacon light
rays.' He feels 'the whole thing ready to tremble, lift, and slip off into outer space
to wander in dark forever through the incandescent galaxies' (*Tsf*, 176). A similar
architecturally-induced daydream causes the inattentive students in *Shamrock tea*
to think that they are about to get into trouble, but Loyola House is no Slate
Street school, and instead of berating them for their wandering thoughts, teacher
Father Brown actually praises them for possessing 'the faculty of visualization to
a high degree'. 'We need boys with imagination', he goes on to say, 'boys who can,
by intense concentration, lift themselves beyond the merely superficial and

mundane' (*St*, 146). Hence the right to appropriate the ivory tower, to assume a position at the top of the literary hierarchy, is given by dint of imaginative power. Carson may have only been an ostensible presence in the Queen's English Department between 1967 and 1971, but he would undoubtedly have attended more regularly, and been awarded a first class degree, if that university had possessed a Faculty of Visualization.

The celebration of the creative faculty in *Shamrock tea* suggests that Carson's own staging of the fight between the barbarians and the civilized has a deeply Romantic heritage, and – somewhat ironically – the poet that springs most readily to mind in this context is the one already occupying the debris at the back of Carson's. For Keats the sophisticated exemplar much-loved by twentieth-century university English departments was also Keats of the cockney school of poetry, the anti-establishment figure criticized for having fanciful ideas above his station, the man who famously championed the instinctive and sensual imagination against the dictats of empiricism, arguing that, where 'the dull brain perplexes and retards' ('Ode to a nightingale'), 'what the imagination seizes as Beauty must be truth, whether it existed before or not'.[13] Too much *Shamrock tea* can make you start seeing unlikely correspondences everywhere, I realize, but this shared emphasis on the free imagination is further suggested by another Keats / Carson coincidence. The imaginative powers of the protagonists in Carson's book qualify them to undertake its central quest, which involves their use of van Eyck's 'Arnolfini Double Portrait' as a portal to fifteenth-century Bruges. Keats's letters reveal that he also took great pleasure in paintings that seemed 'particularly hospitable to the poet's "curious" imagination', art that allowed him to 'glimpse a new and strange world' and to be absorbed 'into the pictured scene'.[14] Both of these writers deserve their places in Crawford's big tent of modern poets, then, joining all of those others who have struggled in their different ways to accommodate primitive imaginative instincts within sophisticated social and educational contexts. A third occupant of this tent seems on the face of it just as unlikely an ally, but Ezra Pound's desire, 'with his method of the luminous detail to have poetry, not academia, govern knowledge'[14] is not so far removed from Carson's annexation of established educational power through his attention to luminous details such as the beautiful tracery of glass and cast iron in the imagined Loyola House, the

---

13 *The letters of John Keats*, ed. Robert Gittings (Oxford, 1970), 37. 14. See Martin Aske, 'Still life with Keats', in Michael O'Neill (ed.), *Keats: bicentenary readings* (Edinburgh, 1997), 129–43, 130, 131 and 141. **14** Crawford, 183.

mirror in the Arnolfini portrait, the dome of the Belfast Central Library, or the 'mysterious moonlit space' of the Vice Chancellor's garden at Queen's University.

Implicitly, both Pound and Carson are suggesting that it is the responsiveness of the poetic imagination – a capacity not acquired through rote learning or taught by academics – that gives one the right to claim the position of authority, although the work of both poets also indicates that such assertions are not in themselves sufficient to effect a change of the guard. The imaginative insurrection has to take place in terms understood by the very *ancien regime* that is being overthrown, hence Crawford describes Pound as bent not only on out-imagining the professors, but also on 'out-professoring' them;[15] and just as Pound promoted himself as a walking 'Ezuversity', so Carson not only imaginatively assumes the seat of learning, but also occupies and transfigures its language. As he had done in the *Pocket guide to Irish traditional music*, Carson has great fun parodying professor-speak in *Shamrock tea*, with my own favourite example being the following learned discourse by Father Brown:

> Do sit down and make yourselves comfortable, he said, and help yourselves to the tea and Jaffa Cakes. An excellent product, if I might venture, in which we experience a trinity of gustative experiences, as the sweet viscous orange centre is sandwiched between the hard dark bitter chocolate upper layer and the sponge biscuit base. Its name always recalls to me the Jaffa Gate of Jerusalem, by which one enters that city when visiting the Church of the Holy Sepulchre. (*St,* 145)

The satire is not exactly biting here; rather this is the sort of waggish, sympathetic pastiche that scholars themselves often produce as a therapeutic diversion. Like Father Brown, Carson not only takes pleasure in the 'primitive' thing described, but also in the incongruously 'sophisticated' means of description, accentuating what are actually some of the better qualities of academic discourse: celebration ('an excellent product'), modesty ('if I might venture'), inclusiveness ('we experience'), lateral thinking ('recalls to me the Jaffa Gate'), experience and urbanity ('by which one enters the city when visiting the Church of the Holy Sepulchre'). By the time we reach the end of *Shamrock tea*, things have gone a stage further: we find not mock-academia here, but something almost unrecognizable from the real thing. The main text is followed by a bibliography that contains over fifty titles (and these only 'selected sources'), with specific references on numbered pages acknowledged at the end (*St,* 304–8). The author

15 Ibid.

may limit himself to crediting influences here, but nevertheless this move has something in common with Eliot's 'Notes on the Waste Land': a radically disruptive, iconoclastic display of imaginative verve is being followed, almost apologetically, by the self-effacing and authenticating stamp of academia, the dutiful provision of an evidential basis for the 'argument'. Indeed, you could argue that Carson out-professor's the professorial Eliot: there is no sense that this appendix is intended as either spoof or filler.

Where the poetic imagination was once envisaged as a means of escape from the world of rote learning, as well as a means by which revenge might be taken on that world, now it accords the right to the levers of power, potentially transforming the educational system into something radically new. The sophisticated appropriation of both the place and the discourse of learning in prose works such as *The star factory* and *Shamrock tea* demonstrates that Carson has moved beyond the polemical and rhetorical habits that characterize much of his early poetry and music criticism, indicating a growing appreciation of the Jekyll and Hyde nature of the modern writer's cultural identity. Nowhere is this developing appreciation and self-awareness more evident than in *Opera et cetera*, although a glance at this book's list of contents, with its liberal sprinkling of Latin, might appear to suggest that it is now the sophisticate who holds sway, that the educated voice is in control of this volume. After all, Latin remains indelibly associated with the rote learning of a traditional, dryasdust education, the acquisition of this dead language being the sort of 'academic exercise' that causes the schoolboy in Tony Harrison's 'Rhubarbarians' to utter profanities of frustration. But Carson is too solicitous of his envisaged reader's patience to force anything on us, and not only does he provide notes advising that translations of the Latin phrases 'can be found in *Chambers twentieth century dictionary*', he even goes to the trouble of reprinting these translations, thus saving us the bother of looking them up. Carson's choice of dictionary itself says something of his values and cultural allegiances. In *Last night's fun* he gestures fondly to his '*Chambers*, which is so well-thumbed it has nearly acquired a thumb-index' (*Lnf,* 150); elsewhere in the same book he offers a footnote musing on the appropriateness of this dictionary's name, 'with its implications of legal wranglings in book-lined inner sanctums, of precedents and antecedents, of rooms within rooms' (*Lnf,* 140). Perhaps he is drawn to the Johnsonian wit that can still be found in *Chambers*,[16] perhaps its reputation with

---

16 Amusing definitions in *Chambers* include 'Jaywalker' ('a careless pedestrian whom motorists are expected to avoid running down') and 'mullet' ('a hairstyle that is short at the front, long at the back, and ridiculous all round').

crossword-solvers and scrabble-players recommends it to a poet much drawn to wordplay. Whatever, this book is preferred to the 'official' reference work of the academic establishment, the *Oxford English dictionary*; Carson's discomfort with all-things-Oxbridge can be sensed in *Shamrock tea*, where he describes a 'Loyola House uniform [...] the navy blue blazer over the crisp white shirt, draped with the Oxford Blue tie striped with Cambridge Blue; the charcoal grey trousers. Black Oxford shoes rested on the floor. As I donned the immaculate ensemble, I felt myself becoming another person.' (*St*, 77) By his democratizing gestures Carson distinguishes his own use of untranslated foreign diction from that encountered in both the educational system and in the poetry of high modernism: clearly he does not share Pound's patrician disregard for the 'common reader'.

Having said this, it would certainly need special pleading to argue that *Opera et cetera* is an unsophisticated book of poetry. Yes the poems are littered with the bric-a-brac of everyday experience, but for every familiar 'Pyrex bowl' there is an unfamiliar 'logical palabra' (*Oec*, 26), for every 'Elastoplast' there are 'Coulomb interactions' (*Oec*, 34). I want to end this discussion by looking at one such record of the split personality, a poem in which – on first inspection, at least – Carson-the-sophisticate appears to be determining the direction of events:

Auditque vocatus apollo

We were climbing Parnassus. My guide kept asking
    me 'how a man can
Penetrate through the lyre's strings'. I tried to think
    of a silly answer, and a can-

Can dancer's disembodied legs sprang to mind, or the
    patent ostrich-egg-
Slicer of a harp. *Our mind*, he said, *is split.* Too
    true. Like he was Quee and I was Queg –

One of those guys. Orpheus. Apollo. Rilke. Ahab. Dick.
    And climbing Mount
Olympia is like that: enquiring for the whale that
    disappears beneath its fount-

Ain spray. You think you've reached the summit when
    another distant crest
Appears to challenge you. *Quo Vadis?* Something like that.
    I asked if we could rest.

I don't know why I started this. One summer doesn't
    make a swallow.
Suddenly, the jangling of a lyre. I cried, *Who's there?*
    He says, *It's me. Apollo.* (*Oec*, 39)

Chambers twentieth century dictionary will only take you so far with this poem, which is the sort that sends academic poetry critics scurrying to the library (or increasingly the internet) in order to source allusions. Most of these are literary, and the texts are academically-sanctioned highbrow – no place for *A nostalgic look at Belfast trams since 1945* here. It appears that, from the start, the narrator is seeking elevation in more ways than one. When he describes himself as 'climbing Parnassus', the speaker locates himself on the path of an 'official' or mainstream poetic tradition ultimately leading back to the Muses and Apollo. This seems a surprising invocation, as one would expect a rollicking Irish poet to owe fealty to the 'passionate music' of the more rebellious and disorderly Dionysus – but more of this later. At this stage in the poem, the main thing to recognize is the speaker's apparent aspiration to conquer and claim the cultural high-ground – much as Carson once occupied the superior turret of the Lanyon Building at Queen's. His guide on this path is Rainer Maria Rilke: the short translation from Rilke's third 'Sonnet to Orpheus' only reinforces the sense that we are treading on hallowed turf here, and that the central concern of this poem is with lofty aesthetic ambitions. Yet Carson also chooses to repeat the German poet's phrase 'our mind is split', which confirms our sense of the difference between narrator and guide, whose divergent attitudes have already been indicated by the former's irreverent desire 'to think of a silly answer' to Rilke's profoundly serious question, and by his transmogrification of the transcendent lyre into (first) a 'can- / Can dancer's disembodied legs' and (second) an ostrich-egg-slicing harp. Sophisticated and idealistic aesthetic aspirations, it would seem, still require mocking barbaric responses.

    This narrator can hardly be described as Rilke's passive acolyte, then, but nor is he a mere scoffer. The split mind suggests a certain internalization of these tensions, an impression that is reinforced by the next area of allusion in the poem.

Carson's textual splitting of 'Quee' from 'Queg' emphasizes the already-divided personality of the *Moby-Dick* harpooner, a man who can be comfortably accommodated neither in the 'civilized' world of America, nor any longer in the 'savage' Polynesian society from which he has sprung. Here we see the tension that elsewhere forms a suppressed undercurrent in Carson's work clearly rising to the surface; we also see how this writer has gained an increasingly subtle awareness of his own ambiguous status as sophisticated barbarian. The allusion hints at a degree of nostalgia for a lost idyll of 'natural' identity: Queequeg cannot claim his royal birthright because he has been defiled by his contact with the 'sophisticated' Americans. This chimes with the touch of belligerence that can be heard in the deliberately crass, throwaway phrases 'One of those guys' and 'Something like that': Carson is flashing his 'man-of-the-people' credentials at us here. There is, however, a sincerity and pathos about the following lines, wherein the speaker finds his own imagery of tantalization with which to record the poetic frustration voiced by Rilke in the sonnet to Orpheus:

> You think you've reached the summit when
> > another distant crest
> Appears to challenge you.

But we should also recognize a difference in attitude here: Rilke's question at least leaves open the possibility that there may be a profound artistic solution; Carson's formulation appears to offer a more sceptical recognition of the futility of such quests for perfection and elevation. 'Appears' is a carefully chosen, carefully placed word: it bears the same double-meaning as Heaney has elsewhere conveyed by the phrase 'seeing things', although where Heaney often seeks to disclose the mysterious in the mundane, Carson usually does the opposite, sowing a seed of doubt about the genuineness of the aesthetic challenge confronting the narrator. In truth, we have already been alerted to the potential spuriousness of the venture when, for some reason, Parnassus suddenly turns into Mount Olympia (which isn't even in Europe, let alone Greece).[17] This glaring error suits the freewheeling inexactness of the poem, indicating that we shouldn't take this speaker too seriously. More importantly, it also suggests that he knows he is on the wrong path. *Quo vadis* indeed.

Such self-examination contributes to a tone that is, ultimately, less belligerent-barbarian than self-deprecating sophisticate. The overall impression left by

---

17 Mount Olympia is in Washington State, USA; Olympia, birthplace of the Games, is on the Greek Peloponnese; Mount Olympus, home of the gods, is in central Greece.

'Auditque vocatus Apollo' is not so much one of nostalgia for a more innocent and unified native consciousness than of a clear-eyed recognition of hybridity. But that is not to say that Carson is left sitting on the fence in this poem, for while he may share Rilke's symbolist ambition for a form of creative writing that approaches the condition of music (and shares his fears that such ambitions may never be realized), he – as we have seen elsewhere in his writing – has a very different kind of music in mind. Apollo, as I have suggested, is the wrong deity for this poet; Orpheus's lyre is a less suitable instrument for his purposes than, say, Joe Cooley's accordion. We know that Carson sees music – or to be more precise, Irish traditional music – as a model of authentic artistic expression, and he sees the improvisatory and serendipitous variations of this music as suggesting methods by which such authentic expression might be achieved. When the speaker asks his guide if they can rest (a suitably musical term), he symbolically gives up the highbrow quest; reflecting poignantly on his artistic achievements and ambitions, he amusingly and creatively garbles Aristotle's swallow aphorism in the best tradition of the Irish vocalist. But the very act of giving up the quest results in the music suddenly flowing: not aetherial harmonies, the 'gust inside the god' of Orpheus's instrument, but a more discordant 'jangling' sound that transforms the Greek lyre into something more distinctly Gaelic, a vehicle for the 'passionate music' that Rilke counsels us to forget. And when Apollo does put in an appearance, he does so in a less than elevated guise: not so much god of poetry as Greek-next-door, indigenous male rather than transcendent deity.

The poem's argument runs as follows, then: the presiding spirit of art will respond, breathing musical life into poetry, only when he is addressed in the appropriate way; this appropriate way is not necessarily that of one's celebrated forebears (however much one might admire their work). The approach that Carson takes in 'Auditque vocatus Apollo' – one which eschews crude polemics, recognizes the usefulness of literary allusion, but nevertheless confirms a commitment to the demotic – is a persuasive one. By producing such a sophisticated defence of primitivism, Carson ensures that he cannot be regarded as one of 'those poets and critics who would seek to ignore or deny the fact' that 'the course of modern poetry and the development of modern academia are, for better or worse, deeply intertwined',[18] but should rather be seen as one who, on facing up to this fact, has recognized and defined his own distinctive aesthetic identity, and in so doing has found an authentic voice.

18 Crawford, 18–19.

'Faery lands forlorn': reading tradition in the poetry of Ciaran Carson

PATRICIA HORTON

In his two essays 'The Argentine writer and tradition' and 'Kafka and his precursors', Jorge Luis Borges provides a suggestive model for thinking about tradition in the poetry of Ciaran Carson. Borges is a good starting-point for a number of reasons. First, as I discuss in detail later, there are significant points of comparison between Borges's work and that of Carson, a sense of a shared cultural perspective. Even a cursory glance at 'The Argentine writer and tradition' gives some indication of a common ground. In the essay Borges attacks the notion that the Argentine writer is isolated from the rest of Europe and cannot, therefore, have access to European traditions. Rather, he reclaims Argentina's marginal status, its difference, as positive and empowering in that it enables writers to 'handle all European themes, handle them without superstition, with an irreverence which can have, and already does have, fortunate consequences'.[1] Not only does Borges allude directly to the Irish writer in his essay, presenting his/her situation as analogous to that of the Argentinean writer, but his refusal of containment and his rejection of traditional categories and boundaries resonates powerfully in Carson's own writing. My second reason for turning to Borges is that his radical and anarchic theory of tradition in 'Kafka and his precursors' seems particularly appropriate to Carson's work. Having considered Kafka's work alongside a series of random writings, Borges concludes:

> If I am not mistaken, the heterogeneous pieces I have enumerated resemble Kafka; if I am not mistaken, not all of them resemble each other. This second fact is the more significant. In each of these texts we find Kafka's idiosyncrasy to a greater or less degree, but if Kafka had never written a line, we would not perceive this quality; in other words, it would not exist. The poem 'Fears and scruples' by Browning foretells

---

[1] Jorge Luis Borges, *Labyrinths: selected stories and other writings*, eds. and trans. Donald A. Yates and James E. Irby (London, 1970), 218. Hereafter, abbreviated to *L* and page references incorporated into the text.

Kafka's work, but our reading of Kafka perceptibly sharpens and deflects our reading of the poem. Browning did not read as we do now. In the critics' vocabulary, the word 'precursor' is indispensable, but it should be cleansed of all connotation of polemics or rivalry. The fact is that every writer creates his own precursors. His work modifies our conception of the past, as it will modify the future.[2]

Positing tradition as fluid and unpredictable, Borges's model allows us to think more creatively about the workings of tradition in Carson's poetry and about his relationship with his literary predecessors. This essay will use Borges's notion of tradition to concentrate on a single idea in Carson's work, his ongoing fascination with the relationship between the real world and alternative realities, the world of the imagination, of dreams, nightmares, and altered states of consciousness. In its approach to and exploration of this relationship, Carson's poetry assembles its own tradition, bringing together literary precursors such as Keats, De Quincey, Rimbaud, Baudelaire, and even Borges himself, writers seemingly random, but linked to Carson and sometimes to one another in their preoccupation with perception, vision and visionary states, and in their exploration of the relationship between reality and imagination.

In 'The Irish for no' Carson sandwiches together references from Heaney and from Keats's 'Ode to a nightingale' (*Ifn*, 49). Carson has spoken of his use of Keats in the poem as an attempt to explore 'how the romantic agony – that is the Romantic desire to transcend reality, to escape from the awfulness of life, and the recognition that such transcendence is impossible – fits into a context of brutality and political violence'.[3] Neil Corcoran, in his 1991 essay, 'One step forward, two steps back', reads the poem as a critique of the 'luxuriance of Keats's ode' and as a negative 'judgement on the sensorial opulence of Heaney's early work'.[4] This reading captures well Carson's parodic stance towards Heaney, but it fails to see how the allusions might reveal a more complex and profound response to Keats than Corcoran has allowed for.[5] There is, I would argue, a degree of artistic

---

2 Borges, 2.   **3** Ciaran Carson, interview with Frank Ormsby, *Linen Hall Review* 8:1 (1991), 6. The phrase 'romantic agony' is, in fact, the title of a book on Romanticism by Mario Praz which takes as its subject the darker side of Romanticism, its concern with sadism, masochism, perversion, eroticism and satanism. While this is not, I think, the sense in which Carson uses the phrase in the above sentence, it is interesting that it is to these aspects of Romanticism that Carson frequently turns. **4** Neil Corcoran, 'One step forward, two steps back: Ciaran Carson's *The Irish for no*,' in Neil Corcoran (ed.), *The chosen ground: essays on the contemporary poetry of Northern Ireland* (Bridgend, 1992), 214.   **5** I would argue that Heaney's own interpretations of Keats in, for example, 'The fire

sympathy between Carson and Keats, a shared sense of 'the frustrations of living in a world where language is elusive, beauty is eroded, and transcendence is impossible'.[6] But Carson's sense of kinship with Keats works at a deeper level as these remarks from Carson make clear: 'I love Keats … The world of the Odes is made "real" in language. Is it the real world? In 'The Irish for no' I have lines from Keats turning up beside a Black & Decker drill. Is that the real world? Is the language in which we write about the Troubles, a reflection of their reality? Or "unreality"?'[7] As I will go on to show, Carson has an abiding attraction to Keatsian uncertainty and to Keats's probing and blurring of the boundaries between dream and reality, illusion and truth, waking and sleeping.

From his earliest work, Carson has been preoccupied with the idea of boundaries. Poems throughout his early collection, *The new estate and other poems*, probe the relationship between past and present ('An early bed'), primitive and civilized ('The great Fitzpatrick'), the traditional and the new ('The new estate'). More particularly for my purposes, Carson's poems explore a Keatsian dilemma: the conflict between reality, and with it ideas of entrapment and constriction, and dreams, imagination and the promise of escape. In 'The half-moon lake', for example, the speaker broods on the death of a child in a lake. He reads the boy's death as a desire to escape 'into the reversed world / Of his dreams, hoping that life there might/ Prove otherwise'. It is deliberately unclear whether the drowning has been an accident or suicide:

> Was the faultless mirror shattered
> By the thin boy diving for the moon
> Of his own face rising through the water? (*Tneop*, 29)

The poem is an early example of Carson's ongoing obsession with mirrors and images, and with representation more generally. Here the boy's reflection represents a sense of selfhood from which he has been estranged. This interpretation is borne out in the lines 'Deep/ In the unseen water it is possible/ He lies, with himself at last asleep' (*Tneop*, 29). Death brings peace and fulfilment in the re-uniting of the split self.

i' the flint: reflections on the poetry of Gerard Manley Hopkins,' in which he describes Keats's writing as feminine, sensual and luxuriant and somehow remote from the real world, have come to control discussions of Keats in relation to Irish poetry. See Heaney, *Preoccupations: selected prose 1968–1978* (London, 1980), 79–97. **6** Mary Fitzgerald-Hoyt, 'Grounding Keats's nightingale: Ciaran Carson's *The Irish for no*,' *Canadian Journal of Irish Studies* 19: 2 (1993), 76. **7** Ciaran Carson, interview with John Brown, *In the chair: interviews with poets from the North of Ireland* (Cliffs of Moher, 1992), 144.

'The half-moon lake' is one of a cluster of poems in *The new estate* that deal with a child longing for escape from a present which is portrayed as harsh and disturbing. These lines, for example, from 'An early bed', in which a child seeks escape from the anger and authority of his father, are deeply reminiscent of 'The half-moon lake' in their desire for a freedom which is clearly associated with death: 'I held my breath/ And tried to sink below the surface/ Of myself, into somewhere else' (*Tneop*, 19). This idea of constriction and the necessity for escape is expanded in various ways in the collection. In 'Engraving from a child's encyclopaedia', one of several poems about paintings, photographs and engravings in the collection, there is a sense that any representation catches only part of the truth and that the engraving is a form of entrapment that fixes the fluid moment in a frozen image. This poem represents an attempt to transcend the fixity of the image and to imagine the details that have been left out in the engraver's portrayal:

> Some other life persists: the *roches moutonnées*,
> For example, might perhaps be taken
> For black sheep, resting furtively on pinnacles
> Of ice, after their long journey. One of the human
> Figures is seated, looking towards them.
> Is he counting them, is he asleep?
> All three are lost in contemplation.
> They seem a long way from home. (*Tneop*, 26)

Recognizing that representations are partial and selective, the imaginative faculty allows the speaker to explode the 'reality' the engraving is supposed to represent. In 'The alhambra' the 'clouds/ Of boiling steam' in the laundry become for the speaker an imaginative entry into an Other world that is clearly linked to the cinema next door, the Alhambra of the title. Like imagination, cinema is a window onto a world of possibility: 'It is here I will/ Kiss a girl who will never be my wife, watching/ The *Titanic* founder for the second time/ Through cascades of broken ice'. Via the imagination, the speaker becomes a time-traveller, witnessing not just the sinking of the *Titanic* but 'the Fall of Rome' and 'the death of Al Capone'. The moment of escape is fleeting, however, for the speaker is 'washed back into daylight,/ To the laundry – sea-foam on the lens,/ Shirts and underwear revolving/ In my struggle to escape the glass' (*Tneop*, 43). That word 'glass' is important, suggesting not simply 'reality' and the mimetic but also the hourglass – time itself. As Carson puts it elsewhere, 'glass is an aspect of death' (*Tsf*, 273).

The final lines I have just quoted from 'The alhambra' call up Keats's 'Ode to a nightingale' where the nightingale's voice is described as one that 'oft-times hath / Charmed magic casements, opening on the foam/ Of perilous seas, in faery lands forlorn'.[8] Like Carson's own poem, Keats's 'Ode to a nightingale' reminds us that dream experience is fleeting – in both poems the speaker is returned to the real world which imposes limits and constraints on the imagination. As with Carson, Keats's poetry pitches between visionary impulses – the imagination, in his description, is like 'Adam's dream – he awoke and found it truth'[9] – and an awareness of the impossibility of transcendence. Escape is always hampered by knowledge of suffering and pleasure is inseparable from pain – in 'the very temple of Delight/ Veil'd Melancholy has her sovran shrine'.[10] Poems like 'La belle dame sans merci' make clear Keats's reservations about the dream experience and in *The fall of Hyperion* the poet is warned that 'None can usurp this height …/ But those to whom the miseries of the world/ Are misery, and will not let them rest'.[11] The route to the dream world is fraught with pain, anxiety and despair, and such feelings constantly vex and hinder the dream state. The Keatsian echo in Carson's 'The alhambra' also reminds us that Keats asked complex questions about reality and truth. It is perhaps his knowledge of his impending death that makes the notion of the real especially nebulous for Keats. By November 1820 he already felt he had passed out of the real world and was leading 'a posthumous existence',[12] and about the same time he wrote to Charles Brown asking 'Is there another Life? Shall I awake and find all this a dream? There must be we cannot be created for this sort of suffering [sic]'.[13] This questioning of the real is implicit in poems like 'Ode to a nightingale' which ends with the speaker wondering 'Was it a vision or a waking dream?/ Fled is that music:– Do I wake or sleep?'.[14]

While Keats is concerned with the blurring of dream and reality, it is rather to de Quincey that we turn for an exploration of the darker side of the dream experience, its potential to turn into nightmare. De Quincey shares with Keats a concern with altered states of consciousness, but is linked more particularly to Carson in his concern with the instability of the urban landscape and of the subject within it. For de Quincey the city is both a territory of gothic nightmare and a space of endless possibility and fluidity. His *Confessions of an English opium-*

8 John Keats, *The poetical works of John Keats*, ed. H.W. Garrod (Oxford, 1939), 258.   **9** John Keats to Benjamin Bailey, Saturday 22 November 1817, *The letters of John Keats*, ed. Maurice Buxton Forman, 2nd ed. (London, 1935), 68.   **10** Keats, *The poetical works*, 275.   **11** Ibid., 511.   **12** Keats to Charles Brown, Thursday 30 November 1820, *The letters of John Keats*, 526.   **13** Keats to Charles Brown, Saturday 30 September 1820, *The letters of John Keats*, 520.   **14** Keats, *The poetical works*, 260.

eater, a narrative poised between dream and nightmare, stands as a major precursor to Carson's work. The hallucinogenic experience de Quincey undergoes through opium disrupts spatial and temporal certainties, and turns London into a labyrinthine structure:

> And sometimes in my attempts to steer home-wards, upon nautical principles, by fixing my eye on the pole-star, and seeking ambitiously for a north-west passage, instead of circumnavigating all the capes and head-lands I had doubled in my outward voyage, I came suddenly upon such knotty problems of alleys, such enigmatical entries, and such sphynx's riddles of streets without thoroughfares, as must, I conceive, baffle the audacity of porters, and confound the intellects of hackney-coachmen. I could almost have believed, at times, that I must be the first discoverer of some of these terrae incognitae, and doubted, whether they had yet been laid down in the modern charts of London.[15]

Here, the city is a utopian space of endless possibility and discovery. Later, de Quincey will suffer the nightmare aspect of this dream experience when he is tormented by, what he calls, 'the tyranny of the human face' – 'now it was that upon the rocking waters of the ocean the human face began to appear: the sea appeared paved with innumerable faces, upturned to the heavens: faces, imploring, wrathful, despairing, surged upwards by thousands, by myriads, by generations, by centuries: – my agitation was infinite, – my mind tossed – and surged with the ocean.[16] De Quincey's nightmares are dominated by architectural manifestations 'of endless growth and reproduction' that distort both space and time:

> Buildings, landscapes, &c. were exhibited in proportions so vast as the bodily eye is not fitted to receive. Space swelled, and was amplified to an extent of unutterable infinity. This, however, did not disturb me so much as the vast expansion of time; I sometimes seemed to have lived for 70 or 100 years in one night; nay, sometimes had feelings representative of a millennium passed in that time, or, however, of a duration far beyond the limits of any human experience.[17]

Under the influence of opium, the mind becomes terrifying and labyrinthine, almost like the city itself, a dark Gothic space into which the opium-eater is plunged.

---

15 Thomas de Quincey, *Confessions of an English opium-eater and other writings*, ed. Grevel Lindop (Oxford and New York, 1985), 47–8.   **16** Ibid., 72.   **17** Ibid., 68.

In common with de Quincey, Carson's dreams and nightmares are bound up with architecture and the city. In an interview with Frank Ormsby, Carson gives a gloss on this:

> For years I've had a series of recurrent dreams about Belfast – nightmares, sometimes, or dreams of containment, repression, anxiety and claustrophobia … often, I'm lost in an ambiguous labyrinth between the Falls and the Shankill; at other times, the city is idealized and takes on a Gothic industrial beauty. It's a landscape I know almost better than the waking city: so at times I'm disappointed that the complicated scenery of the dream world is not to be found on the 'real' map. But then, the real world sometimes throws up details that are contiguous to the dream. Often, they are just as surreal, as shocking and bizarre, as nightmares. Perhaps the poems I write are located somewhere between the two worlds.

Carson faces a comparable ambivalence to de Quincey when faced with the city. Its multiplicity and instability are both a source of terror and a source of elation. Figuring variously as ruins and labyrinth, Belfast is literally the 'collapsing city' in Carson's poetry (*Ifn,*, 33). As a space in which buildings and streets disappear, and in which hidden alleyways and staircases suddenly appear, it acts as the perfect Gothic setting, poised somewhere between dream and nightmare, memory and reality, between the conscious waking world, altered states of consciousness, and the unconscious. In such a setting the phantasms of memory and the ghosts of the past flit between, and are sometimes more real, than the actual inhabitants of Belfast. Carson's poems probe the boundaries between dream and nightmare, between the real and the surreal, but unlike de Quincey, Carson is much more self-conscious in his presentation of the city, and of Belfast in particular, as a Gothic space. In a poem like 'Night patrol', for example the speaker explains how

> the whole Victorian creamy facade has been tossed off
> To show the inner-city tubing: cables, sewers, a snarl of
> Portakabins,
> Soft-porn shops and carry-outs. (*Ifn*, 34)

That 'creamy façade' seems to refer to the respectable, public face of Belfast beneath which lies the city's unconscious, its dark double. That public face is connected to a Victorian decency, but beneath it lurks a lurid underworld of sex shops and seedy bars. The underbelly of Belfast is a seething mass of entrails, the dark innards of that 'Something many-toothed, [and] elaborate' stirring at the heart of Belfast in 'Smithfield market' (*Ifn*, 37). In its nightmare aspect Belfast is a world of 'Zig-zag stairwells' (*Ifn*, 32) where buildings suddenly bubble up out of nowhere – like the greengrocers' shop in 'Clearance' (*Ifn*, 32) – or more commonly the site of disintegration, unravelling and unstitching. The nightmarish quality of this cityscape manifests itself in the 'dark umbilicus of smoke … rising from a heap of burning tyres' (*Ifn*, 36), or the '[m]aggots' that 'seethe between the ribs and corrugations' of the ammunition dump (*Ifn*, 37). It manifests itself, above all, in the indiscriminate and disturbing violence which runs throughout Carson's poems, in instances like 'the Belfast business-man who drilled/ Thirteen holes in his head with a Black & Decker' (*Ifn*, 50).

Carson's representations of Belfast draw heavily on the idea of the labyrinth. This is appropriate for several reasons: first because Belfast is being continually destroyed and reconstructed, and is therefore physically unknowable and often unfamiliar; second because Carson's *flâneries* awaken memories which disrupt spatial and temporal certainties and therefore defamiliarize Belfast; and finally because Belfast exists as an underworld which is inhabited by something monstrous – 'Something many-toothed, elaborate, stirred briefly in the labyrinth'. In 'Belfast Confetti' there is no escape from this labyrinth – 'I know this labyrinth so well – Balaclava, Raglan, Inkerman, Odessa Street – / Why can't I escape?' (*Ifn*, 31). The result is complete disorientation and breakdown – 'What is/ My name? Where am I coming from? Where am I going?' (*Ifn*, 31). Yet the city's ability to defy 'definition, order, structure' can also be an exhilarating experience allowing for the possibility of subversion (*Tsf*, 15). In *The star factory*, we are told that 'streets named after places form exotic junctures not to be found on the map of Empire: Balkan and Ballarat, Cambrai and Cambridge, Carlisle and Carlow, Lisbon and Lisburn, and so on through Madras and Madrid, till we eventually arrive, by way of Yukon, at the isles of Zetland, whereupon we fall off the margins of the city' (*Tsf*, 8). Carson's only means of control over the city is narrative itself – 'Now that I can see the city's microscopic bits transfixed by my attention, I wonder how I might assemble them, for there is no instruction leaflet; I must write it' (*Tsf*, 15). Writing is a means of creating order although the form and structure of that order come in infinite variations.

A similar fascination with the unconscious and with altered states of consciousness can be found in Rimbaud and in the French symbolists more generally. That Carson is attracted by this aspect of their writing is evident in two poems from *First language*, 'Le bâteau ivre' and its companion piece, 'The ballad of *HMS Belfast*', and from his translations of poems by Rimbaud, Baudelaire and Mallarmé in *The Alexandrine plan*. In these translations Carson is clearly stimulated by a common *fin de siècle* context – *The Alexandrine plan* was published in 1998 – and by the subversive and rebellious role adopted by the three French poets. Above all, Carson is drawn to their relentless and often doomed pursuit of the visionary and the transcendent, the realm of the ideal, which can be reached through sensation, memory, death, the halluncinatory and, crucially, through poetic language. While I concentrate on Rimbaud in this essay, there is no doubt that Carson is also strongly drawn to the figure of Baudelaire. They share fascination with the city as a gothic space, a preoccupation with time and with the power of memory to conquer time and an ironic perspective on the poet's predicament. In particular, Carson is drawn to Baudelaire's poem '*Correspondances*' – he translated it in both *First language* and in *The Alexandrine plan* – in which the speaker-poet has the ability to intuit and interpret the sacred and mystical world of the ideal, to experience the sense of harmony (represented here as synaesthesia) and linguistic fullness of that world and to transmit something of this vision to others through poetry. Carson experiences a similar longing to Baudelaire for the infinite and the eternal, a longing for connectedness. There is something of this desire in Uncle Celestine's description of what will happen when the inhabitants of Belfast finally consume Shamrock Tea: 'They will see the world as it really is, a world in which everything connects; where the Many is One, and the One is Many. There will be no division, for everything in the real world refers to something else, which leads to something else again in a never-ending hymn of praise. The world is an eternal story' (*St*, 236). Clearly this is playful, tongue-in-cheek, but it is indicative of an impulse in Carson's work towards connectedness, though a connectedness that can accommodate difference. This strand in Carson's poetry is evidenced formally in his attraction to oral narrative – webs of endlessly digressing and multiple narratives, but all connected, even if that is sometimes by the most flimsy of threads – and more generally in his attraction towards a diffusion of boundaries or barriers, particularly those represented by the conscious ego. It is perhaps for this reason that Carson is drawn to the figure of Keats, a poet who, like him, knows 'the magical connective power of nicotine' (*Ffa*, 102–3) and who continually attempts to transcend the limits of self, embracing the notion of the poet as a 'camelion'.[18]

18 Keats to Richard Woodhouse, Tuesday 27 October 1818, *The letters of John Keats*, 206.

These tendencies are also one aspect of Carson's attraction to Rimbaud and, more particularly, to the poem 'Le bâteau ivre'. The poem is Rimbaud's ultimate expression of his notion of the poet as 'voyant' or visionary, a state which Rimbaud believed was achieved by a 'disordering of all the senses'. In a letter to Georges Izambard he elaborates on this – 'The sufferings are enormous, but one has to be strong, to be born a poet, and I have discovered I *am* a poet. It is not my fault at all. It is a mistake to say: I think. One ought to say: I am thought … *I* is someone else'.[19] This is the poet as visionary who reaches beyond the banal reality of the everyday through the dislocation of the mind and arrives at 'l'inconnu', 'the unknown'. In 'Le bâteau ivre' the poet, like the drunk boat, surrenders his mind to the intoxication of his visions. The mind is liberated from the bounds of everyday reality and transported into a hallucinatory world. This delirious voyage of the senses is, however, short-lived and the poem ends accepting failure, and longing for death. Carson's 'The ballad of HMS *Belfast*' is a version of 'Le bâteau ivre'. It translates Rimbaud's poem into a Belfast context and makes language its central concern. The poem drunkenly imagines the ship HMS *Belfast*, a symbol of Ireland more generally, leaving her moorings in old Belfast and embarking on a surreal journey. The poem is an *aisling*, a traditional Irish form of vision poetry typically used to express nationalist sentiments. This vision, like that experienced by the speaker in Rimbaud's 'bâteau ivre', is an intoxicating voyage in pursuit of 'the Future: new Empires, Realms of Gold, and precious ore/ Unheard-of since the days of Homer' (*Fl*, 72). It becomes clear, however, that the reality of the voyage – 'We grew languorous with grass and opium, the *kif*, the very best of draw/And sprawled in urinous piazzas' (*Fl*, 74) – is very far from the ideal world that has been imagined. The poem ends with the speaker finding himself back in 'grey Belfast' aboard what is now the 'prison ship Belfast', a recognition not simply that the vision itself has been illusory but that, like all visions and ideals that are adhered to rigidly and exclusively, it can be constricting and limiting. The poem seems to argue that Ireland cannot throw off its connection with Britain and the English language. This interpretation is borne out in the first version of the poem which appeared in *The Times Literary Supplement*:

> I lay bound in iron chains, alone, my aisling gone, my sentence passed.
> Grey Bélfast dawn illuminated me, on board the prison ship Belfást.[20]

19 Rimbaud's credo is very similar to Keats's definition of the 'poetical character': 'it has no self – it is every thing and nothing – It has no character … A Poet is the most unpoetical of any thing in existence; because he has no Identity, he is continually in for – and filling some other Body.' Keats to Woodhouse, 227–8.   20 Ciaran Carson, 'The ballad of HMS *Belfast*,' *Times Literary Supplement*,

What we see here, and what is missing from the version of the poem published in *First language* are the accents on the word 'Belfast'. In Irish the emphasis falls on the second syllable of the word, while in English the emphasis falls on the first. These lines, like *First language* more generally, reveal the ongoing tension in Carson's work between two kind of inheritance, Irish and English. Carson's bilingualism has been an enabling condition, giving a feeling of 'in-between-ness', of things being 'neither/ One thing nor the other' ('Loaf', *Bc,* 15) summed up in the words 'or rather', a phrase which 'if you're brought up bilingually … is a fundamental thing. Anything can be told this way or that.'[21] There is, too a sense in which this can be disabling, a 'schizophrenic' condition to use Carson's word, manifesting itself in a tendency towards the hybrid forms of the grotesque; images of the dismembered body which are used to reflect psychic discontinuity and fragmentation; and related to these the gothic motif of the double.[22]

Carson's concern with duality and multiplicity of identity is apparent form his earliest work in, for example, 'The half-moon lake' and is, as we have noted in 'The ballad of HMS *Belfast*', intertwined with Carson's bilingual condition. These concerns surface again in the poem 'Jawbox' where the poet explores 'schizophrenic' conflicts over language and accent through the Jekyll/Hyde motif. Crossing the border between Northern Ireland and the Republic of Ireland, the speaker experiences a feeling of entrapment, and of annihilation, which reminds him of childhood desires for escape:

> his child's body, hunched in the dark alcove underneath
> The sink, sulking, tearful, wishing he was dead. Imprisoned by so many
> Small transgressions, he wants to break out of the trap. He's
>   caught between
> Bel*fast* and *Bel*fast, in the accordion pleats between two
>   lurching carriages
> Banging, rattling, threatening to break loose … (*Bc,* 92–93)

The dualities of Jekyll and Hyde, English and Irish, the face and its mirror image, proliferate in the poem. While such dualities threaten a coherent sense of self, at

---

27 August 1993, 7. **21** Ciaran Carson, interview with Rand Brandes, *Irish Literary Review* 8 (1990), 84. **22** Hugo Hamilton's *The speckled people* (London and New York, 2003), which tells the story of one boy's experience of a multiple linguistic inheritance, is a powerful and disturbing exploration of the relationship between language, national identity and home. Given that these are key concerns in Carson's work, it would be interesting to compare how both writers treat these themes.

the same time, the dominance of one over the other results in terror and brutality. In the poem Hyde, who is associated with Irishness, with brutality and violence, with the dark side of the unconscious, triumphs, and the final lines of the poem depict Jekyll being choked to death. This schizophrenia is a sickening, frightening condition where the sufferer must live in fear of what would happen if '[t]he coupling snaps' (*Bc*, 93).

It is perhaps in Borges, also a bilingual speaker, that we find the clearest parallels to Carson's work for ways of thinking about, describing and structuring reality and about how this relates to language. Both Carson and Borges are suspicious of fixed rigid structures and share Keats's notion of negative capability, that ability to be in 'uncertainties, mysteries, doubts, without any irritable reaching after fact and reason'[23] Both writers are also concerned with upsetting linear time sequences, and with time as an unpredictable force working on a series of radically unstable and shifting planes. In 'Tlon, Uqbar, Orbis Tertius' Borges describes how '[o]ne of the schools of Tlon goes so far as to negate time: it reasons that the present is indefinite, that the future has no reality other than as a present hope, that the past has no reality other than as a present memory'.[24] Borges's writing insists that the reality we experience is only one version of the many kinds of reality that are being lived in different times and places:

> He believed in an infinite series of times, in a growing, dizzying net of divergent, convergent and parallel times. This network of times which approached one another, forked, broke off, or were unaware of one another for centuries, embraces *all* possibilities of time. We do not exist in the majority of these times; in some you exist, and not I; in others I, and not you; in others, both of us.[25]

Borges even goes as far as to suggest that the real itself is an illusion, that the world and its inhabitants are mere projections of someone else's dream. 'The Circular Ruins', for example, tells the story of a man who wants 'to dream a man … dream him with minute integrity and insert him into reality'.[26] The dreamer succeeds in doing this, only to discover that he himself is 'a mere appearance, dreamt by another'.[27] The world itself is an illusion, and so are we. Yet if Borges is aware of the possibilities of such multiple perspectives, he is also aware of the problems. In several stories he dwells on the awfulness of a world without

---

23 Keats to George and Thomas Keats, Sunday 21 December 1817, 72.   **24** Borges, 34.   **25** Ibid., 53.
26 Ibid., 73.   **27** Ibid., 77.

structure, without some kind of order. Thus, in 'Funes, the Memorious' Funes cannot forget anything, and since he cannot forget he becomes 'the solitary and lucid spectator of a multiform, instantaneous and almost intolerably precise world'.[28] In 'A New Refutation of Time', then, Borges accepts, albeit unwillingly, our inability to deny the existence of time or reality:

> Our destiny (as contrasted with the hell of Swedenborg and the hell of Tibetan mythology) is not frightful by being unreal; it is frightful because it is irreversible and iron-clad. Time is the substance I am made of. Time is a river which sweeps me along, but I am the river; it is a tiger which destroys me, but I am the tiger; it is a fire which consumes me, but I am the fire. The world, unfortunately, is real; I, unfortunately, am Borges.[29]

Carson follows Borges in scrambling chronologies and linear time. 'For if', as the speaker in 'Ambition' argues, 'time is a road'

> It's fraught with ramps and dog-legs, switchbacks and spaghetti; here and there,
> The dual carriageway becomes a one-track, backward mind. And bits of the landscape
> Keep recurring. (*Bc*, 27–8)

Involuntary memory is often Carson's guide, because it disrupts temporal constructions, obliterating the gap between past and present in the moment of remembering – 'Every time that *Blue Grass* / Hits me, it is 1968' (*Ifn*, 21). Memory will not allow the telling of a linear narrative, for it moves from object to object according to its own internal logic, in much the same way as an oral narrative, which although it has a narrative to tell, can take as many different versions as there are people. Tunes, like stories, attract Carson because, as he says, they 'invent their own dimensions' – they have no 'final version' and like Belfast itself they elude any definitive narrative – 'If the city is a piece of music, it depends on who's playing it, who's listening; and you are not the person you were a week ago.' (*Lnf*, 33). Yet, like Borges, Carson is aware of the dangers of entire dislocation, surrender to the heady, vertiginous process of time. Like language, and like identity, time needs some kind of structure. We must 'try to piece together the exploded fragments' even what we create is temporary and contingent (*Bc*, 108).

---

28 Ibid., 94.   **29** Ibid., 269.

Borges and Carson share three common metaphors for describing these structuring processes – the map, the labyrinth and the library.

Both Borges and Carson treat maps with suspicion. Maps are partial and inaccurate and give only selective details about any territory – 'No, don't trust maps, for they avoid the moment: ramps, barricades, diversions, Peace Lines' (*Bc*, 58). They are also bound up with power – a fact that is made clear in the poem 'The brain of Edward Carson' where Edward Carson's vision of Protestant Ulster is represented as an attempt to impose his own rigid framework on Ulster – 'The map of Ulster opened up, hexagonal and intricate, tectonic:/ Its shifting plates were clunked and welded into place by laws Masonic' (*Fl*, 30). For Carson, Belfast is a kaleidoscope of images which shift according to the perception and the perspective of the viewer. 'Question Time' provides a good example of how our understanding of the city is a continuing negotiation between past and present, memory and reality. A description of the present-day city gives way to a Belfast of childhood, the Belfast of the mind's eye, as the speaker in the poem is inter-rogated. Only his ability to remember this old Belfast proves his identity and guarantees his safety. Stopped by a few locals who are suspicious of his movements back and forth through various areas of Belfast, his replies to their questions take the form of a map, a map 'which no longer refers to the present world, but to a history, these vanished streets; a map which is this moment, this interrogation, my replies' (*Bc*, 63). This sense of the 'symbolic map' – a map of the city plotted according to memory – is expressed eloquently by Borges: 'Through the years, a man peoples a space with images of provinces, kingdoms, mountains, bays, ships, islands, fishes, rooms, tools, stars, horses, people. Shortly before he dies, he discovers that the patient labyrinth of lines traces the images of his own face'.[30]

Given Carson's growing concern with language it is perhaps not surprising that he has become increasingly interested in the idea of reality as text. Again Borges is clearly a precursor and Carson has recently acknowledged his significance in interview.[31] Borges often constructs reality as a text or library, and equates both with labyrinths. Thus in 'The garden of forking paths' Stephen Albert says 'Ts'ui Pên must have said once: *I am withdrawing to write a book.* And another time: *I am withdrawing to construct a labyrinth.* Every one imagined two works; to no one did it occur that the book and the maze were one and the same thing.'.[32] Or perhaps more pertinently in 'The library of Babel' where Borges describes the universe as a library which is simultaneously a labyrinth 'composed of an

---

30 Jorge Luis Borges, *Personal anthology*, ed. Anthony Kerrigan (London, 1968), 203. The phrase 'symbolic map' is borrowed from Eamonn Hughes.   **31** See Brown, 148.   **32** Borges, *Labyrinths*, 50.

indefinite and perhaps infinite number of hexagonal galleries'.[33] The meaning of the library, like the secret of the universe, is unknown though the speaker has, in his youth, 'wandered in search of a book, perhaps the catalogue of catalogues'.[34] In this library everything, in all its permutations, has already been written:

> Th[e] thinker observed that all the books, no matter how diverse they might be, are made up of the same elements: the space, the period, the comma, the twenty-two letters of the alphabet. He also alleged a fact which travellers have confirmed: *In the vast Library there are no two identical books.* From these two incontrovertible premises he deduced that the Library is total and that its shelves register all the possible combinations of the twenty-odd orthographical symbols (a number which, though extremely vast, is not infinite): in other words, all that is given to express, in all languages.[35]

While Carson's work registers a sense of terror in the face of multiple selves and languages, increasingly his poetry has come to revel in multiplicity and difference, in our inability to map or pin down the shifting, kaleidoscopic nature of language, the city and reality. In *First language* Carson is particularly concerned with the limits and possibilities of language, and with translation. Both ideas come together in the key trope for the collection, that of Babel, the biblical story which charts the loss of a common language and a common speech and the subsequent proliferation of languages. After Babel all human communication is necessarily mediated through acts of translation, whether it is within a single language or between languages. With its aspiration to unity and stability Babel is, for Carson, analogous to the imperialist desire to dominate and colonize, and in its attempt to build a unitary state – one people, one language – Babel is comparable to the ideology of unionism and nationalism. What Carson is at pains to emphasize, and this is not a new concern for him, are the links between language and power, and how language can be used to imprison people in particular kinds of narratives. There is in Carson's poetry a sense of impatience and anger with a language that has been imposed from above. For Carson, authority is linked to print and to a sense of the official. This is what is at work in the poem 'Stone hand', a nightmarish vision of Belfast in which the 'civic colossi' descend from their plinths and walk the streets.[36] They speak in the 'lapidary

33 Ibid., 78. **34** Ibid., 78–9. **35** Ibid., 81. **36** Ciaran Carson, 'Stone hand,' *Irish Review* 15 (Spring 1994), 110–11.

images of Parliament and Empire'. Interested only in maintaining the status quo, they are not open to what Carson refers to here, and in 'Second Language', as the '_che serà_' of language (_Fl_, 13).

Babel is, however, not only a symbol of totalizing power structures, but also of humanity's birth into multiplicity and difference, and into uncertainty of meaning. It tells of our continual 'need … for translation inadequate to compensate for that which multiplicity denies'.[37] What Carson seems to be at pains to do in _First language_ is to stress that translation permeates every aspect of our lives, that it is, to quote John Goodby, 'an ontological condition'.[38] This is evident in poems such as 'Apparat' where a bomb disposal expert searches for the correct 'language' or code which will defuse a bomb (_Fl_, 29), or '_Correspondances_' where it is the 'verdurous babble' of Nature which we try to interpret (_Fl_, 39). In the same way, 'On not remembering some lines of a song' highlights how our ability to remember is dependent on finding the 'switch between the _off_ and _on_, the split chink/ Through which you peer with half an eye/ And glimpse the other, time-drenched world' (_Fl_, 27). The past is another language and remembering is an act of translation between past and present. This is reminiscent of Borges's 'Pierre Menard, Author of the _Quixote_' which also explores the movement between past and present as an act of translation. It tells the story of Pierre Menard whose intention it was to rewrite the Quixote – 'He did not want to compose another _Quixote_ – which is easy – but the _Quixote itself_. Needless to say, he never contemplated a mechanical transcription of the original; he did not propose to copy it. His admirable intention was to produce a few pages which would coincide – word for word and line for line – with those of Miguel de Cervantes'.[39] Menard's tactic is to try as far as possible to be Miguel Cervantes, which involves forgetting the history of Europe between the years 1602 and 1918, and other such impossible tasks. Menard fails, of course, but he leaves three fragments, the ninth, twenty-second and thirty-eighth chapters of _Don Quixote_. The speaker compares Menard's _Quixote_ with that of Cervantes and concludes: 'Cervantes's text and Menard's are verbally identical, but the second is almost infinitely richer'.[40] Although not a word has been changed, the _Quixote_, simply through the passing of time, becomes a new and richer text.

While Carson is open to the possibilities of difference and translation, he does, however, see how this can lead to relativism and a meaningless multiplicity. This

---

37 Jacques Derrida, 'Des tours de Babel', _A Derrida reader: between the blinds_, ed. Peggy Kamuf, trans. Joseph F. Graham (Ithaca, New York, 1985), 243. **38** John Goodby, _Irish poetry since 1950: from stillness into history_ (Manchester, 2000), 295. **39** Borges, _Labyrinths_, 65–6. **40** Ibid., 69.

concern is at the heart of 'Sonnet' (*Fl*, 44–5). The sonnet form, one of the most coherent and structured of poetic forms, is stretched to breaking point in Carson's poem, and we are left with what is practically twenty-eight lines from which we struggle to elicit some kind of unified meaning. It is an appropriate symbol of the destruction of Babel for as we wander through the ruins of the sonnet form, we find ourselves in the labyrinth of language, Carson's own idiolect, which we struggle to translate into a language we can understand. While there is a certain amount of playfulness here, this can be read an attempt to show what can happen when Babel is pushed to its most extreme conclusion. The result is a complete breakdown of meaning and communication.

Although it may seem that with *First language* we have travelled quite a distance from Keats and de Quincey, it is in both poetry and prose subsequent to this collection that Carson most explicitly engages with these Romantic writers. *The twelfth of never, Fishing for amber* and *Shamrock tea* are parodic visionary epics in which Carson relishes, mocks and interrogates dreams, visions and all manner of hallucinogenic trips. The three texts explore the comic, wondrous and at times monstrous territory where visions, madness, death and creativity feed off one another. At the heart of all three books is the desire to 'cleanse the doors of perception' (*St*, 93). This is not simply a negative impulse, not simply a desire to dispel illusions and to strip away inherited and limiting systems – although that is there in abundance – it is also a constructive one. As I have argued, Carson is entranced by the world of dreams and visions and by the way in which their 'exploration or representation involves the creation of hitherto unattempted modes of expression'.[41] Carson is clearly in agreement with Aldous Huxley's comments in *The doors of perception*, a text on which he clearly draws in *Shamrock tea*:

> Every individual is at once the beneficiary and the victim of the linguistic tradition into which he or she has been born – the beneficiary inasmuch as language gives access to the accumulated records of other people's experience, the victim in so far as it confirms him in the belief that reduced awareness is the only awareness and as it bedevils his sense of reality, so that he is all too apt to take his concepts for data, his words for actual things.[42]

---

41 Christian La Cassagnère, 'Dreams', *A handbook to English romanticism*, ed. Jean Raimond and J.R. Watson (Basingstoke, 1992), 97.   42 Aldous Huxley, *The doors of perception and heaven and hell* (1954; London, 1994), 12.

Given Carson's concerns in these three books, it is not surprising that Keats and de Quincey, as well as Coleridge, have significant parts to play. In the chapter entitled 'Opium' in *Fishing for amber*, for example, de Quincey's *Confessions of an opium-eater* is clearly being used as a model. Carson is drawn to the 'irregularity' of de Quincey's narrative and the account Jan Both gives of his own opium-taking mirrors the rhythm and structure as well as the strangeness of de Quincey's account.[43] One crucial difference, however, is that while the experiences recounted – and importantly they centre around the dissolution of the ego, its openness to penetration by and absorption into 'foreign bodies' – are part of the pains of opium, a source of terror and anxiety for de Quincey, they are relished by Jan Both.

Coleridge and Keats are to the forefront in *The twelfth of never*, a collection that while it revels in the magical and fantastic, is clearly concerned with showing how visions and ideals can delude, isolate and destroy those who succumb to them. Coleridge's 'Kubla Khan' as well as Keats's 'La belle dame sans merci', poems that explore the role of the unconscious in the creative process as well as the dangerous and destructive power of the creative vision, are much in evidence in this collection, providing Carson with an opportunity to explore Ireland's political unconscious as well as the way in which Ireland has been used as a vehicle for all kinds of spurious visions. Keats's 'La belle dame sans merci', for example, acts as a model for 'The rising of the moon' (*Ttn*, 19) and '1798' (*Ttn*, 39) where the speaker in both poems encounters a femme fatale who embodies a vision of Ireland. In 'The rising of the moon' – the title is taken from a traditional ballad that celebrates the heroism of the United Irishmen – the speaker is seduced in stanza one by 'an old colleen', a figure whose 'nettle-green' eyes and revolutionary zeal link her with Ireland and Irish republicanism, but 'the madder red skirts of her liberty' and her description of Ireland as the helpless childlike Hibernia implicate her strongly in empire and imperialist enterprises – 'madder red' is associated with royalty, with the red coats worn by the British Military from the early 1700s to 1855 and with the poppies (reminding us of the Opium Wars in which Britain and later France participated) that appear later in the poem. Carson keeps this imperialist context to the fore by bringing a traditional Irish love song, 'the Rose of Tralee', into play in stanza three. Written

---

43 I use the term 'irregularity' deliberately – in his introduction to the pains of opium de Quincey comments, 'I have not been able to compose the notes for this part of my narrative into any regular and connected shape' (62). Limitations of space forbid a detailed exploration of the two sections to which I allude, but I would direct readers to *Fishing for amber*, 194–8 and *Confessions*, 73–4.

by William Pembroke Mulchinock, a wealthy Protestant merchant, the song is a lament for Mary, a Catholic peasant girl and the Rose of Tralee, whom he loved and who died of tuberculosis when he fled to India to serve with the British as a war correspondent after he was wrongly accused of murder. For Mulchinock Mary represents truth, honour and beauty and is a comfort and solace to him during the war. More broadly, she is the embodiment of a romantic, sentimental and nostalgic vision of Ireland, a vision that the song continues to sustain for the millions of tourists who visit Ireland every year. In the second half of the poem the speaker comes into contact with the 'old colleen' – 'I saw her again' – though in this second meeting she has metamorphosed into the dead Mary. With her 'grass-green lips' and her 'bloodless hand[s]', she gently rebukes the speaker for his desertion – '*You might have loved me for eternity*'. Although Mary adopts the guise of an Ireland betrayed and abandoned, a victim, the poem alerts us to the fact that her hands are far from 'bloodless'. Around the 'clear crystal fountain' where she appears 'poppies, not potatoes, gr[o]w in contraband'. The 'poppies' not only indicate that 'Mary' is caught up in imperialism and the opium wars that were raging at the same time as the famine, they also imply that the romantic nationalist ideals she embodies have a narcotic effect and foster addiction and dependence in those who come into contact with them. What Carson seems to be at pains to stress in the poem is the interdependence between the ideologies of nationalism and imperialism, particularly their reliance on war and violence, and the way in which visions of liberty and national ideals perpetuate the imperialist systems they seek to undermine. Abandoned and weak, The Rose of Tralee is another version of Hibernia and of the ambivalent 'old colleen' of stanza one whose 'nettle-green eyes' remind us of Mary's 'grass green lips'. Whether it be revolutionary republicanism, imperialism or romantic nationalism, the ideologies the three women represent lead to the same bleak conclusion: death.

A similar set of concerns is at the heart of the poem '1798'. The femme fatale in this poem is, from the start, associated with war, and 'the Papal Spanish wine' on her 'pallid lips' show that she is in collusion with Catholicism and fascism. She is also clearly a figure for Ireland and her association with fairy lore, her fears of betrayal and her aspiration to a pure language and identity reinforce her connection to the ideology of romantic nationalism and, more broadly, to fascism. Carson's title for the poem, '1798', is deeply ambivalent. To the extent that the poem is indicative of the way in which republican ideology can degenerate into or is a mask for a much more sinister romantic nationalism, the title works ironically, reminding us that republican thinking in Ireland is still largely dependent on romantic nationalist ideas and ideals – 'Two centuries have gone, yet she and I abide'. But the poem may be more optimistic and affirmative. The phrase 'Two centuries have gone' in the last stanza clearly locates the poem in 1998, the year in which the Good Friday Agreement. This certainly forms part of the context in which the poem was written. With this in mind, the end of the poem becomes more ambivalent. The 'snowy blossoms' remind us not just of Easter and the Easter Rising but also recall the flurries of snow that fell around Good Friday when the Agreement was signed.[44] While that word 'abide' carries with it a strong negative charge and emphasizes the endurance of the ideologies Carson has been describing, there is a positive charge in the last stanza which comes from the poet opening up a gap between the reader and the Ireland described in the poem. The speaker and his lover are 'Like emblems of a rebel song no longer sung,/ Or snowy blossoms drifting down the mountainside'. The 'snowy blossoms' of the last line carry redemptive overtones, as though the Agreement just might hold out the possibility of fulfilling the potential that surfaced briefly in 1798.

While Carson is clearly suspicious of visions and the ways in which they can be used, his poetry retains a longing for the ideal, an impulse towards the ineffable, the eternal and the transcendent that leads him to challenge conventional ways of thinking, seeing and speaking. The following passage from *Fishing for amber*, in which Carson meditates on translation, sees that impulse come to the fore:

> Translation is a kind of monster, and its seeming master is a Dr Frankenstein, whose Creature gets to recognize himself in the distorting language mirror of a puddle. He also sees the stars down there, in the deep bottom of beyond, and he weeps at the sight of his face ... He moves in the aura conjured up by John Keats, in his 'Ode to a nightingale': 'Darkling I listen; and for many a time/ I have been half in love with easeful death' –

> > O for a beaker full of the warm South,
> >   Full of the true, the blushful Hippocrene
> >   With beaded bubbles winking at the brim
> >   And purple-stainèd mouth,
> >   That I might drink, and leave the world unseen,
> >   And with thee fade into the forest dim – (*Ffa*, 206)

---

44 The weather was an important part of the mood in the period when the Good Friday Agreement was being negotiated, as Henry McDonald and Patrick Wintour point out in an article in the

Carson's description of translation as a monstrous Frankenstein, a grotesque imperfect copy of the idealized human form is significant because, as a bilingual speaker, Carson identifies strongly with the figure of the double and with hybrid figures, such as the poet in Baudelaire's 'The albatross' whose 'gawky gorgeous wings impede his walking' (*Fl*, 39). Given its intrinsic doubleness, then, translation might be seen as one of Carson's preferred forms. Importantly, these comments from *Fishing for amber* take us back to where we started, back to Keats and back to the poem, 'The half-moon lake', and the longing to glimpse 'the stars down there in the deep bottom of beyond' which is at the heart of Carson's writing. Equally important, however, is Carson's recognition that our time-bound human condition and the 'distorting mirror' of language make it impossible for us to access that realm. As I have shown, Carson's conflicts and desires around dreams, visions and ideals resonate powerfully in other periods and contexts, in the work of writers such as Keats, de Quincey, Rimbaud and Borges, yet it is to Keats that Carson most frequently and consistently turns. As this comment from an interview in 2002 shows, Keats's dilemmas and questionings continue to influence and inform in significant ways Carson's explorations of the relationship between language, reality and transcendence:

> Catholicism deals with the ineffable. Or used to. As a Catholic, you experience certain things which you cannot explain or, perhaps, you are not meant to explain. You know, as a Catholic, that the language of men is ultimately doomed because it can only refer to 'all ye know on earth'; whereas the ultimate reality – for Keats as well – is death, and what lies beyond it … The Catholicism of my childhood seems more ornate, more otherworldly, than today's version. The Latin Mass has gone, and with it a whole concept of language. Latin may have been incomprehensible to the majority of Catholics, but it was universal. It purported to express the mystery of liturgy, of eternal truth. Perhaps that's a more interesting idea than vernacular accessibility. As if language can express things beyond language.[45]

Observer on 12 April 1998: 'outside, the unseasonal icy winds and flurries of sleet and snow gave a sense of unreality'.   **45** Carson, interview with Brown, 146.

Carson's carnival of language: the influence of Irish and the oral tradition

FRANK SEWELL

> What is happening [...] is the rebirth or re-connection to the oral tradition. And the new Irish poetry draws much of its strength from contact with that tradition. Muldoon, Meehan, Carson, Durcan, in these four particularly [...] one hears in the background, one senses or discerns in the patterning of both language and experience, elements of both the old and the new traditions.[1]

It is widely known that the poet, author and musician Ciaran Carson, who writes in English, was brought up in an Irish-speaking household in Belfast. In this paper I aim to show some of the ways in which the Irish language and his own bilingualism[2] have had a profound effect on the poet's thinking, his vision and, consequently, his work.

Carson makes repeated references in his prose to a wide variety of Irish language dictionaries that a-muse and inspire him. He once wrote: 'you can see I use dictionaries. The language is too big for me' (my italics).[3] Here, he was writing of the English language as 'too big' for him. In another sense, however, it is evidently not enough for him, as he uses dictionaries in the plural, and likes to word-search in several languages, sometimes simultaneously:

> I would say the word *horse* over and over to myself; then the Irish word, *capall*, which seemed more onomatopoeically equine, yet with its ghost of English cobble, and then I'd mentally feel the bumps of the cobblestoned street ...
>
> Thinking now about those slate-blue cobbles, *cobalt* comes to mind, from the German *Kobold*, a demon, for this deep blue substance was

1 Theo Dorgan, 'Looking over the edge', in *Irish poetry since Kavanagh*, ed. by T. Dorgan (Dublin, 1996), 148. 2 'I was reared bilingually: for my parents, Irish was a second language, which they spoke exclusively at home. So I think Irish was my first language, by a short head.' Ciaran Carson, 'The other', in *Strong words: modern poets on modern poetry*, ed. W.N. Herbert and M. Hollis (Tarset, 2002), 234–5, 234. 3 Ibid., 235.

supposed by German miners to be a mischievous and hurtful metal. Cobalt-60 is a radioactive isotope. I remember cold-war talk of Cobalt bombs. The word creates a fall-out.[4]

This is typical of Carson and of his poetic practice: he sounds words out (and / or looks them up) for their layers of meaning within, say, English, then associates them by sound or sense with words from the same, or from another, language (often Irish). The sound-alike words found by association seem to stick to, or connect with, the original word in what may seem an arbitrary or post-modern, but certainly a highly imaginative and creative fashion.

This method or technique, derived partly from Carson's own early bilingualism, was confirmed for me when I attended a writing workshop led by the poet himself. He declared in the course of the workshop that, as a writer, he felt like a Hollywood director to whom words presented themselves like actors at a screen test. The writer's/director's task, he said, was to select and, in some cases, pair the words together into an original poem/film. Taking on the pose and persona of a cigar-toting Groucho Marx-like director, Carson then very comically acted out a scenario in which wanna-bes 'Moon' followed by 'June' auditioned for a place in his poem/film. The next set of actors/words to audition for a part were (Mr) Velcro and (Miss) Day-Glo who were far more interesting individually (both being, in this case, new-fangled words, each syllable of which held layers of meaning and multiple associations) and as a pair (not least, of original rhymes). One can just imagine Carson beginning to get carried away with the various possible ramifications of the Latin-sounding first syllable of Vel-cro alone. In any case, Velcro and Day-Glo were hired, Moon and June fired.

A casual glance at Carson's poems reveals how such a selection (or attraction?) procedure must have occurred during the creation of some of the startling juxtapositions and far-fetched, sometimes multilingual, connections and rhymes that characterize his unique body of work. For example, the poem that sets the tone and formal technique (of long-lined, rhyming couplets) for *Opera et cetera* (1996), and which prefaces the volume, is 'Eesti':

> *Their eyes and the holes in their hands were nailed into*
> *my gaze,* quod erat demonstrandum:
> *Digits poised and pointed towards their hearts. They*
> *are beautiful Panjandrums [...].*

4 Ibid.

This red-letter day would not be written, had I not
wandered through the land of Eesti.
I asked my Father how he thought it went. He said to
me in Irish, Listen: Éist.

(*Oec,* 7–8)

If Metaphysical poets were known for the yoking together of disparate ideas or images, Carson (as in the above example) seems to yoke together similar-sounding words from disparate contexts, languages and regions, forging (in the Joycean sense) truly international poems that, he would be glad to say, could end up anywhere.

He is a strong believer, for example, in the idea that a poem should take, first, the writer and, second, the reader, through a journey of linguistic and imagistic exploration that stimulates the mind and senses with surprise and wonder at where, when and how the trip proceeds and, indeed, winds up (see 'Loaf', for example, *Bc,* 15). But how is such a daunting criterion to be met?

> Anything I've written under the auspices of poetry involves a word-search, an exploration; and I don't know what I'll say until it's said. It's a discovery. In poetry, the destination of the journey should remain unknown until one arrives. Then one is pleasantly surprised. 'Poetry is what gets lost in translation.' Perhaps, but poetry is itself translation, carrying a burden of meaning from one place to another, feeling it change in shape and weight as it travels. Words are a shifty business.[5]

A shifty business, maybe, but one important consequence of Carson's early and, in his case, enabling double-exposure to 'the Irish [language] of the home'[6] and the English language of the street, is a clear sense from early on that there are *at least* two ways of saying and, therefore, of seeing everything.[7] Consequently, throughout his work and indeed characteristic of it, is a marked pluralism, including linguistic pluralism, a constant sense of diverse languages, dialects and registers being playfully brought together[8] in, sometimes, the most illuminating ways.

---

5 Ibid.   **6** Niall McGrath, 'Ciaran Carson: Interview', *Edinburgh Review,* 93 (1995), 64.   **7** Carson favourably quotes W. R. Rodgers as saying, 'Nothing pleases me so much in writing as to be able to sit on both sides of the sense, and if there were six sides I would sit on them all.' See Carson, '1940–49: Beagles, horses, bikes, thighs, boats, grass, bluebells, rickshaws, stockings', in *Watching the river flow: a century in Irish poetry,* ed. N. Duffy and T. Dorgan (Dublin, 1999), 81–6, 83.   **8** Carson views Denis Devlin's poem 'Memo from a millionaire' as 'a very Irish poem, if being Irish means to

For example, at a time when some were saying 'no' or (in triplicate) 'never' to political compromise or flexibility, and shoving these words down the throat of Belfast and Ulster to claim that not they but *Belfast* and *Ulster* were constantly saying 'No', Carson was reflecting on the lack of any single, too-simple, too-black-and-white word for either 'yes' or 'no' in Irish. The Russian language, for example, may have its 'da' and 'nyet', but Irish (as Russian does in other contexts) affirms or negates a verb only by repeating it. Thus in answer to a brief question such as 'is it?', one answers, in Irish, (affirmatively) 'it is' or (negatively) 'it isn't'. With this in mind, Carson writes:

> We were debating,
> Bacchus and the pards and me, how to render *The Ulster Bank – the Bank*
> *That Likes to Say Yes* into Irish, and whether eglantine was alien to Ireland.
> *I cannot see what flowers are at my feet*, when *yes* is the verb repeated,
> Not exactly yes, but phatic nods and whispers. *The Bank That Answers All*
> *Your Questions*, maybe? (*Ifn*, 49)

This poem, 'The Irish for no', ends with an image of an 'unfed cat' who 'toys with the yin-yang of a tennis ball, debating whether *yes* is *no*'. Carson's poem suggests that in the turning of that ball, as with the rotation of the earth under one's feet, there is (or should be) a world of possibility, some room for negotiation at least, beyond flat or deadly absolutes. Otherwise, the alternative (as presented in the poem) produces totally dysfunctional individuals and societal relationships: Juliet haranguing Romeo, cops committing suicide, and businessmen practising extreme self-harm.

As well as offering Carson another angle on, and vocabulary for, life as it was in the north of Ireland (mainly during the Troubles from 1966 until recently), Irish plurilingual and sometimes macaronic traditions of storytelling and music, offered the poet a range of narrative strategies and techniques such as (arguably) his characteristic long line (of mostly eight full beats). This use of the longer than average poetic line has been attributed to the acknowledged influence on Carson of the American poet C.K. Williams.[9] It is more than likely, however, that Carson, as a traditional musician, fine flute player and singer, was equally, or also, influenced by the expansive phrasing of oral storytelling[10] and by the eight-beat

play about with a language not wholly yours'. Ibid., 85. **9** Eamonn Grennan, 'American relations', in Dorgan (ed.), *Irish poetry since Kavanagh*, 102. **10** 'In Carson the nightmare of Belfast at war is mediated in a scarifyingly inventive narrative voice, half traditional seanachie [seanchaí] and half musical phrases of traditional tunes. He certainly came to enjoy the wriggle-room, the possibilities for twisting, turning, doubling back and sidetracking that a longer line makes possible. Such flexibility, requiring extended length of line (sometimes, stanza and poem as a whole), is even seen in the tenses of the verbs employed: 'I think all the longer poems begin in the present tense, suggesting that their stories are being told now; but of course they then proceed to go and shoot off all over the place, drifting backwards and forward through time.'[11]

By contrast, Carson's early collection, *The new estate*, was (on hindsight) a strong but formally conservative volume, reflecting the poet's learning of his craft from predecessors such as Seamus Heaney. Many of the poem titles could have been Heaney's, and Carson covers a range of subject matter reminiscent of Heaney and John Montague: for example, with poems on his namesake St Ciarán, the Celts and O'Carolan.

Carson, in this volume, also translates or, rather, 'adapts' three 'Early Irish' lyric poems (*Tne*, 1,30,39). Such poems, in general, tend to be characterized, in Heaney's words, by their 'suddenness and richness', by their 'compact and concrete "steel-pen exactness"', by 'the tang and clarity of a pristine world full of woods and water and birdsong [which] seems to be present in the words.'[12] Heaney's discussion of this part of the Irish literary tradition (in a 1978 RTE broadcast, later to appear in his first collection of essays *Preoccupations*) leads him directly to the same 'sharp tooth of winter' poem that Carson adapted in his own first volume just two years earlier: the ninth-century poem 'Scél lemm dúib', often published in English as 'Winter':

Original	*Anon (mostly literal)*	*Heaney*	*Carson*
Scél lemm dúib:	News I bring:	Here's a song –	News to tell:
dordaid dam,	bells the stag,	stags give tongue	the stag bells –
snigid gaim,	winter snow,	winter snows	summer goes,
ro-fáith sam;	summer past;	summer goes	winter snows.

→

street-wise urban wide-boy, whose tonal stratagems and shifts chronicle a world in constant disintegration.' Terence Brown, 'Out of Ulster 2: Heaney, Montague, Mahon and Longley', in T. Dorgan (ed.), *Irish poetry since Kavanagh*, 60–70, 69. **11** Frank Ormsby, 'Ciaran Carson interviewed', *Linen Hall Review*, 8: 1 (1991), 5. **12** Seamus Heaney, 'The God in the tree: early Irish nature poetry', in *Preoccupations: selected prose 1968–78* (London, 1980), 181.

Original	Anon (mostly literal)	Heaney	Carson
gáeth ard úar,	wind high and cold,	High cold blow	[omits stanza]
ísel grían,	low the sun,	sun is low	
gair a rith,	short its course,	brief his day	
ruirthech rían;	seas run strong:	seas give spray	
rorúad rath,	russet bracken,	Fern clumps redden	Bracken, bright red,
ro-cleth cruth,	shape awry,	shapes are hidden	an unmade bed;
ro-gab gnáth	wild goose raises	wildgeese raise	usual as ice,
giugrann guth;	wonted cry;	wonted cries	wild goose's voice.
ro-gab úacht	cold lays hold	Cold now girds	Cold holds
etti én,	on wings of bird	wings of birds	the wings of birds –
aigre ré:	icy time:	icy time –	has seized my words,
é mo scél.[13]	this I heard.[14]	that's my rhyme.[15]	so ends my tale.

(*Tne*, 39)

What's noteworthy regarding Carson's adaptation of this poem is his daring-do in switching the order of lines three and four in the first stanza, perhaps to emphasize that the speaker is back in winter once again. The reminder may be necessary since he completely omits stanza two. This omission itself may be down to the fact that Carson was unhappy with his own version of stanza two, but really it would be difficult (centuries after the poem was written) to avoid cliché in any translation of this stanza: thus, drastically but surgically, Carson removes it altogether, which says something, in my view, about his abhorrence for cliché.

In stanza three, Carson prefers 'bracken' to 'fern', the former having more local associations in real and linguistic terms perhaps – 'bracken' has more of an Ulster-Scots thwack to it than the softer, more English-sounding 'fern'. As for 'wonted cry' (or 'cries'), the phrase would only ever be used ironically in a Carson poem, as the tone is somewhere between Victorian and high-faluting. The middle lines of stanza three (Carson's stanza two) are intriguing; here Carson seems perhaps to personalize the natural imagery but if one pays careful attention to his punctuation one sees that line two goes with line one, and line three with line four, keeping the focus for now, anyway, on the natural world.

13 See James Carney, *Medieval Irish lyrics with The Irish bardic poet* (Dublin, 1967, 1985), 10.
14 Ibid. 15 See Heaney, 'The God in the tree', in *Preoccupations*, 182.

In his last stanza, however, Carson makes explicit what is implicit in the other versions: that this is a mood piece, reflecting also the condition or situation of the teller of the tale, who (in all versions) reminds us of his presence in the first and last line of the poem. There can't be any doubt but that he too (the speaker – one imagines a monk or hermit) is caught in the grip of winter, which Carson makes crystal clear by adding 'has seized my words'. There is no point in arguing whether it is better to imply or clarify in the case of a translation such as this; Carson or any of the translators might well translate the poem entirely differently today or tomorrow again, just as Carson has done with Seán Ó Ríordáin's 'Malairt'.[16] However, the main point is that Carson's and Heaney's contemporaneous preoccupation with 'Scél Lemm Dúib' / 'Winter' with its still chilling sense of being locked in a dumbfounding winter, seems on hindsight to recall the zeitgeist of the mid-to-late 1970s in the north east of Ireland.

Regarding matters of form, it is also worth noting the comparative looseness of Carson's distant ghostly echo or chime between the ls in the last stanza: 'holds' in line one, and 'tale' in line four. The expected rhyme does not occur here. Instead the poet seems to have extended the rhyming pattern in this one stanza to span across the poem as a whole so that the very last word, 'tale', rhymes with 'bells' and, in particular, 'tell' in stanza one, line one; while 'holds' (stanza four, line one) chimes with 'snows' and, in particular, 'goes' (stanza one, line three). This short adaptation from early Irish could, therefore, be said to provide early signs of Carson's formal inventiveness and flexibility.

Carson himself has said that he became frustrated (both as a reader and writer) with poetry after the publication of *The new estate* (1976). Two years later, he published a slim pamphlet of poems called *The lost explorer* (1978), but there was a gap of nine years between that and the publication of his second major collection *The Irish for no* in 1987. The frustration and delay was due to Carson's increasing sense that poetry often seemed dry, lacking in urgency and excitement[17] compared to his other loves: traditional storytelling, ballads and music. In 1986, for example, Carson published *The pocket guide to Irish traditional music*, a work that directly influenced both his return to poetry and, he said, the very 'shape and structure of *The Irish for no*'.[18]

---

16 Carson, '1940–49', in *Watching the river flow*, 81–6, 86. Compare his version of Ó Ríordáin's 'Malairt' here with the version in *First language*, 38.   **17** Ormsby, 'Ciaran Carson interviewed', 7. I also acknowledge the excellent research contained in Daniel McAllister, 'Subversion in the poetry of Ciaran Carson' (undergraduate dissertation, University of Ulster 2002), 4.   **18** See Ormsby, 'Ciaran Carson interviewed', 7.

The latter, in the words of poet and critic Ruth Padel, established Carson as a 'major poet', and 'introduced everyone to his long, reeling, liberating line, wonderfully musical and teeming with tumultuous anecdote, history, observation, humour and passion'.[19] Here is an example of what Padel means:

Horse Boyle was called Horse Boyle because of his brother Mule;
Though why Mule was called Mule is anybody's guess. I stayed there once,
Or rather, I nearly stayed there once. But that's another story.
At any rate they lived in this decrepit caravan, not two miles out of Carrick.

('Dresden', *Ifn*, 11)

The narrator of this poem soon gets sidetracked by reflections upon loosely related items such as shop bells, nuggets of old news from the Middle East or Mullaghbawn,[20] before arriving via various extremes of circumlocution at Dresden (the poem's title, by now probably forgotten by the much diverted and entertained reader), and finally wandering off again at the end:

I might have stayed the night, but there's no time
To go back to that now; I could hardly, at any rate, pick up the thread.
I wandered out through the steeples of rust, the gate that was a broken bed.

('Dresden', *Ifn*, 16)

Even that 'broken bed', one senses, is another story for another night but for now the breathless storyteller (note the semi-colon between 'now' and 'I' above, where one would normally expect a full stop) has left his audience / readers breathless and in need of a timely break before the next tale is woven, song sung or tune taken up.

The *craic*, the characters (Flynn, McGinty, etc.), the numinous details ('steeples of rust') and many diversions of Carson's opening poems in *The Irish for no* prompted the Irish language poet Nuala Ní Dhomhnaill to reflect on a lack that she had been noticing in poetry and fiction, and which Carson, too, must surely have felt and now, to some extent, solved:

---

19 Ruth Padel, 'The Sunday poem', in *The Independent on Sunday*, 23 May 1999, 13.   **20** Home of John Campbell 'whose storytelling suggested some of the narrative procedures of some of these poems'. See the title page verso of *Ifn*.

I read contemporary Irish writing [...] with an ever-growing feeling of grievance. A nagging sense [that] 'there is something missing, only what the hell is it?' I have always known that this dissatisfaction on my part was a result of my being a product of a largely oral tradition [...] a life which was only partially and even then, very imperfectly, reflected in literature.

What a relief it is then to open Ciaran Carson's *The Irish for no* and in the first four poems to be arrested by something utterly familiar but until now never encountered within the covers of a poetry book – the authentic voice of the good 'seanchaí' [...]. It is all here; the long seemingly haphazard, spoken, line; the miraculous non-sequiturs; the additive rather than subordinate clauses, the repetition of the just said, the transitions due to memory and association rather than due to any formal or linear logic, the vast repertoire of a good seanchaí, captured once and for all, permanently, on the printed page. The structure of these poems is that of an organic thing, a tree perhaps, with the subplots branching off here and there [...]. Yet each poem is immediately recognizable as a distinct entity and most important of all alive alive-o. I am not so mean to suggest that these poems are mere transcripts of oral speech [...]. Their art is rather that of a successful mimicking of oral techniques within the much more formal framework of a printed poem. What can seem at first to the unwary reader to be a rather aimless meandering can turn out to be as craftily plotted as a good whodunit.[21]

Ní Dhomhnaill recognizes and elucidates exactly where Carson is coming from and what he is tapping into: namely, the oral tradition of which she herself is a product. She may not have known it at the time but, in a sense, Carson was partly, at least, a product of the same tradition. His father, known to Belfast Irish speakers as Liam Mac Carráin (the Gaelicized version of Carson), was a much-loved and respected seanchaí-like figure, whose own self-penned miscellany of poetry, ballad and prose tales was published in 1986 as *Seo, siúd agus eile*.[22] One story from his father's book is translated and included by Carson in *The star factory* (143), a text in which the Irish-speaking father figure and yarn-spinner looms large;[23] as does the Irish language in general.

21 Nuala Ní Dhomhnaill, 'The English for Irish', a review of Carson's *The Irish for no*, in *Irish Review* 4 (1988), 116–18.   **22** Liam Mac Carráin, *Seo, siúd agus eile* (Dublin, 1986), his third published book, a text which mixes genres, interspersing tales with poems and songs.   **23** Carson would also have encountered other seanchaí figures through his studies (including Irish) at St Mary's Christian

WHAT'S IN A NAME?

Carson's father, Liam Mac Carráin, was a remarkable figure in the Belfast Irish-speaking community: an author of three books, a teacher and storyteller, his range of interests (based on my personal acquaintance with him) included not just Irish Gaelic arts and culture but Scots Gaelic and, significantly, Esperanto. In *The star factory*, Carson recalls how his father explained in a BBC Radio Ulster interview that he 'used to hide in' the Irish language, that the language offered him a form of 'sanctuary' or shelter, an escape route to what sounds remarkably like a 'saol eile' / 'another life or world' in the Donegal Gaeltacht, a haven for the northern Irish (*Tsf*, 106).

For Carson himself, the Irish language does not so much offer a 'saol eile' as a 'súil eile' / another eye with which to view the world; a 'teanga eile' / another language or (literally) tongue with which to speak of the world around him. Unlike, the mid-twentieth-century poet Seán Ó Ríordáin who felt himself to be, at times, 'torn between two languages' and thus debilitated as a writer,[24] Carson seems to have an imagination, a store of words, images, references, associations, etc. that is only increased and multiplied by his bilingualism, enriched (not confused or diminished) by cross-fertilization.[25] Thus, for example, while he is writing in English, he seems at times to be thinking in Irish or, at least, 'drawing thoughts' from the 'well'[26] of Irish as much as from the well of English:

> I, too, hide in language, within this book; in this respect, at least, I am my father's ilk, or *macasamhla*, as it is in Irish, literally, 'the son of a resemblance', hence copy or type, as in *mac leabhair*, a copy of a book. So we have the expression, *'gurab leis gach leabhar a mhac'*, 'to every book belongs its copy'. (*Tsf*, 106–7)

Crossing the stepping-stones of language from 'ilk' to *'macasamhla'*, and using the non-linear, associative logic of the side-tracking seanchaí, leads Carson to

Brothers Grammar School, at various Gaeltachtaí and, later, through his work and contacts as a musician and as Traditional Arts Officer for the Arts Council of Northern Ireland.   **24** See F. Sewell, 'Seán Ó Ríordáin: Joycery-Corkery-Sorcery', in *Irish Review*, 23 (Winter, 1998), 42–61.   **25** To what extent this is due to the fact that Carson writes in English, as opposed to the minority language, Irish, is beyond the remit of this essay. In the meantime, it's worth noting Ní Dhomhnaill's comment that 'in moment's of despair at what I do [writing in Irish], I like to console myself that Irish is to the culture of this island, North and South, as the yeast is to bread. It may be invisible but it is what makes it rise.' Ní Dhomhnaill, 'The English for Irish', 117.   **26** 'I have drawn from the well of language many a thought which I did not have and could not put into words.' G.C. Lichtenberg quoted by W.H. Auden, *Secondary worlds* (London, 1968), 122.

continue the above narrative with the traditional tale of the birth of copyright law in Ireland: King Diarmuid's pronouncement 'to every cow its calf' / 'to every book belongs its copy'. Drawing from the well of Irish vocabulary ('mac') and from seanchaí storytelling techniques (including digressions) part-learnt from his father (*Tsf* 1), therefore, influences not only the content of Carson's work but also the non-linear structure.

There is a fine example of Carson senior's storytelling masterfully translated in the 'White star street' section of *The star factory* (143–47). In his father's Irish language text version of the folk-tale, the main character, Liam is referred to throughout solely as 'Liam'. The story is introduced, however, with the following (slightly tongue-in-cheek and certainly rhetorical) paragraph:

> Tá scéal Liam na Sopóige (Liam an tSolais, Bhulaí an Laindéir) le cluinstin le blianta fada i mbéaloideas na hÉireann, agus leoga tá leaganacha den scéal le fail in Albain, sa Bhreatain Bheag agus i Sasain féin. Níl a fhios agam cé acu Gael, Gall nó Breatnach a bhí ann mar Liam ach seo an leagan den scéal a bhíodh ag m'athair.[27]

> The story of Liam of the Lamp (Will o' the Wisp, Jack o' Lantern) has been heard for years in the folklore of Ireland, and of course there are versions of the story to be found in Scotland, Wales and even England. I don't know whether Liam was Irish, English or Welsh but here is the version of the story that my father used to tell. [my translation]

Ciaran Carson omits this oral-style preamble from his translated version in *The star factory* but seems to have decided to incorporate the plural possibilities regarding Liam's identity and origin into the array of names which he uses for this one character. The result is not only humorous and realistic (in terms of dialogue etc.), but it makes Liam sound like both a 'Protholic and Catestant' at once (*Fl*, 71). For example, no less than seven variations of the main protagonist's name[28] are given by Carson (*Tsf*, 143–7):

(1) Will Gallagher (the most repeated version throughout, used by the narrator)
(2) Willie Gallagher (used in conversation by the devil)

---

27 Mac Carráin, *Seo, siúd agus eile*, 45.   **28** The Irish language name Liam corresponds with William, in English. The former is traditionally seen as an almost emblematic Irish and Catholic name; the latter as an almost exclusively Protestant name, not least since William of Orange.

(3) Billy Gallagher (used in conversation by the devil)

(4) Liam (used by the narrator)

(5) Bill Gallagher (used in conversation by the devil)

(6) William (used by the narrator)

(7) Liam Ó Gallchóir (used by the narrator at the end of the tale with a sense of it being his full and grand title)

Moreover, if his dad's version raised the possibility of Liam's origins being Irish, English or Welsh, Ciaran Carson's researches in *The star factory* (following *his* version of the tale) span Dinneen's and McCionnaith's Irish dictionaries, the *OED*, and *Brewer's dictionary of phrase and fable*, and find numerous early references to a character comparable with 'Liam na Sopóige' in Shakespeare and in Russian and German 'superstitions', among other sources. It seems, as a result, that Liam na Sopóige / Gallagher could well be (a relation, at least, of) not only 'Will-o'-the-wisp' or 'Jack o' Lantern' (as Carson senior suggested), but also 'Friar's Lanthorn', 'Spunkie', 'Fair Maid of Ireland', 'Walking fire' or, in Russia, 'Wandering fire' (*Tsf,* 147–49) ....

Meanwhile, Liam's nemesis, the devil has six different appellations in Carson senior's version: '*An Fear Thíos*' (the man below), '*an diabhal*' (the devil), '*Lúsaiféar*', '*Sátan*', '*Fear na gCrúb*' (the hoofed man), and '*An Fear Dubh*' (the Dark, or Black, One). Ciaran Carson adds a full six more names to the list in order to double the levels of comic irreverence:

1) the Devil (used in conversation by Will, and by the narrator)

2) His Satanic Majesty (used by the narrator; an allusion to the Rolling Stones)

3) Lucifer (used in conversation by the devil himself)

4) Satan (used by the narrator)

5) Mephistopheles (used by the narrator)

6) The Cloven Hoofed One (used by the narrator)

7) Your Man (used by the narrator)

8) The Lord of Flies (used by the narrator)

9) Old Nick (used by the narrator)

10) The Black Prince (used by the narrator)

11) Old Scratch (used by the narrator)

12) His Black Nibs (used by the narrator)

Carson's *The star factory* provides many instances of the poet reading in one language and thinking in two or more. For example, he takes delight in the surname 'Rang' which suitably belongs to an instructor in stamp-collecting: suitably, because the primary meaning of 'rang' in Irish is 'class', linked also to 'rank' or 'rung', as Carson muses (*Tsf,* 31) with what Heaney calls an 'illumination by philology'.[29]

The text also demonstrates that the two languages, Irish and English, don't just interact in the poet's mind but in reality, past and present. Carson repeatedly ponders such interactions, especially when they take an unexpected turn that might defeat some expectations or presuppositions: thus he provides a footnote to remind us that the Gaelic type used in the first Irish stamps, was the very type that Elizabeth I commissioned 'for the first Irish translation of the Bible, by William Bedel, in 1681–85' (*Tsf,* 32).

Carson seems to be fascinated by such moments when the two cultures, Irish and English, overlap or engage, though generally don't see eye to eye. Thus he selects and quotes the following excerpt for discussion:

> Until the creation of the Irish Free State in 1921, Ireland had always used our British stamps, but then fresh arrangements had to be made. At first the British stamps were simply overprinted with the words 'Saorstat Eireann', but in 1922 a newly designed issue came into use. Some of these bore a map of the whole of Ireland – and that, of course, is hardly correct, since the six Northern counties are not in the Free State at all, but remain part of the United Kingdom. It is many years since those stamps were issued, but the error has not yet been put right. – T. Todd, *Stamps of the Empire,* 1938 (*Tsf,* 32)

Mr Todd's imperial certainties are hilarious here: 'the error' and 'put right'? It very much depends on your viewpoint what the error is, and how it might be put right. Carson's writing repeatedly reminds us (if we need reminding) that viewpoints other than our own are not only possible but actively exist and need to be acknowledged:

> There's no final way of saying here is how it is. There isn't finally an answer to the objective structure of the world. So that what is going on here, in terms of how things are expressed and things are said with

---

29 Heaney, 'Further language', a lecture given at the American Conference for Irish Studies, QUB, 26 June 1995 <http://www.findarticles.com/p/articles/mi_qa3822/is_199710/ai_n8772944>, 7, accessed 8 Sept. 2006.

absolutes, that there's only one way, it has to be this way or that way; from a very early age I understood that it's not like that.[30]

One of the recurring highlights of *The star factory* is Carson's ability to reflect dispassionately upon an astonishing range of reference, to visit an array of vantage points, aided in part by his early immersion in two languages and subsequent study of others. A case in point is his elucidation of 'lillibulero', the title and part-chorus of an anti-Catholic marching song with, according to *Chambers dictionary*, a 'meaningless refrain'. Carson juxtaposes Chambers' 'definition' with the fact that 'lillibulero' is agreed, as he puts it, 'at least in Ireland' to be a corruption of '*(an) lile ba léir é, ba linn an lá*' which translates as 'the lily was plain to be seen, and the day was ours' (*Tsf*, 42). He then adds, with characteristic relish, that he has since heard of 'a new twist to the derivation [...] Breandán Ó Buachalla has a most plausible theory that *Lile* refers to the astrologer William Lilly (1602–81), who made accurate prognostications about the outcome of the Jacobite wars' (*Tsf*, 42). What is notable here is that Carson recounts the various theories, possible interpretations and associated tales; but he does not fret in any 'essentialist' manner over which version is correct, absolute or authoritative. Instead, he enjoys the Babel-onian, demotic possibilities and associations that abound in such a richly enigmatic and layered word as 'lillibulero'.

Interestingly, in his own poetry, he had also earlier indulged in his own similar 'corruption' of English language morphemes in a kind of answer to 'lillibulero': '*ocularity a moiety blah skiddery ah disparity*' ('Bagpipe music', *Fl*, 51), suggesting that if the repeated l's and b's of 'an lile ba léir é' in Irish sound odd or comical to the English-accustomed ear, so too may the repeated 'ity' in many English words to non-English ears. It's all a question of perspective as Carson's 'Bagpipe music' points out, a poem that continues a long line of Irish macaronic verse.[31] Importantly, Carson's playing about with a language not wholly his[32] is not a matter of mere linguistic or cultural revenge but of optimistic 'diplomacy',[33] placing English and Irish etc. on the one ballad sheet and on the one level dance floor. If culture is 'a conversation between equals',[34] Carson is putting the two

---

30 McGrath, 'Ciaran Carson: interview', 64. 31 See, for example, Aogán Ó Rathaille, 'Ar choileach a ghoideadh ó shagart maith' / 'A good priest's stolen cock', in *An duanaire, 1600–1900: poems of the dispossessed*, ed. S. Ó Tuama and T. Kinsella (Mountrath, 1981, 1990), 147. Here English is used for comic effect in an Irish language poem. 32 Carson, '1940–49', in Duffy and Dorgan (eds), *Watching the river flow*, 85. 33 Diplomacy (the 'exchange' of gifts, words, language, places) in poetry, Ireland and politics, is the main theme of Carson's '1940–49' essay. Ibid., 81–6. 34 James Stephens, 'The outlook for literature with special reference to Ireland' (1922), in M. Storey (ed.), *Poetry and*

main languages of Ireland into a very musical conversation just as his own poems 'Bagpipe music' and 'Snow' form an *'agallamh beirte'* / duet with Louis MacNeice's original poems[35] of the same name: '*scrake nithery lou a mackie nice wee neice ah libralassie ...*' (*Fl* 53).

Carson stands 'in religious awe' (*Tsf,* 43), he tells us, of even the most 'banal' of placenames ('Milltown', *Tsf,* 43) and chilling of personal names: 'the word-bubble ambiguities of "Michael Stone" rub up against each other like pebbles, accidentally contiguous on a huge beach' (*Tsf,* 42). On several occasions he has returned to wonder at the etymology of Belfast city's name (see 'Farset', *Bc* 47). In *The star factory,* he adds Deirdre Flanagan's comments to the mix of glosses. Flanagan refers to earlier 'authoritative' scholars, and in true scholarly fashion backs up her own theory with reference to supporting sources across the centuries. Note, however, the degree of caution with which Carson presents her view: 'she [Flanagan] then draws our attention to numerous sources which *corroborate* her *assertion* that the name of Belfast derives from the ford or sand-bank in the River Lagan' (*Tsf,* 47, my italics). Carson reflects rather on the multifarious meanings of 'fearsad' (thought to provide the 'fast' in Bel-fast) in what seems to be his favourite Irish dictionary: Dinneen, 1927; and in consultation with a walking, talking Irish dictionary, his father, who tells him that in the 1940s, 'fearsad' came to be used to refer to the Axis forces (literally, in Irish, the Axle People). This is a reminder that languages and meanings live, move and change like a river, even Belfast's Farset river: 'The most satisfactory translation of Belfast, according to Deirdre Flanagan, is "approach to ford". I register this meaning tentatively, remembering or peering at the [river] Farset, though I didn't know its name then' (*Tsf,* 48). Carson sounds far from convinced but would probably not be happy with any one definitive or exclusive, single 'translation' of 'Belfast'.[36] Nor would he dismiss so readily out of hand the version/translation that (co-)exists in the folk or popular oral culture: 'without the Farset, the name of Belfast would not be' (*Tsf,* 45).

Carson's 'mapping of the city' of Belfast is much commented upon as is his fascination with maps, or rather maps changing over time like the stamps he discusses in 'The General Post Office' section of *The star factory.* Here his 'religious awe' for names extends to the names of colours and (Indian) states, and

Ireland since 1800: a source book (London, 1988), 178–88, 179.   **35** See Edna Longley, 'Out of Ulster 1: Louis MacNeice and his influence', in Dorgan (ed.), *Irish poetry since Kavanagh,* 52.   **36** The same is true regarding the name of the Falls Road; in Irish, Bóthar na bhFál. Years ago, my inclination was to translate this as 'the road of fences' because 'fál' often means a fence, hedge or barrier. In consultation, Carson reminded me that 'fál' has many other shades of meaning. For example, 'fál' may also be linked to 'the fields' that older Falls Road residents sometimes (used to) mention.

ultimately reflects his wonder at the richness and suggestiveness of words themselves from whatever source:

> I was initially drawn to [...] the stamps of the British Empire [...] their inks of pale rose, carmine, lilac, slate, bistre, cobalt and vermilion; but this was a vast pandemic field, in which the minor Indian States alone – Chamba, Gwalior, Nabha, Faridkot, Sirmoor, Rajpipla, Travancore and Cochin, to name a few – took up some seventy pages of the Gibbons catalogue. (*Tsf*, 32)

Among the colours listed above, one notes the word 'cobalt' again, the multilingual associations of which Carson discusses at length elsewhere.[37] Among the selected states, one notes the exotic but also Gaelic-sounding 'Gwalior' and 'Travancore' as well as the post-colonial ironies of 'Sir-moor' and 'Raj-pipla'. This is all familiar territory for the reader of Carson's urban, postmodern brand of *dinnseanchas*[38] / the lore of places and their names:

> Familiar territory now, well, almost, for going down the Kashmir Road into Bombay Street – burned out in '68 ... I was there in my mind's eye, one foot in the grave of that Falls Road of thirty years ago, inhaling its gritty smoggy air as I lolled outside the door of 100 Raglan Street, staring down through the comforting gloom to the soot-encrusted spires of St Peter's, or gazing at the blank brick gable walls of Balaklava Street, Cape Street, Frere Street, Milton Street, saying their names over to myself. ('Question time', *Bc*, 60–63)

The etymology, sound and sense of all these names have an extraordinary appeal for Carson but so too does their rich political/cultural history: even for someone with the most 'latent republicanism' (*Tsf*, 32), Kashmir and Bombay as street-names in Belfast stand as ironic relics of imperialism;[39] similarly Balaklava recalls not just the (military and economic) successes but also the blunders of empire,[40]

---

37 Carson, 'The other', in Herbert and Hollis, *Strong words*, 235.   38 See Ní Dhomhnaill, 'The English for Irish', 118.   39 See also Pól Ó Muirí, 'Dinnseanchas', *Dinnseanchas* (Dublin, 1992) where the same range of street-names are listed as 'iarsmaí na himpireachta' / 'relics of empire'. 40 'General Lord Raglan's ill-phrased orders to Lord Lucan contributed to the destruction of the Light Brigade at the Battle of Balaklava during the Crimean War (1854–1856) [...]. Prior to the disaster at Balaklava, Raglan's habit of phrasing commands as polite requests rather than orders caused confusion and life-threatening delays at the Battle of the Alma.' See 'Changing the world, 1784–1904',

as well as some of the violence inflicted on its behalf and in reaction to it, involving the donning of 'balaclavas'. Carson piles name on name, irony on irony, placing the friendly-sounding Frere Steet in this contrasting list but also the ambiguous Milton Street, named after the author of both *Paradise lost* and 'An Horation ode upon Cromwell's return from Ireland'.

A KIND OF GO-BETWEEN

As a rule, there is an intermediary between society's experience and the individual's psyche – a kind of go-between that can be called culture. If not for that, the outer world of facts and events and the inner world of feelings and thoughts would resemble two interlocutors speaking different languages with no way to communicate. It is precisely culture that serves as an interpreter who helps us to understand what reality tells us and what it asks us about, and who, at the same time, helps us to formulate our own questions and responses in a comprehensive language of symbols. Within culture perhaps the most apt interpreter of this kind is poetry.[41]

Throughout his career, Carson has translated (with a characteristic pluralism) from several languages, and often from Irish: as we have seen, in his first collection, *The new estate* (1976), the fledgling poet adapted (perhaps as apprentice pieces) three early Irish lyrics; subsequently he has translated (for half of his life, he tells us)[42] a poem by the mid-twentieth century poet Seán Ó Ríordáin (*Fl* 38; 1993), as well as numerous poems by his contemporaries such as Nuala Ní Dhomhnaill (1990) and the younger Belfast poet, Gearóid Mac Lochlainn (2002). His continuing engagement with the Irish language is evidenced, therefore, by his numerous and periodic translations of poems (and even prose, *Tsf,* 143) from Irish into English.

A subtle and linguistically sensitive translator,[43] Carson still to this day has occasion to read, tune into (*Tsf,* 106) and, sometimes, speak in Irish but doesn't write in the language, generally. Significantly, however, the first poem in *First language* is in Irish, albeit with a French title: 'La je-ne-sais-quoi'. This lyrical love poem (although it may be read as addressed to the Muse and/or to a lover) contrasts sharply with the poet's other work. He has not, to my knowledge, translated this poem; and without permission, I would not do so either. However,

http://www.national-army-museum.ac.uk/exhibitions/changingTheWorld/page2–3.shtml, accessed 11 Sept. 2006.   **41** Stanislaw Baranczak, a Polish poet, translator and critic, quoted in Heaney, 'Further language', 6.   **42** Carson, '1940–49', in Duffy and Dorgan, *Watching the river flow,* 86. **43** As evidenced by his Emersonian translation of Ó Ríoráin's 'Malairt' as 'Second nature' (*Fl* 38).

it's worth noting at least that the poem plays freely with 'set' expressions, reminding us that nothing is 'set' in Carson's world vision or use of language: thus we get the idiomatic 'i bhfaiteadh na súl' ('in the blinking of eyes') juxtaposed with the more original and, in the context, erotic 'i bhfaiteadh na mbéal' ('in the blinking of mouths'), and the Dylan-esque 'i ndorchadas an lae' ('in the darkness', not of the night, but 'of the day').

On the subject of writing in Irish, or not, Carson has stated: 'I feel at times that the idea that I should write in Irish because it's the language of the Irish soul or something like this is a bit off anyway.'[44] He is too sophisticated a thinker and writer to fall for any such essentialist notion. Instead, he taps into Irish culture in all of its forms and languages, creating a newly-forged and rejuvenating synthesis out of them so that, for example, traditional musical or storytelling techniques may inform the structure of an entire poetry collection, or influence the forms and directions that his poems take.[45]

In this regard, Carson has said that he was 'pleased that some people told [him] they'd read *Belfast confetti* as they would a novel, from beginning to end. Certainly, the intention was to make a very structured book.'[46] The carefully arranged mixing of genres in this collection, especially the combination of prose passages and poems, recalls (in Ireland, at least) the form that many classic tales have come down to us, including *The Táin* and *The children of Lír*. Alternatively, and in an analogy that Carson might prefer, the juxtapositions and formally contrasting sections of some of his volumes recall a session in a céilí house where a song might be followed by a tune then a story, etc. in a whole variety of 'party-pieces'.

The fact, moreover, that he is as likely to allude to, or take his inspiration from, European, British, Japanese or other sources is a measure of the internationalism or, if you prefer, universality of Carson's work. Thus, for example, his early Irish adaptations are counterpointed with other adaptations from Welsh and Greek (*Tne*, 27, 17); while Ó Ríordáin's 'Malairt' / 'Second nature' (*Fl*, 38) is carefully 'mirrored' with Charles Baudelaire's 'Correspondences' (*Fl*, 39). Ultimately, therefore, if a poet such as Ní Dhomhnaill characteristically raids the subconscious to bring back the 'Pinot Noir' or 'real McCoy' of potent poetry,[47] Carson ransacks the

---

44 McGrath, 'Ciaran Carson: interview', 64.   **45** 'Part of my joy [at reading *The Irish for no*] is the quite palpable and undisguised presence of the Irish language throughout this book of poetry in English […] I like to console myself that Irish is to the culture of this island, North and South, as the yeast is to bread. It may be invisible but it is what makes it rise. Hence my understandable pleasure at a book that proves me right.' Ní Dhomhnaill, 'The English for Irish', 117.   **46** Ormsby, 'Ciaran Carson interviewed', 7–8.   **47** Ní Dhomhnaill, 'Comhairle ón mBean Leasa' / 'The heist', *Pharaoh's daughter* (Loughcrew, 1990), 146–7.

dictionar*ies* and language*s* that are available to him ('*Tak, tak*', *Fl*, 64) and, indeed, all around him.

As a writer, translator, and (I would say) linguist, he enjoys slipping in, out of, and between languages; as well as listening out for what gets slipped into and out of all forms of language, including literature, conversation,[48] street-signs and even graffiti. I wish to conclude with one curious example of this which occurs in the poem 'The Irish for no':

> It was time to turn into the dog's-leg short-cut from Chlorine Gardens
> Into Cloreen Park, where you might see an *Ulster Says No* scrawled on the side
> Of the power-block – which immediately reminds me of the Eglantine Inn
> Just on the corner: on the missing *h* of Cloreen, you might say. (*Ifn*, 49)

Carson is no doubt a-mused by the missing, silent 'h' above – a letter that, over time, has slipped into modern Irish much as Carson slips Protestant into Catholic (*Fl*, 71) and vice versa:

> in Ciaran Carson's recent book […] *First Language* – those terms [Protestant and Catholic] have suffered a sea-change by being shipped out in a poem called '*H.M.S. Belfast*' there to become Protholics and Catestants. And these new names have about them the kind of freewheeling, open-ended suggestiveness which has characterized much of the poetry written here [in the north of Ireland] over the past couple of decades. When I think, for example, of Medbh McGuckian's early poem called 'Slips', I think of the way possibility slips silkenly through that very title, like hair, as the poem says, coming down in the middle of a conversation. The vernal promise of a slip in the horticultural sense and the collusion of desire and repression in a slip of the Freudian nature or in a drunken slip of the Protholic or Catestant tongue, such fluidity and unruliness are characteristic of not only McGuckian and Carson, but famously also of Paul Muldoon, whose gift always seems to exercise itself accidentally on purpose, as we used to say when the language was available to us as the carnival we forget it can still be – an entry to further language, a way of putting the muse back into amusement, of turning the language into a slip of a girl awakening to a new self, unabashedly winging it into the future.[49]

---

48 'A lot of poets, it seems to me, are unaware of the beauty and sophistication of "ordinary" speech.' Carson quoted in Ormsby, 'Ciaran Carson interviewed', 7.   **49** Heaney, 'Further language', 7.

Borrowed lines? A reading of Ciaran Carson's American influences

CIARAN O'NEILL

> At the end of the day, I don't think that the impulse behind what I write
> comes from other Irish poets … I read a lot of American poetry.[1]

Writing a review of a selection of C.K. Williams's poetry in 1989, Ciaran Carson's predilection for a yarn triggered a meandering account of his first encounter with the American poet:

> Some time in 1985, I think, the Irish poet John Hughes loaned me this
> book by a hitherto unheard-of (to me) poet: reading it, it struck me with
> the force of revelation. I had not, for various reasons, written any poetry
> for many years; but, for various reasons, (the same ones, maybe) I was, at
> the time, toying with the possibility of writing in a mode which would
> owe something to traditional oral narrative, as exemplified by innumer-
> able characters in pubs throughout the length and breadth of Ireland.[2]

The circumstances in which Carson encountered Williams for the first time were such that he 'had not, for various reasons, written any poetry for many years'. In fact in 1985, Carson had not (with the exception of a pamphlet in 1978 entitled *The lost explorer*) published a book of poetry since his debut volume *The new estate* (1976). The book John Hughes had loaned the Belfast poet – Williams's *Poems, 1963–1983* – acquainted Carson with the American's *Tar* (1983), which as he recounts nostalgically, was 'included in its entirety'. For Carson, this episode proved decisive: 'Within a year of reading *Tar*, I had written a book called *The Irish for no*: I hereby acknowledge a debt'.[3] The publication of *The Irish for no* (1987) saw Carson end what had been an eleven-year-long poetic silence. Williams's influence, as Carson later reiterated in interview in September 2000,

1 'Ciaran Carson interviewed by Rand Brandes', *Irish Review*, 8 (1990), 89. 2 Ciaran Carson, 'Against oblivion', *Irish Review* 6 (1989), 115–16. 3 Ibid.

thus came at a crucial juncture: 'I don't think I could have written *The Irish for no* without his voice. It certainly woke me up from some kind of poetic slumber'.[4]

Williams's long poetic line proved an imperative for Carson's return to writing. Appealing to the Belfast poet's enthusiasm for both story-telling and music, a long line provided the opportunity to experiment with, even fuse the conventions of both 'yarn' and traditional 'reel' in verse. Addressing this Williamsian hallmark on Carson's *The Irish for no*, my aim is to proceed by exploring a small chorus of American poetic voices that appear in, influence, and echo throughout Carson's writing. While I am aware that figures such as C.K. Williams, Robert Frost, and William Carlos Williams rarely feature in 'Carson criticism', my contention is that these poets provide a valuable context for reading Carson's poetry.[5] Below, a poem from C.K. Williams's *With ignorance* (1977) opens my transatlantic study of Carson's work:

> If you put in enough hours in bars, sooner or later you get to hear every
>   imaginable kind of bullshit.
> Every long-time loser has a history to convince you he isn't living at the
>   end of his own leash
> and every kid has some pimple on his psyche he's trying to compensate
>   for with an epic,
> but the person with the most unlikely line I'd ever heard – he told me
>   he'd killed, more than a few times,
> during the war and then afterwards working for the mob in Phila
>   -delphia – I could never make up my mind about.[6]

Only partially quoted above, Williams's poem 'Bob' helps to demonstrate the new proximity Carson came to occupy in the mid-1980s with the American's poetic: 'When I did come back to writing it was through trying to accommodate bar-talk. Speech and slabber ... I wanted to get that into the poetry'.[7] Here Williams's bar scene, the setting for his murky underworld narrative of crime and bravado, offers a model of the potential conversational nuances and depth to 'speech and slabber'. Carson's interest in precisely this type of idiom is seen in 'Cocktails', a

---

4 John Brown, 'Ciaran Carson', in *In the chair: interviews with poets from the North of Ireland (Cliffs of Moher, 2002)*, 147   **5** One notable discussion can be found in Neil Corcoran, *Poets of modern Ireland: text, context, intertext* (Bridgend, 1999). Chapter 10, 'One step forward, two steps back: Ciaran Carson's *The Irish for no'* discusses figures such as Robert Frost's and (more obliquely) C.K. Williams's contribution to Carson's poetry.   **6** C.K. Williams, 'Bob', in *New and selected poems* (Newcastle upon Tyne, 1995), 55–7.   **7** Brown, 145.

poem where the recreation of the narrative momentum or 'onward rush of pub speech'[8] takes hold from the very beginning. As the poem opens, 'the story' is in full swing:

> Bombing at about ninety miles an hour with the exhaust skittering
> The skid-marked pitted tarmac of Kennedy Way, they hit the ramp and sailed
> Clean over the red-and-white guillotine of the check-point and landed
> On the M1 flyover, then disappeared before the Brits knew what hit them. So
> The story went: we were in the Whip and Saddle bar of the Europa.
>
> (*Ifn*, 41)

Carson's Belfast-style (or 'Troubles') renovation of Williams's theme in 'Bob' – the 'epic' storytelling, or in reality, 'bullshit' that is recounted shamelessly in bars – finds in 'Cocktails' an ironic disclaimer attached: 'So / The story went'. Above, the isolated 'So' almost seems deliberately placed, and for a moment reminds one of a similar syntactic arrangement in Robert Frost's poem '"Out, out –"' Here in a cruel episode, a young boy is dismembered and dies as a result of a chainsaw (or 'buzz saw') accident: 'So. But the hand was gone already'.[9] Notable for its display of a similar temperament in the face of tragedy is Paul Muldoon's 'Aisling': 'It's all much of a muchness / In Belfast's Royal Victoria Hospital / a kidney machine / supports the latest hunger-striker'.[10] Of the three, Carson's poem 'Cocktails' is the least pathetic, in that its tragedy is not a mortal, but socio-political one. Implicit in all of these poems however, is a critique of the cultural normality of voicing meaningless buffering rhetoric in the avoidance of moral consequence.

   Continuing to examine Carson's and Williams's exposition of their respective narratives, each is seen endeavouring to mimic the dynamic physiognomy of 'the story'. In 'Bob' and 'Cocktails', each poet, aspiring to the natural rhythm of a verbal rant, engineers a poetic line that pushes toward the margin and past it, spilling consecutively onto the next. This quality is arguably more acute in 'Cocktails'; the break-neck pace of Carson's first stanza allowing punctuation to hardly figure. Williams's approach, on the other hand, is the more measured of the two. In 'Bob', the elongated lines accompany the caustic yet meditative tone in which the poet delivers his moral on a life (mis)spent in bars. In letters to Neil

---

8 Brandes, 82. **9** Robert Frost, '"Out, out –"', *Selected poems* (London, 1973), 90. **10** Paul Muldoon, 'Aisling', *Poems, 1968–1998* (London, 2001), 126.

Corcoran (dated 5 May and 19 October 1989), Carson elaborates on what he regards to be the various facets of this formally experimental long line:

> Storytelling is there; the line breaks are points of suspense, where you want to see what happens next. The length of line is a storyteller's deliberate fast-paced gabble. It's also based around *haiku's* seventeen syllables, and the intention is to have a kind of *haiku* clarity within the line – stumbling-blocks of word-clusters, piling up adjectives, etc.[11]

Oscillating between the modes of 'storytelling' and the Japanese *haiku*, Carson's long line is intended to imitate a 'fast-paced gabble', while retaining the imagistic clarity of the *haiku* form. It is a marriage of traditions, almost, one that is taken a step further in the volume that follows *The Irish for no*. *Belfast confetti* (1989) is a text interspersed with actual *haikus* or, 'stop-gaps … a kind of punctuation'[12] that the poet draws from Japanese writers such as Buson, Basho and others. For some readers however, the arrangement of *Belfast confetti* may have the effect of overstatement; the evocation and prevalence of the *haiku* being otherwise underscored throughout in Carson's sustained use of the long poetic line. Considered from a transatlantic viewpoint, here the poet's gesticulations toward the *haiku* have (as he is surely aware) been made before:

> If Williams is concerned with the revelations of the ordinary and mundane (his namesake, William Carlos, sometimes comes to mind in this context), then these eight-line units, of which the book entirely consists, might be thought of as extended *haiku*; the individual lines themselves, in their nitty-grittiness and poise, make gestures towards *haiku* form, though they are slightly longer than the conventional 17 syllables – typically, about 25 syllables with eight or nine main stresses …[13]

The apparent correspondence between Carson's and Williams's allusions to the *haiku* is something for which the latter poet may take the credit. Beyond the topic of Williams's conspicuous long line, which has so far dominated this early part of my discussion, there is potentially a further dimension to both his and Carson's poetic dialogue. Having seen both poets engaging in reportage, or recycling narratives in the manner of a story-teller, there is at the same time a deep sense of moral responsibility evidenced in their poetry. In 'Cocktails' for instance, Carson

---

11 Corcoran, 181.   **12** Brandes, 88.   **13** Carson, 'Against oblivion', 114.

repeats the story as if he had only heard it, breaking off with the disclaimer, 'So / The story went', and thus refusing to pass judgement. This idea of the poet as outwardly a chronicler of events has continuity in Williams's poem also. In 'Bob', Williams is quite aware of the moral transparency of the many characters he has met in bars over the years, although at the same time is conscious of his own limitations as self-styled profiler, recalling the one who got away; the one he muses, 'I could never make up my mind about'. Showing like Carson, a preference for frankness – 'and when he finally turned away, it wouldn't have bothered me at all if / I'd never seen him again' – Williams leaves the conundrum of whether this peculiar character 'Bob' is for real, available to the reader's choice.

In his review of C.K. Williams, Carson resolves that the American's poetry is like 'the word *tar*... thick, unguent malleable, pungent... manifestly about the world of work and people. Dirty realism, perhaps'.[14] Conversely, one might argue that it is toward a similar 'dirty realism' that one finds Carson leaning in the poetry of *The Irish for no* and *Belfast confetti*. Emanating from a backdrop of 'Troubles' Belfast, Carson's poems can have the quality of a collection of stained vignettes; lucidly relaying the ugly reality of his native city, and sometimes, more directly, the sinister acts perpetrated within it:

They had questioned him for hours. Who exactly was he? And when
He told them, they questioned him again. When they accepted who he was, as
Someone not involved, they pulled out his fingernails. Then
They took him to a waste-ground somewhere near the
        Horseshoe Bend, and told him
What he was. They shot him nine times.

('Campaign', Ifn, 36)

T.S. Eliot once wrote of Charles Baudelaire, 'It is not merely in the use of imagery of common life, not merely in the use of imagery of the sordid life of a great metropolis, but in the elevation of imagery to the *first intensity* – presenting it as it is, and yet making it represent something much more than itself – that Baudelaire has created a mode of release and expression for other men'.[15] This statement is, I think, pertinent, given the 'imagery of the sordid life' of Belfast articulated in *The Irish for no*. 'Campaign' sees Carson following in the tradition of poets like Baudelaire and Eliot in recognizing poetry's particular quality of expressing its own moral reckoning. Carson, who ironically has spoken of 'trying

14 Ibid., 116. **15** T.S. Eliot, '*from* Baudelaire', in *Selected prose of T.S. Eliot* (London, 1975), 234.

to write about the streets of Belfast as a wasteland',[16] has, it seems, found this possible in 'waste-ground(s)' close to home. While 'Campaign' and other poems like it in *The Irish for no* may appear terribly explicit, at times even sensationalist in colour, the poet may argue he has learnt from the mistakes of Seamus Heaney's *North* (1975):

> Heaney seems to have moved – unwillingly perhaps – from being a writer with the gift of precision, to become the laureate of violence – a mythmaker, an anthropologist of ritual killing, an apologist for the situation, in the last resort, a mystifier.[17]

Carson's now notorious review of *North* may perhaps have catalyzed his preference for the 'dirty realism' or 'seeing what's before your eyes' approach[18] that C.K. Williams later proselytised in the 1980s. The 'gift of precision' however, that the Belfast poet criticised Heaney for laying down, was something that Carson – despite the achievement of *The Irish for no* – was arguably not to attain until much later. Another American voice, a different Williams – William Carlos Williams – was to alter Carson's poetic profoundly in *Breaking news* (2003), so that something akin to what Eliot called the '*first intensity*' came into view.

Carson's most recent collection, *Breaking news*, reflects a dramatic rupturing of the long poetic line that the poet had adopted from C.K. Williams in *The Irish for no* (1987). While the argument may exist that Carson has since *First language* (1993) been gradually drifting away from the dominance of the long-lined stanza and increasingly experimenting with alternative forms, the terse bullet-point verse of *Breaking news* nevertheless marks an altogether new arrangement. This decisive stylistic shift from a poetic inspired by C.K. Williams to a form comparable to that employed by William Carlos Williams in *Spring and all* (1923) can be best illustrated by examining what is, in *Breaking news*, a typically arranged poem:

> the road
> to Sevastopol
>
> is paved
> with round-shot

16 Brandes, 79.   **17** Ciaran Carson, '"Escaped from the massacre": *North* by Seamus Heaney', in *The Honest Ulsterman*, 50 (1975), 183.   **18** Ibid., 186.

> the road
>
> from Sevastopol
>
> with boots
>
> that lack feet
>
> ('Siege', *Bn*, 50)

'Siege', written in the context of the imperialist campaigns of the Crimean War (1854–6), is found like many of the poems in *Breaking news* both to pre-empt and to enter into dialogue with Carson's closing long narrative poem, 'The war correspondent'. Explaining the stimulus for his interest in the Crimean conflict, the poet writes in his 'Notes' section: 'This book owes much to the work of the brilliant Anglo-Irish journalist William Howard Russell (1820–1907), who is generally regarded as the father of the art of war correspondence. His dispatches from the Crimea … were especially influential in shaping public attitudes to the management, and mismanagement, of war' (*Bn*, 74). It is worth stating here that prior to the discovery of Russell's work and influence, Carson's consciousness of the Crimea had the strange paradox of emanating from precisely Belfast origins. Indeed, this familiarity had spanned several decades – from Carson's first childhood encounters with local Belfast street names such as 'Balaclava' and 'Sevastopol' which are among many that memorialise battles of the Crimean War. Returning to the example of 'Siege', the implicit gestures that the poem makes toward Belfast are starkly reinforced on the page opposite, in another poem 'Exile'. Here Carson muses: 'night / after night / I walk / the smouldering / dark streets / Sevastopol / Crimea / Inkerman / Odessa / Balkan / Lucknow / Belfast / is many / places then / as now / all lie / in ruins / and / it is / as much / as I can do / to save / even one / from oblivion' (*Bn*, 51–2). As is obvious above, Carson in 'Exile' is writing of a very different war to that of William Russell's generation. In an interview I conducted with the Belfast poet this year (2007), he kindly elaborated on this point:

> Part of my aim in *Breaking news* was to juxtapose contemporary, or near-contemporary Belfast with accounts of past imperial wars in places other than Belfast, and thus to suggest that past imperial wars resemble the imperial wars of the present … Some of the poems are modeled on Carlos Williams' attenuated line, and the visual attraction of the imagery expressed by that line, 'The red wheelbarrow' being the classic example.

> And I wondered how that prosody and visual directness might cope with
> questions of war, whether in Belfast or elsewhere.[19]

The poet's reportage of 'war', in company with Russell's, ultimately develops
from his own eye-witness accounts and the effects which close proximity to
conflict has on the writing process. This proposition sees explication in an earlier
interview in 2003, where Carson further explained: 'The short-lined poems came
out that way in the small hours of the morning, like bullet points, often written
to the sound of a surveillance helicopter over my house in North Belfast. Urgent
monitory rhythms'.[20] Clearly impacting on Carson's aesthetic, the image of the
'surveillance helicopter' and its sound – 'urgent monitory rhythms' – stalk the
pages of *Breaking news* in both their presence and absence. In poems such as
'Home', 'Breath', 'Spin cycle', 'Spin cycle 2', and 'Minus', the poet's references to
helicopters looming over the North Belfast cityscape has at first glance no special
significance other than to denote the British military presence (or what remains
of it post-'Troubles') in the city. Read in the context of Carson's 'Siege' and pieced
together, the cumulative effect perhaps is one closer to what T.S. Eliot calls the
'first intensity'. In *Breaking News*, Carson is 'presenting it as it is, and yet making
it represent something much more than itself'; the chronological context of these
poems is such that the recurring image and rhythms of the helicopter almost
certainly allude to specific events that precipitated one notable security operation
in an area of Belfast local to the poet's home. Here one may recall the loyalist
protest around and ostensible 'siege' of the Holy Cross Catholic primary school
in Ardoyne, North Belfast; a dispute that arose over a particular road, or route
through a contentious zone between June 2001 and January 2002. Topographical
and thematic parallels to the latter crisis, if suggested in 'Siege', see the poet as eye-
witness to a more local row. Meanwhile, the historical carnage of Sevastopol and
the Crimea is remembered in Belfast's street names, and as a not-so-distant past.

The sparse but solid imagery of 'Siege' has its own in-built parallelism,
achieved by way of a subtle syntactic opposition. One sentence describes the
journey toward Sevastopol, the other the departure. Both lines impart the same
frankness, in a neutral and even register. Twelve syllables long, each sentence is
broken into seven and five respectively. In total, the poem could be regarded as
haikuesque, yet there is a sterner influence here. Read William Carlos Williams's
'XXII':

---

19 Ciaran O'Neill, unpublished interview with Ciaran Carson, 2007.   **20** Nick Topping, 'Out of
the pub and into QUB: Nick Topping talks to Professor Ciaran Carson', in *Fortnight*, 420 (2003), 16.

so much depends

upon

a red wheel
barrow

glazed with rain
water

beside the white
chickens[21]

'XXII' (or 'The red wheelbarrow'), found among the pastiche sequence of twenty-seven fragments of poetry and prose that is *Spring and all,* shares something of a resonance with Carson's 'Siege'. Where Carson's poem as recounted, numbers twenty-four syllables; Williams's is composed (after its title) in twenty-two. Notably, 'XXII' comprises of one meandering sentence broken into four parts. 'Siege', mirroring this stanzaic arrangement, is built on a broken couplet. The formal resemblance of both poems is also met in their rhythmic similarity. In terms of syllabic grouping, Carson's stanzas follow a 7/5/7/5 schema, Williams's a 6/5/6/5. A reading of 'Siege' and 'XXII' side by side effects distinct echoes, and Carson's interest in 'how (W.C. Williams's) prosody and visual directness might cope with questions of war'[22] has no doubt helped him to achieve in *Breaking news* the 'precision' he so admired in Heaney prior to *North*. While retaining something of C.K. Williams's 'dirty realism', *Breaking news* has shown Carson to owe a debt to another American poet.

Recently, on 5 May 2005, Carson gave his inaugural lecture as Professor of Poetry at Queen's University Belfast. Selecting as his title '"Whose woods these are ...": some aspects of poetry and translation', the newly appointed Professor Carson opened with a recital of Robert Frost's poem, 'Stopping by woods on a snowy evening'. The lecture Carson delivered that day pondered 'the dreamy alternatives' of Frost's poetry, and by extension, those posed by the very nature of language.[23] Carson appeared lost in fascination. Indeed some years before, the poet had been quoted saying: 'Frost sounds very sane and American ... but the

---

21 William Carlos Williams, *The collected poems, vol. 1 1909–1939* (Manchester, 2000), 224. **22** O'Neill, interview with Ciaran Carson. **23** Ciaran Carson, '"Whose woods these are ...": some aspects of poetry and translation', in *The yellow nib,* 2 (2006), 112–27, 116.

language gets stranger the more you examine it'.[24] On this occasion, Carson had been talking about the American's 'After apple-picking', a poem whose metaphysical and at times hypnotic quality undergoes tantalizing development in 'Whatever sleep it is'. Here, in an interesting if also zany intertextual dialogue with Frost's 'After apple-picking' (from which Carson directly gleans the title of his poem), tribute is paid to the American bard:

> *The pane of glass*
> *I skimmed this morning from the drinking-trough,* he whispers to himself,
> *Melted, and I let it fall and break.* Early frost: the stars are blazing
> Now like snowflakes – stem end and blossom end
>
> Swelling and dimming over the black Alp of the roof. It is an October
> Sort of March, the apples ripened out of season … (*Ifn*, 28)

Besides Carson's choice of title, the pun 'Early frost' alluding to the appearance of 'After apple-picking' in Frost's second volume of poetry *North of Boston* (1914), offers a clue as to where the reader should look when reading 'Whatever sleep it is'. Here is perhaps the significant excerpt from 'After apple-picking:

> I cannot rub the strangeness from my sight
> I got from looking through a pane of glass
> I skimmed this morning from the drinking trough
> And held against the world of hoary grass.
> It melted, and I let it fall and break.
> But I was well
> Upon my way to sleep before it fell,
> And I could tell
> What form my dreaming was about to take.
> Magnified apples appear and disappear,
> Stem end and blossom end,
> And every fleck of russet showing clear.[25]

Examining the excerpts from both poems, one can observe Carson's wilful intent to entwine the American's verse with his own for mesmeric or surreal effect. Such instances of seemingly haphazard poetic citation and 'literary allusion' in *The Irish for no* are motivated (Carson has said) by 'playing around with quotations and

24 Brown, 144.   **25** Frost, *Selected poems,* 69.

stuff, all that English Lit. debris lying around at the back of my mind'.[26] The predilection for literary jocularity which the poet demonstrates in such instances shares certain parallels with the philosophy behind Frost's own writing, as conveyed in 'The mountain': 'But all the fun's in how you say a thing'. Where 'fun' is certainly present in 'Whatever sleep it is', for Carson it is the very strangeness of language, the art of composition and writing that moves him to contemplate Frost. Where Carson in his poem is writing on the composition of a painting – how a piece of art comes together by a series of metamorphoses, its various details being found along the way – Frost by association in 'After apple-picking' deals with the artistic vision from its very inception, the vision of an image whose strangeness haunts his sleep and shapes his dreams. Sharing this curiosity in a speculative interzone between sleep and waking reality, Carson is seen celebrating a similar metaphysicality (albeit tongue-in-cheek) in his final stanza. Here again, the poet playfully elaborates on Frost's poem:

> I see it is an angel, not a man, who has
> Descended, looking faintly puzzled at the poor response of the girl
> To whatever important announcement he has just made ...
> ... And the milkman looks up, momentarily
> Amazed at curtains, wings, gusting from the attic window. He rubs his eyes;
> He is still drowsy with these six days out of seven ... (*Ifn*, 28)

The circumstance is not of one but two visions. The first, alluding to the biblical visitation of the Virgin Mary by the Angel Gabriel, is followed by that of the overworked milkman who bears witness, but 'rubs his eyes' in disbelief and longing for sleep. One might say that Carson is at once dialoguing with and enacting the transcendental theme of Frost's poem. There is also room for an ironic interpretation of Frost's 'For once, then, something', with the Belfast poet nodding toward a similar epiphany motif. The dialogue finds continuity in the opening of Carson's 'The Irish for no', which begins, '*Was it a vision or a waking dream?*' (*Ifn*, 49), in homage to Keats's 'Ode to a nightingale'. Here, in a curious instance of *déjà-vu*, Carson's male suitor or visitor is seen overcoming a building of some height to make his entrance, unequivocally recalling the elevated and vertically dynamic entrance of the angel figure in 'Whatever sleep it is'.[27] As the narrative of 'The Irish for no' appears to gesture back to 'Whatever sleep it is', Carson

---

26 Frank Ormsby, 'Interview with Ciaran Carson', *Linen Hall Review*, 8:1 (1991), 6.   **27** Celestial imagery is recurrent throughout Carson's writing. One scene in *The star factory*, for instance, is

contrives that the poem's language should again share cadences with Frost's: 'And now you rub your eyes and get / acquainted with the light'. This syntactic juxtaposition of Frost's 'After apple-picking' with the title (albeit skewed) of another of his poems, 'Acquainted with the night', is repeated elsewhere in an expanding poetic dialogue with the American poet.

'Z', appearing in the 'Letters from the alphabet' section of *Opera et cetera* (1996), presents one such further case.[28] Seen in the excerpt below, a number of distinct references to Frost's poetry are once more carefully integrated into Carson's text:

> You will hear me fading and droning towards you from
>   the valley next
> To one, for I have miles to go: when I deliver all the
>   letters, that's the text …
>
> Snow is falling fast, my parallels already blurring
>   on the mountainside   (*Oec*, 36)

Carson's splicing of Frost's verse with his own (on this occasion with no italic emphasis whatsoever) is conspicuous for its partial citation of the closing refrain of 'Stopping by woods on a snowy evening': 'The woods are lovely, dark, and deep, / But I have promises to keep, / And miles to go before I sleep, / And miles to go before I sleep'. Allusion is also made in 'Z' to Frost's 'Desert places', which opens: 'Snow falling and night falling fast, oh, fast / In a field I looked into going past'. The rhetorical relationship that Carson's poem shares with Frost's is reinforced by his choice of a physical scene (a snow-filled valley) that inclines towards an uncanny atmosphere and portent. Switching from borrowed snowfalls to borrowed lines, earlier, I sketched Carson's movement from C.K. Williams's long line to an attenuated line as employed by W.C. Williams. This breaking of the poetic line occurs, albeit in a more roguish way in Carson's assimilations of patches of Frost's verse in his poetry. The 'English Lit. debris' that the Belfast poet

---

particularly evocative of the 'Mohammedan angels staggering on tenement roofs illuminated' glimpsed in Allen Ginsberg's 'Howl' (*Howl and other poems*, San Francisco, 1956). Carson writes: 'And in these troubled times, from time to time, angels could be witnessed with their long wing-cases trailing behind them, crawling up the neo-Gothic blackened spires of St Peter's Pro-Cathedral like translucent locusts, or materializing on the airy girders of unfinished office blocks' (*Tsf*, 20).
28 Another example is Carson's poem 'From the Welsh' (*Fl*, 42–3), with its allusions to Frost's 'After apple-picking' and 'Mending wall'.

says he has 'lying around at the back of … (his) mind' might be thought of then, with regards to Frost at least, not as *a heap of broken images* but as *a heap of broken lines*. Ciaran Carson's poetry is a jig-saw that clearly has a number of American pieces.

Alphabets and labyrinths in Ciaran Carson's *Fishing for amber*

JERZY JARNIEWICZ

Let me start with a personal note. Sometime in 1999 Neil Corcoran wrote to me and asked, appropriately in a *post scriptum*, if I knew that there was a Captain Jarniewicz in Ciaran Carson's most recent book. The news surprised me. I had met Ciaran in Poland the previous year, when he came over to take part in the Legnica Poetry Festival. We had exchanged a few letters and postcards since, but he did not mention a word about this 'Polish' aspect of his new book. I felt intrigued if only by the mere fact that my family name Jarniewicz is a very rare name. In fact, it was invented and adopted shortly after the war by my grandfather, who wanted to change his old name for a new one with a recognisably Polish ending, and, which was even more important for him, the one that would be one-and-only, undeniably unique. So he came up with Jarniewicz. There were a handful of Janiewiczes and Jankiewiczes around, but no Jarniewiczes, and even up till this very day there are only ten people bearing this surname, all of them members of my close family. Imagine then my surprise when I learnt from my friend's email that there is one more Jarniewicz – a literary character in Ciaran Carson's new book, *Fishing for amber*. Being sure that Ciaran did not write about me, but only took my name for one of his characters, I was anxious to learn how Carson's Jarniewicz was portrayed. I asked my informant to send me details about him: who is that Carsonian Jarniewicz? What is his role in the book? The answer came straight away: 'no need to worry, he is a voice, he only tells stories'.

After reading the book I realized what made Ciaran Carson choose my name for one of his many storytellers. It was not only the Polish sounding suffix, the Slavonic patronymic – icz, that appealed to the author of *Fishing for amber*, but also the opening syllable: jarn. Carson, as it has already been observed, is capable of reading in one language and thinking in another, no wonder then that he noticed the name starts with a word close to the heart of any devout narrator, as

Carson himself undoubtedly is: yarn. In effect of Carson's etymological *fiat*, my family name, *Jarniewicz*, turned into a Polish/English hybrid, *yarn-iewicz*, and acquired new meaning, denoting now a fictitious Polish sea captain who spins a yarn.

It seems to me a telling story of how attentively Carson looks at words. Also of how words, such as my family name, can enter literature in result of the poet's attention to a linguistic fracture, and in this particular case: to the first syllable which in Polish means nothing, and in English acquires specific meaning. Secret meanings of fragments, forgotten or suppressed stories behind names, foreignness revealing its familiar side, or vice versa – this list of Ciaran Carson's themes is far from completion. This is an important interpretative hint to the readers of Carson's prose: other names that he uses may have similar stories to tell. The problem is that we may not be aware of them. And this is perhaps one of the truths that Carson's prose communicates to us: there are myriads of other stories on which the actual stories told in the book have been founded. What we eventually get to know when we have read *Fishing for amber* is merely the peak of a narrative iceberg.

Carson looks at names as if he were looking at pieces of amber with pine needles trapped in the solidified resin. What's in a name?, one poet famously asked, and five centuries later another poet answers: stories. And other names.

Carson seems to disregard the view, commonly accepted in linguistics, according to which proper names (*nomina propria*) have no meaning. As opposed to common names (*appelativa*), proper names do not refer to any classes of objects, but to individuals. If we know the definition of the word 'chair', we know also which objects belong to that category and can thus be called 'chairs'. On the contrary, John is a person who has arbitrarily been called 'John', so it is not possible to tell who else can bear this name. Though this is still a matter of controversy, most linguists would say that whereas common nouns mean something (or have meaning), proper names only denote, but have no meaning and cannot function as predicates. Strictly speaking, proper names do not belong to any language and consequently lexicographers should not, and do not include them in dictionaries.[1] Proper names are homeless, free-floating, exiled words, and though we associate them with particular languages, these languages do not accept them as parts of their lexicons. In consequence names enjoy incomparable freedom; having no meaning they can acquire various senses and denote any

1 See Chapter 7 in John Lyons, *Semantics*, vol. 1 (Cambridge, 1977).

object. They can travel like coins, or like stories. This is, to use Richard Hamilton's phrase, what makes names so different, so appealing.

In *Fishing for amber,* in his use of my family name, Carson severed the link between the name and its bearer and turned the (proper) name into a meaningful noun signifying a storyteller. This is by no means the only case of such a semantic metamorphosis that can be found in his book. Carson collected numerous stories in which proper names turn into ordinary nouns, wandering from one individual to another, from a person to an object, from one language to another tongue. For example, the name Hyacinthus was transformed into the common noun 'hyacinth', signifying a bulbous plant; and the name Berenice changed into berenice, the strayed hair from the stock of an artist's brush. But Carson also presents the reversed onomastic process of common nouns changing into names, as when he suggests that Berenice was named after her amber hair. These processes of incessant metamorphoses of common nouns into proper names, and proper names into common nouns, are in fact one of the basic mechanisms of Carson's prose that spin off his meandering narratives. For example, the narrative about Dutch painting included in the chapter on Berenice develops into a description of the crinkled surfaces of canvases, which in turn invokes anecdotes about varnish, which subsequently leads the narrator, by means of etymological analyses, to the story of the Queen of Cyrene, Berenice. Berenice's name lost its status of a proper name and in a series of Ovidean transformations – including Spanish *berniz,* Portuguese *verniz,* French *vernis* – reached English as *varnish.* The process continues, developing in a meandering, looping, and labyrinthine manner.

In his highly idiosyncratic, personal collection of stories and anecdotes, Carson retells the myth of how Berenice cut her hair and hung it up in a temple, from where it soon disappeared. She was then told that the winds had taken the hair to heaven, where it forms now the seven stars called Coma Berenices. So – Carson concludes his story – a hair, which strays from the stock of an artist's brush to flaw the application of paint or varnish, is known as a berenice (*Ffa,* 17). It is interesting to see how Carson tells this short story. Let me quote the appropriate paragraph in full. Berenice had cut her hair

> with gold shears and she hung it up in the ophisthodomos of the temple of Arsinoe at Zephyrium, but it vanished the first night, or was stolen; and the astronomer Conon of Samos told the king that the winds had wafted it to heaven, where it forms the seven stars near the tail of Leo, called Coma Berenice. (*Ffa,* 17)

Even a cursory glance at the passage alerts us to the fact that this single sentence includes no less than six proper names: Arsinoe, Zephyrium, Conon, Samos, Leo, Coma Berenice. The reader might like to know who Arsinoe was, or why Conon, the astronomer, an entirely marginal figure in this story, is mentioned by name, and not only by his profession. To the story some names seem superfluous, one can imagine other words put in their place which would make no difference for the reading of the passage. The names look as if they were abstract figures, almost nonsense words, interesting to the poet because of their exoticism and the aura of mysteriousness, suggesting stories which remain beyond our reach.

In this respect, it is not a coincidence that in the passage so studded with proper names, Carson speaks about 'ophistodomos'. How many readers would understand this word, meaning 'an apartment at the back of an ancient Greek temple, corresponding to the vestibule in front'[2]? Though it is spelt as an ordinary noun and included in the English language dictionary, contrary to such words as 'Conon' or 'Arsinoe' or even 'Ciaran Carson' for whom we would search in vain in the *OED*, its function does not differ much from the function of proper names with which Carson's narrative is saturated. Its place in the dictionary of the *English* language is debatable, as is the presence of 'Berenice' and 'Arsinoe' – the word is evidently foreign. In his poetry collection, *First language*, Carson will make astonishing use of such words, foreign and yet belonging to the English language lexicon. In one of the poems from this collection, Carson declares that English is not 'yet a language', and then offers us the following lines:

> Growling figures campaniled above me, and twanged their
> carillons of bronze
> Sienna consonants embedded with the vowels *alexandrite,*
> *emerald,* and *topaz.*

> The topos of their discourse seemed to do with me and
> convoluted genealogy;
> Wordy whorls and braids and skeins and spiral helices,
> unskeletoned from laminate geology.
>
> ('Second language', *Fl,* 10)

---

2 *The shorter Oxford English dictionary on historical principles* (Oxford 1973). The dictionary however spells the word without the 'h'.

The seemingly obvious claim that the poem is written in English has been seriously questioned: how English is the Italian noun 'campanile', or the adjective 'sienna'? How English are Greek 'helices' or Latin 'lamina'? And such words and phrases from the same poem as 'Araphoes', 'Nimrod', 'I-Ching', 'Ad altare Dei', 'che sera', 'fleurs de lys', 'Pharaonic unguents', do they really come from English? The poem looks like a multilingual *bricolage*, an example of the post-Babelian confusion of the tongues, exploding any possibility of a homogenous and pure diction, and unveiling the essentially hybrid nature of English; in fact, of any language.[3]

The sentence about Berenice's hair quoted above is worth paying further attention to due also to its use of paronomasia, one of Carson's favourite devices. When Carson writes about Berenice's lock that vanished, the word 'vanished', uttered and then corrected or qualified by another supposition ('vanished, or was stolen'), appears here because of its phonic resemblance to 'varnish', a word which seems to remain outside the mythological story of Berenice's hair, but which in fact not only sparked off the story but also constituted its conclusion. Varnish, absent in the myth, is already there, echoed in the ordinary English verb 'to vanish'.

Carson delights in flooding his texts with proper names, blurring the difference between their arbitrariness and semantic motivation, between their abstractness and concreteness, vagueness and specificity. This fondness for names finds its extreme realization in long passages which are constituted almost entirely of names – such nominal catalogues, which traditional rhetoric calls *enumeratio*, often have no meaning in the context of the narrative, yet excite the poet by their abstract qualities: in such passages language is set loose, liberates itself from the subjection to meaning and starts acting with its phonic quality and distant, often non-verbal associations. Most catalogues start from a general term, which Carson splits as if he were splitting the atom to release the untamed verbal energy. The initial general term is found unsatisfactory and replaced by an open-ended list of specific nouns, or names, dramatizing the transition from the One to the Many. Among Carson's many catalogues one finds for example a long list of names for roses:

> the inadequacy of 'rose' is evident in the plethora of modern varietal names, of which a small section might represent a grand soirée. The ladies present include Albertine, Diana, Jenny Wren, Maid Marian, Zulu

3 Cf. my article, 'After babel: translation and mistranslation in contemporary British poetry', in *European Journal of English Studies, The New Poetics*, 6:1 (April 2002).

> Queen, Violet Carson, Adelaide d'Orleans, Rose of Tralee, Minnehaha,
> Queen Fabiola, Madam Butterfly, Phyllis Gold, Mistress Quickly,
> Constance Spry, Dorothy peach, Dolly Varden, Isabel de Ortiz, Lady
> Curzon, Baby Betsy McCall, Mrs Sam McGredy, Carmen Talon, Queen
> Nefertiti, Goldilocks, Ma Perkins, Wendy, Stella, Mexicali Rose, La
> Follette, Thumbelina, Lucy Cramphorn, Polly Flinders, Miss France,
> Miss Liberty, Miss Ireland, and Violinista Costa. (*Ffa*, 18–19)

This list is further supplemented by an equally long list of masculine names for
roses. Are we much wiser having read this sentence? What language is it in? What
is the meaning of such a list? Such questions are out of place, since we are invited
not so much to expand our knowledge of the world, but rather to savour these
words, as if they were scent, colour, and sound. Some of the names may sound
comic or ridiculous, others we find pompous, or unashamedly prosaic. Patrick
Kavanagh was right when he said that naming things is an act of love.

The poet's fascination with names demonstrates his urge to maximize the
individualization of his language. The phenomenal world is the world composed
of parts, discrete, unique entities which our mind, or our language, collects in
categories, branding them with general names at the cost of their particularity.
That is the curse of language, or, as Carson called it, 'the inadequacy of rose':
language tends to classify and ignore what is individual. For the poet, trying to
overcome that linguistic annihilation of the multiple world, there seems to be no
way out: the poet has to work with language, with general concepts; radical
attempts to particularize would result in unintelligibility. If language, also the
language of poetry, is to communicate anything, then it has to rise above the
incorrigibly plural world and use categories and general terms. All those poets
who are not terrified by 'the drunkenness of things being various', by the plethora
of individual beings, who do not search for wholes and totalities, would take
recourse to specific nouns whose specificity could lead them to the status of
proper names. To this end Craig Raine has employed a long list of proper names
of sheep in his long poem *The prophetic book* which starts with a declaration 'I will
give you the world that is taken for granted'. Raine proceeds to enumerate all the
unique wonders that the world can offer:

> I will bring you the beauty of facts:
> Southdown, Dalebread, Dartmoor,
> Derbyshire Gritstone, Bluefaced Leicester,

> Herdwick, Hill Radnor, Devon Longwool,
> Beulah Speckled Face, Oxford Down,
> Welsh Mountain, North Country Cheviot,
> do not exhaust the names of our sheep.[4]

It is the beauty of facts, writes Raine, and unfolds a list of names, only to say that it remains incomplete, suggesting perhaps that all such catalogues remain incomplete. In both Craig Raine's and Ciaran Carson's writing there is a conspicuous need to mirror the variety and specificity of the phenomenal world in the variety and specificity of the language in which that world is evoked. It is an impossible, Promethean task to save the individual against the dictatorial power of the species, to save the unique against the tyranny of the general.

It can be claimed that Carson's persistent use of proper names, which derive from, or enter, the lexicon of common nouns, aims at questioning the language's aspirations to build wholes and is the poet's attempt to redeem, and to celebrate the variety of the world by stretching the linguistic substance to its limits defined by individuality. If this unattainable aim is ever achieved we would have the one-to-one correspondence between the word and the object it denotes. Carson tries to approach that state by enumerations and cataloguing. A different tactics was suggested by Stephane Mallarmé who tried to capture the uniqueness of experience by refusing to use names. In a much quoted pronouncement he declared: 'to name an object is to suppress three-fourths of the delight of the poem which is derived from the pleasure of divining little by little: to suggest it, that is the dream'.

In the same chapter in which Carson catalogued feminine and masculine names of rose, illustrating thus the inadequacy of the general term 'rose', he went on to outline a history of the tulip mania in seventeeth century Holland. In his short account, which has many predecessors including Zbigniew Herbert's *The still-life with a bridle* and Deborah Moggach's *Tulip fever*, Carson drew the picture of the world exploding, up to the point of madness, with a variety of new phenomena. The Dutch tulip-madness brought about the emergence from the void not only of numerous new types of tulips, but also of an unprecedented variety of their new colours, which then had to be named. The individuality of the world intensified rapidly, leaving language helpless. 'New shades of pigmentation – writes Carson – became visible daily, and the wordsmiths pored by candlelight over glossaries and ancient flower-treatises, exploring new ways of

4 Craig Raine, *Clay. Whereabouts unknown* (London, 1996), 4.

describing colour' (*Ffa*, 22). The act of giving names to the world did not finish with Adam giving names to the animals, it is an incessant process in which language always tries to keep up with the ever-changing and ever-differentiating reality, always lagging a few steps behind the variety that transcends any lexicon. It can be claimed that Carson's catalogues celebrate the richness of language, but even more so, they testify to the language's insufficiency vis-a-vis reality.

NARRATIVES

Carson's prose is a consistent extension of his interests shown in his poems. When in his second poetry volume, *The Irish for no*, he started employing story-telling as the main structural device of his verse, it was obvious that sooner or later he would arrive at what is generally regarded as the domain of the narrative. But in his prose, as the prose section of *Belfast confetti* shows, he plays a double role. He is a devout *collector*, eagerly looking for rare specimens, curios and absurdities, exciting details and unknown facts. As a collector, he is fond of list-making, itemizing, cataloguing and accumulating.

But he is also a declared *story-teller*, an expert in the narrative craft who finds delight in brandishing the wide range of techniques in which stories can be told. He knows that to make the story more interesting, the story-teller has to manipulate the reader's expectations, by retardation and procrastination, by flashbacks and flashforwards, by splitting the narrative and serialising it, making the listeners wait in excitement for the next installment. Carson, the story-teller, knows that in order to make the flow captivating he has to stop and pause, hence the art of story-telling is the art of interrupting. This is the knowledge of Scheherazade, who managed to save her life, not so much by telling, but by stopping her stories. And the one instrument which no story-teller can do without is not a pen, but the pipe. It is an integral part of the story-telling process when the teller searches his pockets to find it, then unlids the cap, stuffs the pipe with an aromatic mix relinquished from a suddenly disclosed tobacco-pouch, lights a match from nowhere with a click of his thumb and finger, and applies it to the bowl (*Ffa*, 240).

Carson's two roles, that of the collector and the story-teller, and the two main devices of his prose, cataloguing and narrating, may be seen as being at odds. The former stands for the many, for what is unconnected, fragmentary and singular. The language of the collector has a staccato rhythm, its basic figure is parataxis, that is, the style in which 'the members within a sentence, or else a sequence of

complete sentences, are put one after the other without any expression of their
connection or relations except (at most) the noncommittal connective, "and"'.[5]
The main function of parataxis, which I would call possibly the most important
stylistic figure underlying the whole book, is to undermine the very idea of
hierarchy, since in paratactic sentences all constitutive elements are equally
important.

Carson's refusal to respect hierarchies, which emerges in his preference for
parataxis, motivates most of his writing. It is often also directly dramatized: for
example, when in Chapter 11 of *Fishing for amber* Carson moves from his account
of the tulip mania to tell the story of the Prague defenestration which sparked off
the Thirty Years War, he gives two versions of what happened when the three
officials, seized and hurled through the window, somehow managed to survive. 'It
was reported by some that the Virgin Mary had wrapped them in her wondrous
cloak; others claimed a dung-heap had broken their fall' (*Ffa,* 23). Virgin Mary
and a dung heap? Virgin Mary or a dung heap? Carson does not take sides, he
reports the two different stories, one wondrous and miraculous, the other down-
to-earth, practical, no-nonsense. Linked in a paratactic relationship, they have the
same value to a story-teller who can turn them into equally arresting narratives,
just as Chaucer who could put side-by-side the exquisite ribaldry of the Miller's
tale and the elevated romance of the Knight.

The use of parataxis corresponds to the repeated theme of temporal
coincidence – events often of different significance and order are narrated by
Carson only because they happened to take place at the same time. Cause and
effect relationship is replaced by simultaneity and parallelism, which like parataxis
question the notion of hierarchy: as it was once remarked, reading Spinoza is as
important as the smell of cooking that at the very moment comes from the
kitchen or the noise of a typewriter that can be heard from another room. The
poet's mind registers them irrespectively of their objective significance. By the way,
Carson does not fail to notice that Spinoza was born at the same moment that the
tulip mania started. It was also the year that Vermeer and Leeuwenhoek were born
(*Ffa,* 124).

In contrast to collecting, story-telling stands for linking and joining,
constructing wholes and patterns. The language of the story-teller has the *legato*
rhythm, focusing on transitions, some of them abrupt and swift, some of them
delicate, unnoticeable, but always making the listener ask that fundamental

---

5 M.H. Abrams, *A glossary of literary terms* (New York, 1981), 191.

question: what happened next? And leading him or her to the narrative solution, which usually takes the form of death, or marriage, or both.

Narratives create an impression of an ordered world in which everything is linked in a linear, temporal or causal sequence. Things apparently dispersed and fragmented partake in a larger pattern that a narrative always presupposes.

There are other differences between catalogues and narratives. In Carson's catalogues the world disperses, proliferates, 'becomes suddenly rich'. What was One turns into the many just as one simple rose explodes and breaks into an uncontrollable plethora of names. Stories, on the other hand, have an integrating function. Various stories lead to one story that underlies the many. 'Stories are all the same', says Carson, and demonstrates how one story is overwritten on another story, which in turn is overwritten on another, and so on, ad infinitum, in a truly palimpsestic set of narrative layers. Whereas stories lead to other stories, catalogues exist indifferently to other catalogues, parallel or simultaneously. Carson's catalogues represent analysis, that is, dividing and differentiating; narratives tend towards synthesis: they bring together various stories to reveal their essential sameness.

Yet Carson is a subversive story-teller as much as he is a subversive collector. He turns catalogues, that is, arbitrary and incomplete lists, into alphabets, that is, ordered and conclusive sequences that reflect some internal pattern. But he also turns narratives which should lead in a sequence of events from the beginning to the end, into labyrinths, the forking paths, dead-ends, cul-de-sacs, and Chinese-boxes.

As a narratologist, Carson knows well that narratives are only arbitrary artifacts used to order our raw chaotic experience; as Hayden White demonstrated it, the same set of events can be ordered in a variety of ways, as a tragedy, comedy, satire, or romance. There is no one privileged type of narration, but various models which we choose by will. Carson the subversive story-teller reveals this basic arbitrariness of narratives, as much as he is intent on breaking their linear continuity. By doing both Carson tries to move narratives closer to his catalogues, to replace hypotaxis by parataxis, subordination by coordination, *legato* by *staccato*, closure by inconclusiveness, the whole by its parts. Contrary to the subtitle which promises *A long story* Carson becomes a collector of narratives, saying yes to the Many.

ALPHABETS

But neither are Carson's alphabets free from his subversive transformations. In *Fishing for amber* Carson has collected his variegated narrative material, ranging from histories of saints to the account of the tulip mania, from Celtic legends to etymological examinations, from adaptations of Greek mythology to summaries of the plots of Shakespeare's plays. The poet orders this most heterogeneous material in a series of chapters neatly arranged in alphabetical order. The first chapter is called 'Antipodes', the second 'Berenice', the third 'Clepsydra', and so on, till we arrive at the last two chapters called 'Yarn', and, finally, 'Zoetrope'.

Alphabetical order suggests some sort of pedantic encyclopedic work, some rigid taxonomy, with neatly arranged material, properly shelved, labelled, and classified. Starting from A we know, or we would like to believe that we know, where we are heading: B and C and D appear in what looks like a natural – familiar and predictable – order. The world arranged in this manner is tamed; the Many has been put under control, harnessed, framed in a rational clear way as the variety of species in Linnaeus's classification or the variety of chemical elements in Mendeleyev's table.

Any book arranged alphabetically, as a dictionary or an encyclopedia, has a very strong sense of the beginning and the end. What can one expect before A, or after Z? These two letters, defining the work's limits, are in fact synonymous with the absolute beginning and the absolute end, the Alpha and the Omega. And if the book offers us the beginning and the end, it also wants us to believe that in between it offers us everything. There are no other letters in the English alphabet apart from the twenty-six which are present in Carson's book and organize its material. This is Carson flirting with the idea of wholeness and completeness. Yet he is only flirting, since this alphabetical order is arbitrary and far from completion. The straightforwardness and the reliability of the alphabet is only an illusion, the readers of Carson's alphabets find themselves in a labyrinth, or should we rather say: lose themselves in it.

Most of the alphabetically arranged titles of the chapters in *Fishing for amber* are proper names. If we take them as guidelines, introducing us to the themes of the chapters we will feel at a loss. In most cases, the relationship between the title of the chapter and its subject matter is loose and coincidental, or even none. Readers will soon find out that the word appearing in the title has no special significance for the chapter it denotes. Carson sometimes starts the chapter with a story about the character from the title, but then quickly drops it and moves on to another, unrelated narrative. Sometimes the character or object from the title of the chapter emerges only in the very last sentence.

The neat order which the alphabetical arrangement of the chapters makes us expect is thus meaningless – overshadowed and overpowered by the sheer volcanic energy of the flux of Carson's prose. Stability suggested by the alphabetical patterning yields to the nearly cosmic rule of metamorphosis.

FATHER

It seems that in Carson's narrative world there is no guiding principle, no centre that would keep various strands and yarns together, no omphalos that would guarantee the fixity of the world recounted. Such centre is often metaphorized in the figure of the father, the starting point, the name giver. Does this mean that Carson's centreless prose is also fatherless? On the contrary. *Fishing for amber* is dedicated to Carson's father, this surely is a sincere sign of filial attachment, but I would claim that in the general structure of the book the dedication plays an important thematic role. Carson acknowledges the debt to his father, thanks to whom he learnt all these stories. Not by chance Carson's father starts telling his long story at Ciaran's wedding: Ciaran will soon be father himself. His father telling him stories during the wedding, *generating* them, prepares Ciaran to generate other stories, other lives. In this generational sequence story-telling is presented as life-sustaining activity, more so: as synonymous with life. One of the oldest stories of world literature proceeds in the paratactic rhythm of generations: 'And unto Enoch was born Irad; and Irad begat Me-huja-el: and Me-huja-el begat Methusael: and Methusael begat Lamech' (Genesis 4. 18). This sentence can be interpreted as a model of the way in which stories are generated. One story leads to, and begets another story. This mechanism reappears in various guises in Carson's book, not least in the description of a certain Dutch painting of an interior. On the canvas we find one room telescoped into another leading the viewer deeper and deeper into the labyrinthine corridors of representation.

AGAINST THE WHOLE

To conclude, I would like to propose that Carson's catalogues and narratives in their various forms both serve one purpose which is the refutation of the idea of the Whole. The illusion of order created by the alphabet stands for the illusion of the Whole to which all Carson's accumulated facts, stories, etymologies could belong. Yet they do not participate in anything apart from tentative, arbitrary narratives, which themselves break, twist, get fragmented, and end abruptly, revealing themselves to be parts of other narratives which in turn belong to narratives of another order, and so on and so forth. The great synthesis proves impossible. In Carson's world it is not merely impossible, but unnecessary. This sense of fragmentation and of the absence of an organizing whole, identified by some as Carson's postmodernist trait, is shared by many writers. We can find it, for example, in Fernando Pessoa's 'The keeper of sheep 47':

> I saw that there is no Nature,
> That Nature doesn't exist,
> That there are hills, valleys and plains,
> That there are trees, flowers and grass,
> That there are rivers and stones,
> But that there is no whole to which all this belongs,
> That a true and real ensemble
> Is a disease of our own ideas.
> Nature is parts without a whole.[6]

The seemingly obvious distinction between alphabets and labyrinths appears illusory. Whereas in his stories in *Lost in the funhouse* John Barth introduces us to the labyrinths of his postmodern fiction in which, to our pleasure, we soon get lost, in *Fishing for amber* Carson achieves the same effect by leading us into his alphabet, which promises neat order but means delightful confusion. In fact, Carson's alphabets are nothing else than veiled labyrinths.

---

6 Fernando Pessoa, 'The keeper of sheep 47', in *Selected poems*, ed. and trans. Richard Zenith (New York, 1998), 47.

Carson, Heaney, and the art of getting lost

ELMER KENNEDY-ANDREWS

The labyrinth is one of Carson's favourite images: 'I know this labyrinth so well –
Balaclava, Raglan, Inkerman, Odessa Street – / Why can't I escape?' (*Bc,* 23) asks
the speaker in 'Belfast confetti', the wanderer caught up in the violent dislocations
that characterize urbanization. Though assimilated to the city, this *flâneur*-figure
of instability cannot dominate the situation but, instead, loses his initial,
complacent 'self' in a disorienting space productive of hysteria and terror. Not
only does Carson repeatedly describe the city as a labyrinth, but he also likes to
think of the processes of memory, imagination and storytelling as being
labyrinthine. From the metaphor of the labyrinth flow a mythology and aesthetics
which are used to explore the condition of being lost.

Getting lost is not, for Carson, a bad thing. Rather, he follows in the footsteps
of Walter Benjamin, who supplies him with the epigraph for *Belfast confetti:*

> Not to find one's way about in a city is of little interest ... But to lose
> one's way in a city, as one loses one's way in a forest, requires practice ...
> I learned this art late in life: it fulfilled the dreams whose first traces were
> the labyrinths on the blotters of my exercise books. (*Bc,* 14)[1]

As well as drawing a parallel between the labyrinths of city and text, Benjamin
proposes the idea that to be lost is to be fully present, and to be fully present
involves being in uncertainty and mystery. One does not get lost but, rather, loses
oneself, the implication being that it is a conscious choice, a chosen surrender to
otherness. In deliberately installing wandering and disorientation as recurrent
tropes in his writing, Carson becomes what Giles Deleuze and Félix Guattari call
'nomadic'.[2] Narration no longer serves the narrator's need for self-location and
self-affirmation. The narrator deliberately loses his way, breaking the bond
between narration and location that characterizes traditional rooted discourses.

1 Walter Benjamin, 'A Berlin chronicle', in *Selected writings,* vol. 2 (1927–34), trans. Rodney
Livingstone et al., ed. Michael W. Jennings, Howard Eiland, and Gary Smith (Cambridge, MA,
1999), 598. 2 Deleuze, Giles and Felix Guattari, *A thousand plateaus: capitalism and schizophrenia,*
trans. Brian Massumi (Minneapolis, 1987).

Instead of a discourse based on principles of rootedness, linear progression and centredness, Carson specializes in fragmented, discontinuous forms, ways of extending the boundaries of self into unknown or unofficial territory. Digression evokes the sense of suspended time that belongs uniquely to those who wander; it awakens feelings of dislocation, of being in-between, neither here nor there; it violates the reader's habit and expectation; it is testimony to the narrator's desire for, and capacity to make, new meaning. Concentrating on his later writing – the two prose works, *The star factory* (1997) and *Shamrock tea* (2001), and his novel-poem *For all we know* (2008) – I would like to explore the Carsonian labyrinth, and the education he provides us in existential and narrative abandon.

Any of the chapters in *The star factory* could be used to illustrate the digressive, associative structure of the book as a whole. 'Radio Ulster', for example, starts with a childhood memory of a radio in the fifties. But memory quickly blurs into fantasy, the narrative crossing back and forth between different planes of 'reality'. When Heaney writes about listening to the radio as a child (as in 'A sofa in the forties'), he does so in the context of a minutely detailed time and place. But there is no such sense of being earthed in Carson. His writing acts to undo the reliable coordinates of time and place. In typical fantasy-fiction fashion, the narrator imagines shrinking down and physically passing into the magical world inside the radio (as the narrator in *Shamrock tea* crosses into the world of fourteenth-century Bruges through the magic portal of the Arnolfini Portrait).

> I would press my ear against the big warm humming Bakelite body, and mentally shrink myself to walk about its Toltec labyrinth of valves and tubes and crystals, sometimes encountering giant dust-beetles who would scan me momentarily with alien antennae, and then go about their scarab business managing the dark interior. There are many sanctuaries within it, many aisles and transepts, dimly lit by the red glow of votive lamps. A sacristan with a broken insect leg sometimes appears to tend the candles … Sometimes I encounter creatures like myself, but cannot speak to them, since each of us are rapt or lost in private explorations, murmuring before the shrines, or behind the closed doors of confessionals, where one whispers to the priest through a wire grille which smells of brass, nicotine, aftershave, and cassocks. (*Tsf*, 105–6)

The magical world inside the radio is naturalized, perceived in terms of the familiar imagery of a Catholic childhood. The imagined world is described in such minute and vivid detail that it becomes as real as the real world. With various levels of reality dissolving into each other, the reader rapidly loses his bearings: which is more 'real' – the radio's actual valves and tubes and crystals, or the imagined confessional smells of brass, nicotine, aftershave, and cassocks? The image of the confessional leads in the next paragraph to the idea of sanctuary, and the radio programme *Tearmann*, which is Irish for sanctuary, on which the narrator's father has appeared. The sanctuary his father spoke about was the Irish language: 'I used to hide myself within her'. The narrator makes a similar declaration: 'I, too, hide in language'. This, he says, makes him '"a son of resemblance" (*Tsf,* 106), hence copy or type', which in turn leads into a long excerpt from a book by Patricia Lynch, which is an anthology (or a copy of copies) of the lives of the Irish saints. Lynch's book includes the story of Columcille who made a copy of the only extant Book of Psalms against the express command of St Finnian. After recounting this story, the narrator tells us that the book was a present from his father, 'no doubt' because the first section is devoted to Saint Ciaran of Clear Island: 'perhaps he (his father) wanted me to follow in his (St Ciaran's) footsteps, though the path of the Clear Ciaran is straighter than the one I'm taking through this book' (*Tsf,* 113). There follows another excerpt from Lynch's book telling of St Ciaran's journey to the well at Fuaran. The ancient Ciaran 'met other roads but did not look at them' (*Tsf*, 114), and refuses to be distracted by the rich variety of human life he encounters along the way. The story is a little parable of single-minded focus and determination not to get lost – the very qualities that author Ciaran is anxious to dispense with in his narrative. And it is from his father that the narrator has apparently learnt his digressive style of story-telling. He says he can 'remember, or imagine' his father telling such stories, 'losing himself in language, escaping clock time' (*Tsf,* 116). The idea of escaping into language leads to thoughts of literal incarceration, of his father's brief wartime internment, and his Uncle Pat the IRA man hiding beneath the floorboards of a 'safe house'. In this chapter and elsewhere, Carson identifies with 'the underground status' (*Tsf*, 118) of all kinds of underground men – gangsters, IRA men tunnelling their way under the Maze prison, the prisoner in his cell 'escaping into language, as he renegotiates his memory to make a story of his life' (*Tsf,* 116). With these images of tunnelling underground and escaping into language Carson discovers a potent metaphor for the moral and political implications of his own writing practice. By opting for roads not taken rather than official routes, his narrators disengage from conventional narratives and unsettle the received versions of reality. Getting lost is a way of undermining the purported psychological and political mastery of the official narratives, subverting the 'reality' of the official map which is always bound up with power and authority.

Typically, instead of developing these ideas conceptually, the narrator moves on to refer to a children's Hallowe'en story competition in Derry which he happens to be judging at the time of writing the book. He copies out in its entirety one of the stories entitled 'Star Factory', which takes the form of a letter written by a 'Chris McCauley' with an address 'Star Factory, Foyle Road, Derry' (*Tsf,* 118–20). In this embedded narrative, the Chris McCauley narrator tells of losing his football in the grounds of the derelict Star Factory and breaking into the premises to retrieve it. He finds himself in a room full of women making shirts. They turn out to be apparitions, one of whom tells him that if he doesn't get away within half and hour he too will become a ghost like them and all the other little boys who had come looking for their footballs. Again, different levels of reality dissolve into each other. Hailing Chris McCauley as another 'underground man', the narrator expresses his gratitude to the author of this 'missive from the Underground' for permission to reproduce 'Star Factory' in *The star factory.* The story, the narrator confesses, still gives him 'a serendipitous *frisson*' (*Tsf,* 120). By including a footnote on the etymology of the word 'serendipitous', the narrator-Carson foregrounds the pervasively self-reflexive, layering effects of the text. What remains indeterminate, of course, is the status of the Chris McCauley 'Star Factory' story: was it really a fantastical story written by a real Chris McCauley, or is the author Chris McCauley as much of a fiction as the character of Chris McCauley in the story which the narrator-Carson claims to have read for a children's story competition? Carson enmeshes us in a Saussurian network of shifting signification with no absolute terms. If *The star factory* is framed by the image of the father who is identified as source and inspiration of the narrator's storytelling, the ending, with its intimation of death and mutability, dislodges Carson Sr. from becoming a fixed point of reference, and sets the peregrine-postman on his rounds once again, this time within a generational succession of transfer and transformation: 'I hold his free hand to guide him through the story, and we walk its underworld again' (*Tsf,* 292).

A loosely associative structure characterizes not just individual chapters but the book as a whole. Most (but not all) of the chapters take their title from places in Belfast, though the place names do not necessarily provide any significant or central organizing point of reference. The star factory of the title was an abandoned mill, full of Piranesian galleries and decaying structures, which haunted the author as a child, stimulus to and symbol of the imagination:

> Here there were dynasties of paths and directions. Each family would tend towards certain entrances or adits, and the abstract space within was riddled with the swarming wormholes of their past and present; they moved, indeed, like slow illiterate teredos … They had no thread of Ariadne. Of necessity, the story they had entered comprised many stories, yet their diverse personal narratives and many-layered time-scales evinced glimpses of an underlying structure, like a traffic flow-chart with its arteries and veins and capillaries. (*Tsf*, 62)

Carson's city, converted into text, becomes an endlessly fascinating lexical playground in which the imagination is freed from the usual conditions of everyday life. The Belfast Street Directory reminds him of 'how the arbitrary power of the alphabet juxtaposes impossibly remote locations' (*Tsf*, 8), and prompts him to think of himself as a literal bookworm 'ruminating through the one thousand, five hundred and ninety-six pages of the Directory in teredo mode, following my non-linear dictates, as I make chambered spirals in my universe, performing parabolas by browsing letters and the blanks between them' (*Tsf*, 8). In the textualized city, reality is readily manipulable, space is fluid, and time no longer exists as a linear progression. In the attempt to possess experience as fully as he can, Carson explodes the moment, opening up its labyrinthine subtexts. The childhood memory of being sent out during class-time on an errand is important for the several minutely detailed 'reveries' which accompany the memory. He imagines himself as 'a secret agent, Early Christian Boy assigned to smuggle the Communion Host through Roman lines to a sacrament-deprived catacomb' (*Tsf*, 206). Different temporal contexts overlap, as indicated by the reference to the hostile authorities as 'the police', or in the metaphorical description of the sky being 'blitzed by photographically developed clouds blown in a hurricane into the present … as time collapsed about it' (*Tsf*, 207). In acknowledgement of the elasticity of narrative time as opposed to the rigidity of real-life clock time, the narrator concludes: 'For all these reveries, I was not unpunctual in my return. The time I've taken to describe the mental by ways is much longer than their actual span, for each can be perceived holistically, in kaleidoscopic, frozen moments; and time is telescoped within them' (*Tsf*, 207). He recognizes that 'time spent inside is not equal to the time spent outside' (*Tsf*, 209). This makes the narrator a kind of time traveller: he even compares himself to Prospero, Nemo, and Dr Who in his Tardis, that master of serendipity: 'he (Dr Who) plots a course to an intended destination; almost invariably, he weighs in at the wrong place and the wrong time, in the middle of a local revolution, or an alien invasion' (*Tsf,* 132). The narrator, too, fancies himself as a Time Lord 'flitting though the universe in his dimension-bending vehicle', which is language itself, unconstrained by the strict demands of reason or realism, and ready to lose himself in whatever interesting by ways present themselves.

2

Carson's book of five years later, *Shamrock tea,* more radically undermines the reality of both the narrator (also 'Ciaran Carson') and his universe, constructing an even more densely labyrinthine world through a range of features typical of fantastical literature: the work within the work, the interplay of dream and reality, the journey through time and space, the mirror or double. These are both essential themes – the problematical nature of the world, of knowledge, of time, of the self – and the essential techniques of composition. The usual distinction between form and content virtually disappears. Through a series of mysterious fusions, dismaying time-warps, and multiple shifts of perspective, the normal categories of perception and experience are dissolved and flow in on each other. Operating on a bewildering variety of levels, *Shamrock tea* transports us to a realm where fact and fiction, the real and the unreal, past and future are complementary aspects of the same continuous being.

The book teems with information, allusion and quotation, part of the process of layering the text, and drawing us into its labyrinthine, mysterious world where everything relates to everything else. Carson incorporates commentaries on a plethora of other authors and books, often obscure, sometimes imaginary (such as the untitled 'yellow', 'green' and 'blue' book), making the narrative an intricate interplay of creation and critique. Scholarship, argument and analysis are paradoxically employed to enlarge upon mystery, not resolve it. In the end, Carson's puzzles often appear to be no more than hoaxes carried off with considerable linguistic panache and supported by a wealth of arcane learning. He mocks both knowledge and invention by displaying them lavishly, finally turning them against themselves. Ideas are important only for their aesthetic value. Real-life people – van Eyck, Wittgenstein, Conan Doyle, Father Hopkins, the author himself – become characters within the narrative, but given fictitious life histories, their biography treated as fair game within a cultural universe where fact and fiction have become interchangeable. Identity is treated with the same freedom and fluidity as space and time. Characters mutate into other characters – even the narrator, who 'learned to become another person' (*St*, 297). There are few people in the story to remember or care about. Characters are pawns, and both character and actions are subservient to the author's chess-playing plottings. Setting, too, is indifferent: there is less local colour than in the poetry. The anchoring details of place and historical circumstance are established only in free-floating fragments, exactly as in a dream, the book as a whole offering escape from the usual conditions of the rational, everyday world. In a realistic text, the reader is less likely to get lost, but in a metafictional text such as *Shamrock tea,* where the story has only tenuous connection with reality as it is commonly understood, the reader can all too easily get lost, and all the more easily because the surface narrative can appear so luminously realistic, its pervasive tone so sober and scholarly, so beguilingly reportorial and reliable.

Carson plays with the Berkeleyan idea that concrete reality may consist only of mental realities, that the 'real world' may in fact be only one possibility in an infinite series of realities. The universe we inhabit, we are led to consider, may be already a simulacrum, perhaps a simulacrum in a precession of simulacra that vanish into infinity. The distinction between past, present and future, and between here and there, begins to dissolve. Underlying the notion of the simulacral or library-like universe is the idea that 'everything is connected *sub specie aeternitatis'* (*St*, 260). Fr Brown picks up the trope of the textualized universe introduced in *The star factory:*

> In the beginning, says St Augustine, God spoke the Word, and thus created heaven and earth. All things exist in that Word, which is the Book of Nature, and the Book of Revelation tells us that *the heavens shall be folded up like a scroll.* So in the eyes of God, time and space can be folded up, and things which appear to us to be centuries or miles apart are, in reality, but a parchment thickness away. If we were bookworms, we could eat into those spaces in next to no time. We are not worms, but we can, by way of Shamrock Tea, travel through those wormholes. (*St*, 260).

The opening sentence of the book – 'Perhaps I will return one day to the world I first entered' (*St*, 1) – indicates that the narrator no longer inhabits the same world he once did, though he was 'struck again by how this world and the other lay so close together, tissue-thin, like two adjacent pages in a Bible, yet stuck irretrievably together, never to be opened' (*St*, 300).

Shamrock Tea – both mythical potion and book – opens these stuck-together pages, and makes possible the journey through the wormholes of space and time. The narrator's uncle Celestine quotes from Wilde's *De profundis* – '[I]t is in the brain that everything takes place' (*St*, 234) – and on that basis outlines his revolutionary plan for Ireland: 'Our mission, said my uncle Celestine, is clear. Ireland has been too long divided. It has been said that the border between North and South exists more in the mind than in any geographical realist; we must, therefore, alter that mind-set' (*St*, 235). His plan is to dump large quantities of Shamrock Tea into Belfast's Silent Valley Reservoir (an idea Carson has lifted from Stewart Parker's play *Pentecost*) to bring about a situation where the inhabitants of the city 'will see the world as it really is, a world in which everything connects, where the Many is One, and the One is Many. There will be no division, for everything in the real world refers to something else, which leads to something else again, in a never-ending hymn of praise. The world is an eternal story' (*St*, 236). A revolution of perception can be effected through the agency of this magical substance which 'cleanses the doors of perception' (*St*, 93), allowing people to experience the world with visionary clarity. *The doors of perception* was actually a 1954 book by Aldous Huxley (and the inspiration of Jim Morrison and 'The Doors') detailing his experiences when taking mescaline, and considered to be one of the most profound studies of the effects of mind-altering drugs. Huxley takes his title from Blake's *The marriage of heaven and hell:* 'If the doors of perception were cleansed every thing would appear to man as it is, infinite. For man has closed himself up, till he sees all things through narrow chinks of his cavern'. Under the influence of mescaline, Huxley observed that everyday objects lose their functionality and suddenly exist simply as themselves: 'To be shaken out of the ruts of ordinary perception, to be shown for a few timeless hours the outer and inner world, not as they appear to an animal obsessed with survival or to a human being obsessed with words and notions, but as they are apprehended, directly and unconditionally, by Mind at large – this is an experience of inestimable value to everyone and especially to the intellectual'.[3] The hallucinatory clarity of van Eyck's Arnolfini Portrait, as described in Carson's book, exemplifies the kind of perception identified by Huxley (though, interestingly, it is Vermeer whom Huxley nominates as the painter with a 'cleansed perception of the infinite significance of all things'). Asked if his experience on drugs was agreeable, Huxley replied:

3. Aldous Huxley, *The doors of perception*, http://mescaline.com/huxley.htm. Accessed 8 November 2007.

'Neither agreeable nor disagreeable,' I answered, 'it just is.' Istigkeit –
wasn't that the word Meister Eckhart liked to use? 'Is-ness'. The Being of
Platonic philosophy – except that Plato seems to have made the
enormous, the grotesque mistake of separating Being from becoming and
identifying it with the mathematical abstraction of the Idea. He could
never, poor fellow, have seen a bunch of flowers shining with their own
inner light and all. But quivering under the pressure of the significance
with which they were charged; could never have perceived that what rose
and iris and carnation so intensely signified was nothing more, and
nothing less, than what they were – a transience that yet has eternal life,
a perpetual perishing that was at the same time pure being, a bundle of
minute, unique particulars in which, by some unspeakable and yet self-
evident paradox, was to be seen the divine source of all existence.

In his supreme concentration on the precisely rendered, luminous fragment,
Carson aspires to be one of Huxley's 'knowers of Suchness'; Shamrock Tea is the
symbolic means of producing the kind of person Huxley described as one 'whose
transfigured and transfiguing mind can see the All in every this'.

Carson playfully places himself in the line of such literary drug-connoisseurs
as De Quincey, Coleridge, Baudelaire, Hesse, Benjamin and Huxley. What above
all the psychedelic literary tradition offered Carson was a point of contact with
the philosophical and political possibilities of psychedelia. In *On hashish*,[4] for
example, Benjamin describes his experiments with mescaline and hashish as an
attempt to recover a concept of experience which had become entirely alien to
post-Enlightenment bourgeois society. Benjamin wanted to penetrate the
dehumanized mask of the post-industrial self, to rehabilitate the revolutionary
potential of the irrational, to 'wed "*rausch*" (intoxication, 'rush, 'high') and
rebellion in a "profane illumination"'.[5] For Benjamin, intoxication is not a mere
personal indulgence or unstructured hedonistic revolt, but a messianic project,
undertaken for the benefit of the entire community. Pastiche though it may be,
Shamrock tea has a similarly serious moral purpose. It is not the self-induced
ecstasy of the anti-social drug-user which Carson advocates, but the serious search
for new ways of seeing, new connections to the ordinary world.

---

4 Walter Benjamin, *On hashish*, trans. Howard Eiland et al. (Cambridge, MA, 2006).
http://www.wbenjamin.org/translations.html, accessed 8 Nov. 2007.   **5** See Scott J. Thompson,
'From "rausch" to rebellion: Walter Benjamin's *On hashish* and the aesthetic dimensions of
prohibitionist realism', in *Journal of Cognitive Liberties*, 1:2 (Spring/Summer 2000), 21–42,

Paralleling Benjamin's intention to explore through his drug-taking the range of experience associated with schizophrenia,[6] there is Carson's interest in multiple or disintegrated personality – the condition of 'fugue'. Shamrock Tea takes you out of yourself, answers the longing for otherness, for escape from the world and the usual boundaries of existence, the desire for freedom and flight. Carson's Wittgenstein speaks of '*Sehnsucht,* that Germanic yearning for a world beyond the world' (*St,* 160), and muses: 'Sometimes I think that, for all I know, I might be someone else … It is a condition known as fugue' (*St,* 162). In its psychological context, fugue, according to the *OED* is: '1 the attempt to escape from reality. 2 loss of memory coupled with disappearance from one's usual environments'. Wittgenstein proceeds to tell the story of Ansel Bourne, a carpenter and preacher from Rhode Island who, in 1887, following an unhappy second marriage, drew out his savings from the bank, travelled to Pennsylvania, and, calling himself A.J. Brown, began a new life as a shopkeeper. A few months later, feeling suddenly disorientated and frightened, he reclaimed his old identity and resumed his former existence as Ansel Bourne. Other instances of the 'fugue' state cited in *Shamrock tea* include the story of Mary Reynolds, which the narrator and his school-friend Maeterlinck come across in a book in Loyola House library. *Mary Reynolds of Pennsylvania: two souls in one body,* though not included in Carson's 'Selected Sources' at the end of *Shamrock tea,* is presumably the book *Two souls in one body?* (1927) by Henry Herbert Goddard, Director of the Ohio State Bureau of Juvenile Research to which Mary Reynolds was committed. Mary Reynolds, suddenly in 1811, at the age of nineteen, underwent a mysterious change in personality from a quiet, rather dull religious girl to one who was cheerful, gay and flirtatious. For the rest of her life she oscillated between these two personae. Mixed in with these actual, medically documented instances of multiple personality are Carson's own fictionalized accounts. Using a series of both real and imagined examples, Carson, half-seriously, half-playfully, constructs his own account of the 'fugue' state, which is itself defined by its schizoid confusion of the real and imaginary.

Shamrock tea, with its episodic, multiply embedded narratives, assumes a fugue-like structure, taking fugue this time in its musical sense: 'a musical composition on one or more short subjects, which are developed by successively entering voices and developed contrapuntally' (*OED*). So complex is this orchestration of stories within stories that the reader can easily lose sight of who

http://www.cognitiveliberty.org/2jcl/2JCL21.htm, accessed 8 Nov 2007.   **6** See Theodor W.Adorno, 'Benjamin the letter-writer', in Gary Smith (ed.), *On Walter Benjamin* (Cambridge, MA, 1991), 329–30.

is speaking, and of the status and nature of the narrative that is being relayed, despite Carson's inclusion of helpful markers and reminders. The book begins with the narrator, 'Ciaran Carson' being taken to boarding school at Loyola House by his uncle Celestine. Uncle Celestine tells him of his 'brief relationship with the philosopher Wittgenstein who worked as an under-gardener at Loyola House in the spring of 1949' (*St*, 79). Gradually, the dynamics of the narrative shifts, so that uncle Celestine becomes the immediate addressee or audience, and Wittgenstein takes over as the primary first person narrator, telling in vivid detail of his time as a gardener in Gheel (though the reliability of Wittgenstein's narration is undermined by such incidental asides as 'And there have been times when I have felt I was not far from madness' *St*, 86). A new run of narrative is initiated with the appearance of Fr Brown (who has no apparent connection with G.K. Chesterton's famous detective apart from a shared sacred astonishment at the mystery and surprise of the universe). Fr Brown introduces the Carson narrator to another new boy, Maeterlinck (who has no apparent connection with his famous literary namesake beyond their shared birthplace in Ghent and an interest in dream and fantasy). Maeterlinck's story is largely devoted to his uncle Maurice's story of attempting to locate a book, *The three princes of Serendip*. Eventually tracking the book down to a version by Voltaire entitled *Zadig*, uncle Maurice proceeds to leave the book behind him in a pub, returns to collect it and finds it in the hands of an unnamed man who then offers to tell him the story. The next two chapters of *Shamrock tea* consist of Maeterlinck's retelling of his uncle Maurice's retelling of the man in the pub's retelling of the story of *Zadig*, which is Voltaire's retelling of Walpole's retelling of 'a French translation of an Italian translation made by an Armenian of an alleged Persian original' (*St*, 137)!

As well as specializing in this Russian-doll style of story-telling, Carson further confuses the reader by introducing various devices to radically undermine the ontological status of the narrative. Half-way through, the reader (and narrator) is invited to consider that the events recorded in *Shamrock tea* are already written. Among the books which the narrator and Maeterlinck discover in the Loyola House library is a strange, untitled trilogy, excerpts from which are quoted extensively, and whose relevance is explained by Uncle Celestine: 'You will, of course, have observed that certain passages appear to bear a direct relevance to yourselves; but the books are not mere biographies. Some passages include scenarios that failed to materialize; some describe events as they happened, but not as you remember them; and some are fictions. But all in all, the books contain more truth than other people's memories of themselves, which are constantly

revised to suit their current image of themselves' (*St*, 211). And at the end, the
Carson narrator, who finally reclaims the narrative baton from Uncle Celestine
and others, advises that the events recounted in the book took place in a parallel
reality, a near copy of the world he now inhabits:

> So it was that I found myself in the world I now inhabit. Confused as
> I was for some months, I only gradually learned that it was not the
> same world as that I had left, it was almost identical in most respects.
> (*St*, 296–7).

The world the narrator now inhabits in 1963 is the lunatic colony of Gheel, where
his closest friends 'call themselves by the names they have learned in books' (*St*,
301). He talks with 'Napoleon' and 'Dioscorides', and is visited daily by a person
claiming to be Wittgenstein. The narrator, who is now Maeterlinck, is himself
identified as someone who is probably insane. Having, as he claims, acquired a
position as Director of the Hospice Library in Gheel, he confides that it is out of
the resources of the library that he is preparing to write *Shamrock tea*: 'It struck
me that I might use the resources of this library to construct a believable historical
reality – a world which would differ only marginally from this one' (*St*, 303). He
begins reciting the first few sentences of his new project, which return us to the
beginning of *Shamrock tea* and the opening sentences of the book. The cyclical
structure, reinforced by the recurrence of self-reflecting mirror imagery
('Remember, you are the slave of the man in the mirror, and will be until death
sets you free' *St*, 174), suggests the doomed struggle to escape the given structures
of existence. The unwritten story is always already written, always a copy. The
people in that story are only ever phantoms. The narrator dreams other beings
into existence – Maeterlinck, Fr Brown, uncle Celestine – only to declare that
they are dreams: 'There were several Carsons in Belfast, but no Celestine, or
Berenice, or me. There was no Loyola House; or rather, there once had been a
version of it' (*St*, 298) – which he proceeds to document with reference to George
Basset's (sic – 'Bassett') Directory of County Down of 1886 and C.E.B. Brett's
Survey of the towns and villages of mid Down.

The story we read is both fact and fiction, newly generated and already
written, about to happen and already happened. It is a text with no centre.
Carson's intention would seem to be to coax belief in the patently false using as
much factual evidence, detailed description, historical scholarship and argument
as he can muster to do so, and then telling us it was all a charade. Yet the work

refuses to collapse into mere relativism or absurdism. The symbolic Shamrock Tea (both mythical substance and mythologising book) attests to art's magical powers to envision new possibilities outside or beyond the existing bounds of perception and understanding. For Carson, getting lost within the spirals and loops of his labyrinth is a positive aesthetic event, the application to literary creation of his philosophical outlook. Getting lost is the experience of normal understanding and rational expression breaking down, the moment of heightened awareness when the preconceived ideas and philosophical systems to which a writer may become committed no longer provide reassuring coordinates for understanding and expressing his sense of self or reality. The alternative to getting lost is acceptance of one or another specific dogma. But this principle is an idea and in order to be consistent Carson has to reject it as dogmatic truth, hence the self-cancelling gesture of the book's ending. He is interested, not in fixed and lucid truth but in the ambiguous, indefinite, serendipitous discoveries along the way available to the traveller who deliberately loses himself. This is the truth of the aesthetic moment in which a finally inexpressible reality may yet be intuited. Contradicting the demoralizing idea of reality as a chamber of self-reflecting mirror images is the 'fascinating mirror' (*St*, 259) in the Arnolfini Portrait, which is 'a two-way portal' (*St*, 272). Fr Brown notes: 'The two figures in its looking-glass are about to enter the pictured room from another time and space. They are anyone and anybody. They could be me and you' (*St*, 272). In Carson's fictional world, other worlds are always immanent; the situations he creates are always thresholds to otherness; the resources of his library are inexhaustible; the mundane is magical.

3

Carson's recent work continues to be structured on the image of the labyrinth:

> Halfway through the story of my life
> I came to in a gloomy wood, because
> I'd wandered off the path, away from the light.   (*Ti*, 1)

This, the opening stanza of his translation of Dante's *Inferno* (2002), locates the poet in that space where he wants to lose himself, both literally and figuratively, by following Dante into the 'unsayable' or 'untranslatable', into a textual space which is completely foreign ('It's hard to put words to what that wood was'), but which yet has positive value ('all the good I owe / to it'). In his 'Introduction' to his translation, Carson refers to the contemporary political situation in thirteenth-

and fourteenth-century Florence, to the bloody sectarian divisions, to Dante's exile from his native place which forced him to become a permanent nomad, going 'through nearly all the regions to which the Italian tongue extends, a wanderer, almost begging ... truly a ship without sail or rudder, driven to many ports and straits and shores' (*Ti*, xiii–xiv).

Carson re-writes Dante for contemporary Belfast. He imagines being airborne in the ubiquitous British army helicopter, like Dante riding on the flying monster Geryon, looking down into the darkness of Hell: '"Rings of ditches, moats, trenches, fosses / military barriers on every side": I see a map of North Belfast, its no-go zones and tattered flags, the blackened side-streets, cul-de-sacs and bits of wasteland stitched together by dividing walls and fences ... And we see again the vendetta-stricken courtyards and surveillance towers of Dante's birthplace' (*Ti*, xi–xii). By the end of the poem, Dante's wanderings lead him out of the 'gloomy wood': 'and we emerged to see the stars once more' (*Ti*, 243). Dante's religious faith guarantees his progress from the dark labyrinth of history into the light of Christian salvation. Carson's starlight is of a rather different kind: it doesn't depend on faith in any external agency, but in the transformative power of the imagination. His infernal city is itself also paradoxically a 'star factory' because it is 'a place of the imagination, where history and decaying architecture are turned into stories'.[7]

His novel-poem, *For all we know* (2008) tells the story, or rather stories, of a man (an Irish Catholic writer called Gabriel) and a woman (a half-French, half-English musician called Nina) who meet in a second-hand clothes shop in Belfast sometime in the 1970s. A bomb goes off. The two become lovers. Their love affair unfolds in an atmosphere of constant surveillance, fear and paranoia. Moving between past and present, and back and forth across often indeterminate European terrain, the lovers speak of their 'double lives' and their 'translations' of each other. With the structuring of the work into two parts, Part Two acting as a kind of re-versioning of Part One (the 35 poem titles in Part Two exactly repeating those in Part One), we are immediately aware of the absence of an authentic original, the need always to think otherwise about the text we are reading. Carson says he thought of the relationship between the two lovers, how they come to know each other, misunderstand each other and (mis)translate each other and the events around them, as a 'journey into a mysterious forest of language and translation', which references *film noir*, Cold War thriller, the art of the fugue, and fairy story:

7 Dust-jacket of *The star factory* (London, 1997).

We travelled towards the dark forest and reached it by nightfall.
Snow was in the air, but not here, where no stars could be seen.

('The story of the chevalier', *Fawk*, 44)

Among the various mythical, archetypal and fairytale connotations of the 'dark forest' is the Garden of Eden, where the innocence of 'belief' is forfeit, and the only reality is that guaranteed by sense experience:

And so we lost ourselves in the dark forest of language
believing in nothing which might not be governed by touch

or taste, the apple bursting indescribably with juice.

('On the contrary', *Fawk*, 18)

'Proposal' replays the story of the Garden of Eden in a technological age: 'You were one of the first to go for an Apple, when they / first came out, you said, it must have been the year whenever, // 1984' (*Fawk*, 29). '1984' marks the Fall of humankind: it is the year in which Orwell set his dystopian vision of totalitarian organization and pervasive surveillance, and it is (wrongly) cited in the poem as the year which saw the first appearance of the Apple computer (that was 1976). The poem suggests the relationships among mechanized state power, the new digital technology, art and speech in the construction of contemporary reality:

… Stuck, you'd click on the Option button
whereupon up popped a menu of possible answers

through which you dropped down until it took your mind to the end
you so desired, the Tree of Knowledge looming within reach.

All too soon you were plucking data from the air, making
documents, files and spreadsheets, putting your life in order.
We'd climb into bed to the noise of a helicopter
To bury ourselves under the clothes to muffle the beat
With the beat of our synchronized hearts.

New technologies of state power, surveillance and discipline, symbolized by the panoptic gaze of the helicopter, produce new technologies of writing. Within the strict outline of the sonnet form, the poem elaborates a new digital poetics in which optionality, fractality, serendipity and virtuality react against the forces of state authority and the totalizing narratives of conventionalized or official discourse to create new possibilities of meaning generated out of and beyond the sacred texts of religious myth and regional history. Yet the suggestion of freed speech is darkly stimulated by recognition of the potential death of the author: 'you'd speak temptingly of the serendipity / of the Apple, how it seemed to put words into your mouth / to say what you wanted to say but could not until then'. 'Temptingly' and 'seemed' (like 'All too soon') raise a doubt: the Apple is the occasion of Original Sin if you allow a machine to 'put words into your mouth'. The sestet, reorienting our attention away from the new technologies of communication and control, and overlaying the 'beat' of the helicopter with 'the beat of our synchronized hearts', suggests that despite the creation of virtual worlds reality still matters; that physical closeness, personal contact, and affection have not disappeared from a mechanized world.

The copy-version of 'Proposal' in Part Two works the other way around. It starts by emphasizing presence, body, sense experience in the description of the man and woman eating a Discovery apple, and ends by intimating the 'terra incognita' that opens up once 'we threw away the core':

> You offered me a Discovery. This time I could taste
> Your mouth from it through the juice. We took bite for bite from it
>
> Until we finished it as one. We threw away the core.
> Then we asked things of each other we'd never asked before.
>
> (*Fawk*, 78)

In this particular pair of poems, the counter-narratives of new media politics inform and interact with a traditional metaphysics of presence, just as formally the novel-poem as a whole creates multiple, transactive spaces within and between its two parts.

To structure his account of the journey through the dark forest, Carson again draws on the compositional principles of the fugue, the most complex of contrapuntal forms, in which a main theme or subject is laid down, then sounded imitatively by a succession of other 'voices' in different keys. In this sense, fugue is a style of composition rather than a fixed structure, a style in which restrictions create freedom for the composer by directing his efforts. Similarly, Carson, recognizing that his 'novel of sorts' gestured towards a sonnet sequence (since all the poems consisted of 14, 28 or 56 lines) and the line itself is 14 syllables, felt that 'this constraint was a great help'. Like the structure of a fugue, the poem emphasizes process, its unity coming from the repetition of themes, images and motifs. The dual meaning of fugue in Latin, depending on conjugation – *fugare*, to chase, put to flight, and *fugere*, to flee – must also have attracted him. In the sequence, one 'voice' chases another in a series of rapid thematic fragments, while implicit in the two lovers' attitudes is a desire for freedom and escape from fixed identities. Part Two reprises key ideas, images or phrases from Part One, or indeed from other poems, not only those by Carson but by other poets, in a round of polyphonic and/or polysemic fugal process.

The idea of the labyrinth relates less closely to any specific physical place, namely, the city of Belfast, than in previous work. Traversing a range of locales (Belfast, Paris, Berlin, Leipzig, Dresden), cultures and languages, the poet suggests a deterritorialized cultural space liberated from the bo(u)nds of nation or place. Within this phantom, carnivalized space, traditional categories of identity dissolve and the speaker is redefined by his/her contact with the other. The dialogue between the man and woman forms an important element of the contrapuntal effect of the sequence. In the poem's heterological discourse the referents of 'I' and 'you' are constantly shifting in the moves from direct to free indirect speech. Similarly, the pronominals 'he' and 'she' mutate, at one time referring, not to the two lovers as they usually do, but the woman's 'uncle' and 'aunt' ('The anniversary'). The speakers occupy a space where language shifts fluidly, where they must 'translate' each other: 'You're not from around here, I said. No, from elsewhere, you said. / As from another language, I might have said but did not'. At times they feel compelled to identify the agreed '*lingua franca*'. Linguistic communication is often tenuous (symbolized by failed telephone connections), at times breaks down and is replaced by gesture (a kiss), smell (perfumes), appearances (clothes) as means of disclosure, the signifier becoming more strongly identified with externals. Constantly they dream or talk themselves into other selves: 'If I'm you, who are you?', the man asks the woman at one point. In the dark labyrinths of Carson's poem sequence, identity slips and slides, the disturbance throwing the whole symbolic order into question. A recurrent figure of the poem's uncanny returns is that of the doppelganger, the fetch or shadow self, which betokens a sinister form of bilocation, the elusiveness of selfhood.

Identity has uncertain boundaries, it is mobile, a constant process of translating, adapting or re-cycling the past. In 'Pas de deux', the woman is caught up in an elaborate exchange economy symbolized by the list of names of second-hand clothes shops which have helped her construct a self-image: 'Second time round', 'Double exposure', 'Déjà vu', 'New to you', Second début', 'Turnstyle', 'Another time', 'Generations', 'Good byes'. Signifiers are constantly on the move: 'second hand' slides from the clock face to a kind of clothes shop, to the name of a second-hand clothes shop; 'Je reviens' is the name of a perfume and the final unfulfilled promise made by the woman to the man before she goes off to her death in a car accident on the road to 'Nevers'.

The fugue structure disowns any idea of closure. As Carson explains, echoing the words of Glenn Gould, the renowned composer and interpreter of Bach's fugues: 'In musical terms / the fugue must perform its often stealthy work with shifting // melodic fragments that remain perpetually in / abeyance, or unconsummated' ('In the Dark', *Fawk,* 108). The last poem, 'Zugzwang', the title referring to a blocking move in chess which renders any move by an opponent disadvantageous, reaffirms the value of re-making and re-starting, the endless process which dissolves past and present in the eternal present of continuous creation:

> as the quilters make a pattern of their remnants and rags,
> and the jersey, unravelled, becomes a new skein of wool
> …
> so I return to the question of those staggered repeats
> as my memories of you recede into the future.

The imagery recalls his poem 'Patchwork', which offers an emblem of stitching and mending, the poem itself a patchwork made out of fragments of memory and speech, that is, something new made out of old bits and pieces.

4

There were, of course, various guide-books on the art of getting lost which Carson had to hand. He follows Flann O'Brien's postmodernist lead in *The third policeman* (written 1939, published 1967) in playing with reality and ideas of recursivity, and constructing strange, virtual worlds which tend towards pure fantasy. Like O'Brien, Carson casts his narrative in the form of a quest, the object of which – the magical shamrock tea – is strongly redolent of O'Brien's 'omnium', literally everything that one desires. O'Brien's demented narrative, spiralling into hilarious terror and grotesquerie, is more wildly comic than Carson's gentler whimsy, but both stories share a weirdly matter-of-fact tone which seems removed from conventional moral and psychological concerns. The two works are populated by a similar kind of character, which we might designate the subtly mad, obsessed with theories and secret knowledge. The lengthy footnotes and references in *The third policeman*, and the bibliographical 'sources' so minutely detailed in *Shamrock tea,* are narrative devices which not only mock academic obsessions, but destabilize our usual ontological assumptions. O'Brien has said that the weird, alternative world he has created was meant to be an image of hell: no such dark intent lies behind *Shamrock tea*. Rather, Carson aims to bring us through the worm holes which give access, not to some other world, but to a more lucid, more colourful version of our own.

The writer who would seem to have had the most significant influence on Carson is the Argentine magic realist Luis Borges. The typical furniture of Borges's world reappears in Carson's: labyrinths, libraries, mirrors, doubles, games. Both writers are fascinated by the human capacity for fiction-making, reminding us that we live in fictions, and that the dividing line between dream and reality may not be at all easy to draw. Both specialize in strange, haunting narratives which occupy a twilight zone between fact and fiction, dream and reality. What begins as apparently conscientiously researched erudition may take us into such remote and obscure corners of knowledge that it is impossible for us to tell where arcane erudition ends and fantastical invention begins. Consequently, we enter a liminal space of uncertain knowledge, from whose strange depths we are periodically returned to a recognizable daylight world. Borges's story, 'Tlön, Uqbar, Orbis Tertius', opens with 'I owe the discovery of Uqbar to the conjunction of a mirror and an encyclopaedia',[8] alluding to two sources of knowledge which are central to Carson's aesthetic: the reflective model symbolized by the mirror, and the taxonomic model represented by the encyclopaedia. The narrator comes across a reference in an encyclopaedia to an unknown country called Uqbar, with a note that the literature of Uqbar 'was one of fantasy and that its epics and legends never referred to reality, but to the two imaginary regions of Mlejnas and Tlön'.[9] Later, the narrator discovers *A first encyclopaedia of Tlön*, with the inscription '*Orbis Tertius*' on its first page. The narrator finds himself holding 'a vast methodical fragment of an unknown planet's entire history'.[10] This fantastic land represents an idealistic alternative world freed from the accepted

---

8 Jorge Luis Borges, *Labyrinths* (London, 1970), 27. **9** Ibid., 29. **10** Ibid., 31.

constructions of reality. The narrator concludes that Tlön is 'the invention of a secret and benevolent society',[11] and considers its attraction as a basis for a 'brave new world':

> Almost immediately reality yielded on more than one account. The truth is that it longed to yield. Ten years ago any symmetry with a semblance of order – dialectical materialism, anti-Semitism, Nazism – was sufficient to entrance the minds of men. How could one do other than submit to Tlön, to the minute and vast evidence of an orderly planet?[12]

In these lines Borges signals warning as well as hope for the future. Tlön stands for the power of human invention, the work of a 'benevolent' society. But in the references to conditions in 1940, the year in which the story was written, he also suggests how any system, however potentially liberating it may first appear, can all too easily fossilize into dangerous orthodoxy and be taken as absolute truth – including Nazism. Carson constructs his narrative worlds with the same kind of ironically scrupulous precision in the handling of bibliographical, circumstantial and other supporting materials: what is different is that Carson's fascination with human inventiveness as the hope of the future never darkens in quite the same way into anxiety about either the illusion of final meaning (as in 'Tlön, Uqbar, Orbis Tertius') or the absence of final meaning (as in 'The library of Babel').

Both Borges and Carson are obsessed by man's rage for order, the need for abstraction, classification, the coherence of (narrative) patterns. Corresponding to the architecture of labyrinths and libraries (a library being a kind of labyrinth, suggestive of the idea that we are surrounded by a limitless network of significance), are the curious lexical structures – theories, encyclopaedias, directories, religious beliefs, ideologies, stories – which have been constructed down through the ages in the effort to organize perception, experience and understanding. The labyrinth with its multiplication of possible paths and choices is, for both Borges and Carson, an image of the possible proliferation of varying realities in time as well as space. There are many different worlds, and any system of classification, no matter how well established, is still no more than a 'fiction'. Again, Borges is profoundly conscious of the nightmarish extremes to which man's need for structures may lead him. At first the Library of Babel inspired 'extravagant happiness' as 'all men felt themselves to be the master of an intact and

---

11 Ibid., 39.   **12** Ibid., 42.

secret treasure', hoping that 'a clarification of humanity's basic mysteries'[13] might be found. However, 'inordinate hope' changes to 'excessive depression',[14] and what we are left with at the end is an image of the madness and desperation of the sad, Kafkaesque figures who occupy this dreadful labyrinth of words. While the human species may be on the verge of extinction, the narrator opines, 'the Library will endure: illuminated, solitary, infinite, perfectly motionless, equipped with precious volumes, useless, incorruptible, secret'.[15]

With his image of the universe as a vast library containing all the books which have ever been written and will ever be written, Borges gave us one of the most famous images of twentieth-century literature. This imaginary, endless library is a symbol of the kind of excess of information with which we are all too familiar on the Internet, with its welter of information which can be neither easily organized nor verified. Carson's own postmodern textual practice has anticipated, paralleled, and clearly been influenced by developments in the new electronic media which, in seeking to free the text from the constraints of materiality, have revolutionized the agenda for critical and cultural analysis. Re-deploying key principles of the new digital aesthetics, the Carson text – open, nonlinear, non-hierarchical, 'dimension-bending', multivoiced – resists domination by any single, unitary or totalizing narrative or perspective. It represents a challenge to the conventional discourses that govern our understanding and representation of history and identity. The Carson text occupies the in-between spaces of becoming, the interstitial or 'contact' zones between the established discourses, opening up new doors of perception, new imaginative hyperlinks, leading us via an endless proliferation of new relationships into the chimerical 'terra incognita' of the unbounded and the uncoded. As an analogue to the electronic text, the Carson text foregoes 'real presence' for its own kind of 'liberation technology'[16] which operates through techniques of escape from, or subversion of, the tyranny of the existing constructions of reality. Fixity gives way to the unstable, fluid representation which characterizes the electronic text. The text is never self-sufficient or whole, but always virtual, always provisional and porous. Carson aspires to a kind of textual freedom analogous to that represented by the literally unbound electronic text, which can be linked to and become part of any other text networked with it. As a virtual programme, the Carson text asserts the possibility of its own multiple realization: instead of the text as completed whole,

---

13 Ibid., 82.   **14** Ibid., 83.   **15** Ibid., 85.   **16** J. David Bolter, *Writing space: the computer, hypertext and the history of writing* (Hillsdale, 1991), 21.

we have the text as polymorph or hypertext (hyper-'beyond', 'over'), the kind of text which supposedly derives from and leads to other texts. As a dynamic discursive organization with multiple links and pathways to other texts, the Carson text reminds us that meaning is never singular and fixed, but always multiple and variable. He delights in processing into his text all kinds of variants and variations, related explanatory or illustrative or contextual matter. In this way, he seeks out fault-lines in familiar terrain, crosses borders, breaks up consecrated ground, suggests roads not taken, questions the official maps, interrogates received identities and concepts of home, identity, history. Refusing the reassuring offer of coherence and closure, he reproduces the virtual text's exhilarating promise of possibility and immunity from restraint, its fantasy of freedom, its representation of fluid alternative realities.

5

For Carson, lostness refutes the authority of discourse, defies the systematization of the world, and leads to a deterritorialization of dwelling, knowledge and identity. His mobile form of story-telling no longer departs only to return. Home and away can no longer be taken as simple binary opposites. Shuttling back and forth between different worlds, negotiating between disparate discursive realms and borderlands, he undoes the stable points of both departure and destination, showing how it is possible to be both at home and away at the same time. The narrator's traditional sense of mastery of his world and his materials is unsettled. He becomes unmoored, as do his conceptual coordinates. Carson's postmodern fascination with the subversive power of lostness contrasts with another model – or, rather, models – of poetic lostness that are found in the poetry of Seamus Heaney: the Romantic which, like the postmodern, is a paradoxical narrative of losing oneself to find oneself, and the Modernist, which presents an '*unheimlich*' counter-narrative.[17]

In early poems such as 'The peninsula' and 'The plantation', Heaney sets out the typical Romantic itinerary which is intended to lead to self-discovery. It tells of the traveller's deliberate effort to get lost and, through the process of 'making strange', discovering a new visionary power:

---

17 For the general theorised distinctions between Romantic, Modernist and Postmodernist models of lostness, I am indebted to John Zilcosky, 'The writer as nomad', in *Interventions*, 6:2 (2004), 229–41.

And drive back home, still with nothing to say
Except that now you will uncode all landscapes
By this: things founded clean on their own shapes,
Water and ground in their extremity.
('The peninsula')[18]

You had to learn to come back
To learn how to lose yourself,
To be pilot and stray – witch,
Hansel and Gretel in one.
('The plantation')[19]

Heaney travels only to return: 'I grew out of all this / like a weeping willow / inclined to / the appetites of gravity' ('Kinship'). In an early autobiographical essay entitled 'Mossbawn' – the name of the farm on which he grew up – he lays claim to natural identity with the land:

> I would begin with the Greek word, *omphalos*, meaning the centre of the world, and repeat it, *omphalos, omphalos, omphalos*, until its blunt and falling music becomes the music of somebody pumping water at the pump outside our back door.[20]

Heaney emphasises rootedness in place and community, in a sacred, feminine landscape. Displaced from origins, from family and community, from a traditional folkloric ethos and magical world-view, he seeks to reconstitute himself in a literary culture through which he attempts to recuperate and re-enter the 'first place' of childhood. But the project of reclaiming his inheritance and 'restoring the culture to itself' is complicated by his awareness that the centre or point of origin which he seeks may in fact be a void: 'The bogholes might be Atlantic seepage. / The wet centre is bottomless' ('Bogland'). The bogholes are an image of a round opening in the ground, but the space which opens up, though associated with the '*omphalos*', is bottomless (quite unlike Carson's 'wormholes' which give access to endless exciting new possibilities of connection and relationship). Heaney's excavations in his celebrated bog poems lead not to restitution and recovery but to the innermost recesses of the Irish necropolis

---

18 Seamus Heaney, *Opened ground: poems, 1966–1996* (London, 1999), 21   19 Ibid., 39.   20 Seamus Heaney, 'Mossbawn', in *Preoccupations: selected prose 1968–1978* (London, 1978), p. 17.

where he draws our attention to the unconscious pagan and violent barbarian drives within the diseased psychopathology of Catholic Ulster. In these poems, which take the form of a prolonged imaginative engagement with the powers of darkness, Heaney pursues the hidden, telluric aspects of language, psyche and race sensibility, probes his own deepest fears and the most tabooed knowledges – the wild unruly energies – within the community. His occult journeyings in these dark labyrinths leave him lost and disconsolate, unable to complete the Romantic journey towards self-knowledge:

> Out there in Jutland
> In the old man-killing parishes
> I will feel lost,
> Unhappy and at home.[21]

Never really losing his way, he returns, uncannily, over and over again, to the same ground, the same conflicted feelings of civilized outrage and atavistic identification, unable to reclaim a *Heim* that is not *unheimlich*: 'I am Hamlet the Dane / skull-handler, parablist, / smeller of rot // in the state, infused / with its poisons, / pinioned by ghosts / and affections / jumping in graves / dithering and blathering'.[22] The Romantic lost-and-found story mutates into a Modernist narrative of what Zilcosky calls '*unheimlich* returns'. Unable to disorient himself sufficiently to bring about a redemptive re-visioning of self and world, Heaney's uncanny experience confirms the modern subject's difficulty in getting truly lost. His persistent sense of social obligation, of 'being mired in attachment' ('The First Flight'), prevents him from letting go and trusting to the unpredictable, self-justifying power of the imagination.

'The underground', recycling the images of 'The plantation', figures the poet as a lost Hansel in an Irish forest. The poem invokes Hansel's return home through the wood with the help of the moonlit trail of white pebbles which he had laid. The fairy-story is re-enacted in Heaney's subterranean passage through an imperialist history, symbolized by the London Underground. For Heaney, the track back out of the underground labyrinth is charted by his poetry, an idea reinforced by the return of the lyric Orpheus from the Underworld. But, as the edgy expectancy of the final stanza suggests, Heaney has not yet completely emerged from the dark forest:

21 *Opened ground*, 66.   **22** Ibid., 104.

> To end up in a draughty lamplit station
> After the trains have gone, the wet track
> Bared and tensed as I am, all attention
> For your step following and damned if I look back.[23]

Once again, rather than embrace a potentially regenerative Romantic lostness, he opts for a poetics of Modernist *angst*.

In the title poem of his most recent collection, *District and circle*, the poet is again situated in the flashing, noisy world of the London Underground. Struggling for space and balance, he yet seems to be borne back ceaselessly into the past. The language of the 'first world' permeates the present. 'District' is a word Heaney more commonly uses to refer to the familiar ground of the home parish. 'Circle' obviously relates to the '*omphalos*', the natal origin ('the black O / in *Broagh*). Holding on to a train strap described as 'a stubby black roof-wort' (*Dc* 18), the poet is quite literally clinging to the past. As he is transported through 'galleried earth', he imagines the ghost of his father ('the only relict of all that I belonged to') recalling him to the pastoral Irish Eden from which he has been expelled. This is not an image of a poet who operates confidently in the labyrinths of a rapidly accelerating modernity, but one longing to reclaim an elusive wholeness that he imagines existed in the past.

The more intense the feeling of displacement from origins, the more urgent the effort to re-establish connections with the source, and the more tenacious his faith in poetry's redemptive capability. Heaney's quest for an '*omphalos*', increasingly shadowed by awareness that the centre is fictive, leads him to 'a space utterly empty, / utterly a source'.[24] The earthly home, however desecrated or disfigured by violence, loss and death, can yet be transformed through imagination and writing into what he calls in the brilliantly simple yet evocative phrase 'a placeless heaven'. Going back to childhood, he recalls a place outside his bedroom window where a much-loved chestnut tree was cut down:

> ... [I]t was not so much a matter of attaching oneself to a living symbol of being rooted in the native ground; it was more a matter of preparing to be unrooted, to be spirited away into some transparent, yet indigenous afterlife. The new place was all idea, if you like; it was generated out of my experience of the old place but it was not a topographical location. It

23 Ibid., 213. **24** These lines occur in 'Station island III', *Og*, 248, and again in 'Clearances VIII', *OG*, 314.

was and remains an imagined realm, even if it can be located at an earthly
spot, a placeless heaven rather than a heavenly place. [25]

Heaney loses himself – 'unrooting' himself from the world of time and place –
only to discover 'a bright nowhere' in which emptiness is transformed into
plenitude, time into timelessness, absence into presence through the power of
memory and imagination. The mythical centre, the *omphalos,* is re-discovered in
the super reality of the text. Heaney's earlier re-territorializing aesthetic, which
assumed a sectarian landscape of conflict and division, and which was concerned
with 'bedding the locale' and 'restoring the culture to itself', is replaced by a *de-*
territorializing aesthetic, implying a more inclusive consciousness than anything
envisaged by cultural nationalism.

Continually, however, his experience of Romantic lostness is undercut by
doubt, replaced by Modernist self-consciousness. The possibility of redemption
and personal epiphany is glimpsed in 'Casualty', where forgetfulness of self is a
prerequisite of the desired re-location:

> As you find a rhythm
> Working you, slow mile by mile,
> Into your proper haunt
> Somewhere, well out, beyond … [26]

The poem juxtaposes images of return and circularity associated with community
('The common funeral / Unrolled its swaddling band, / Lapping, tightening / Till
we were braced and bound / Like brothers in a ring') against the sense of freedom
and transcendence contained in the images of linear departure and movement
away, 'Somewhere, well out, beyond …'. Significantly, 'Casualty' ends, not with
this affirmation of productive lostness, but with the return of the repressed, the
voice of conscience recalling the speaker to the concerns of home, a reassertion of
the poem's motif of treadmill circularity:

> Dawn-sniffing revenant,
> Plodder through midnight rain,
> Question me again.

25 Seamus Heaney, 'The placeless heaven: another look at Kavanagh', in *The government of the tongue*
(London, 1988), p 3.   26 *Opened ground,* 157.

Heaney, that is, epitomizes the experience of the modern subject who feels inhibited about giving himself over to the experience of lostness, of going 'somewhere, well out, beyond' the known limits. But in his more Romantic turns, and in Carson's postmodernism, the de-territorialized and disorientated condition of being lost becomes the ground of identity, the necessary condition of writing. In these modes, Heaney loses himself to find himself as a transcendent subject, while Carson loses himself to find himself as a perpetually nomadic author.

Acoustic Perfume

ALAN GILLIS

The inferno of Dante Alighieri (2002), *Breaking news* (2003), *The midnight court* (2005), *The Táin* (2007) and *For all we know* (2008) already suggest a prolific five years for Ciaran Carson. However he has also, during this time, written two novels: *X + Y = K* and *The pen friend*.[1] Admittedly, we might be on safer grounds if we refer to these as 'prose works', because they certainly stretch the conventions of what a contemporary novel entails. But, then again, perhaps we shouldn't straightjacket a form that was once more amorphously understood. What is a novel if bereft of novelty?

X + Y = K and *The pen friend* are marked by overt stylization and formal exactitude. The former comprises three sections ('X', 'Y' and 'K'), each thirteen chapters long. Section X begins with a Belfast writer visiting London on 9 April 2002, the day of the Queen Mother's funeral, to discuss with his editor a proposed book on the 'Goligher story'. The Goligher circle was a Spiritualist group that held séances in Belfast, and whose principal medium was Kathleen Goligher, 'an attractive young girl of about seventeen'.[2] These séances were analysed between 1915 and 1921 by William Jackson Crawford, a lecturer in Mechanical Engineering from Queen's University. The Goligher story thus pits empirical science against the paranormal. Section 'X' further interweaves this Goligher story with the unnamed first-person narrator's observations on art, London, migraines, and his Belfast background.

Section 'Y' then abruptly shifts to a third-person narration set in Belfast, 1974, concerning someone named Kilpatrick, who may or may not be the same character who narrated Section 'X' (they share the same birthday and migraines). To discuss these migraines, Kilpatrick visits a 'Consultant Phenomenologist' called Fitzwilliam, who entices him to work for a surveillance project named 'Farset' (a word central to Carson's riffs on the etymology of Belfast).[3] Farset, we are told, is a pun on 'Farsight', the code-name of a CIA surveillance project from

1 *X + Y = K* was completed in 2003, *The pen friend* in 2006. At the time of writing, both novels are unpublished. In what follows, all citations refer to manuscript copies. For access to these manuscripts, and for generous permission to cite from them, I owe a debt of gratitude to Ciaran Carson. 2 *X + Y = K*, 17. 3 See 'Farset' in *Belfast confetti* , 47–9.

the Cold War. Farset is using Farsight's surveillance techniques in Belfast, techniques aimed at accessing 'the matrix': a realm of traces in which 'any and all information about any person, place or thing might be obtained'.[4] Kilpatrick's migraines, it seems, give him special access to this matrix, while these unusual surveillance techniques, the narration points out, make the Farset 'an extended séance'.[5] Section Y ends with Kilpatrick unable to stop his parents' murder in a café bomb in Belfast.

If Section 'X' is broadly fact and Section 'Y' fiction, Section 'K' is concocted of both (like much of Carson's work, both this novel and *The pen friend* explore what the difference is). Section 'K' alternates between the first-person and third-person, as the protagonists of 'X' and 'Y' morph into someone referred to as K, while we are brought back to London on 9 April 2002. Section 'K' expands upon the earlier infatuations with art, Spiritualism and surveillance (K is meeting his editor about a proposed book 'having three sections of thirteen chapters each' on the Goligher story). However, K's motives for being in London on the day of the Queen Mother's funeral become more strange and troubled as things draw to a close.

Meanwhile, *The pen friend* begins when a first-person narrator receives an unexpected and cryptic postcard from an old flame, which sparks a series of reveries about their relationship. Each subsequent chapter is addressed to the ex-lover, provoked by the continued receipt of her postcards. In obvious respects, then, *The pen friend* is more streamlined and straightforward than $X + Y = K$. Yet the narrator's reveries on the relationship are spun into ambitious meditations upon memory, art, comprehension and misunderstanding. Moreover, it becomes clear that each of its thirteen chapters begins with a postcard and ends with a perfume; in between, each chapter plays out developing variations on similar themes in a similar order, so that its structure according to a pre-ordained template is unusually prominent.

The plot of $X + Y = K$ and *The pen friend*, like that of their predecessor *Shamrock tea*, is pitched through an evolving compendium of facts, concepts and possibilities. One of the most novel aspects of these works is their eschewal of conventional verisimilitude in terms of character and dialogue. For example, the precocity of the children in *Shamrock tea*, and the erudition of their exchanges with their Uncle Celestine, forms a key element of that work's head-spinning fantasia. Playful erudition is itself a central facet of these three books. However,

---

4 $X + Y = K$, 175. **5** Ibid., 192.

they are certainly more plot-driven than the glorious hotchpotch of *Fishing for amber*, or the magic lantern memoir of *The star factory*, or the free-wheeling variations of *Last night's fun*, although they remain golden treasuries of ideas, as well as of stories.[6]

In *Shamrock tea* the ideas are as recherché as the tales are tall, and $X + Y = K$ partakes of this ambience. And while *The pen friend* lacks this fabular element, it is still intricately continuous with its predecessor. Almost immediately, on receiving his first postcard, the narrator launches into a description of fountain pens with an incongruously manic intensity of detail. Fountain pens – as *objets d'art*, as commodities, as technical marvels, as the vessels of writing – then become a primary theme of the novel. This epistolary love story thus immediately announces its oddity to the reader: this is pedantic love. The narrator's reveries – he works in an art gallery – are perpetually sieved through a focus on art and aesthetics (with a particular interest in pens and perfume), and on his Belfast background.

With more than a nod and a wink to $X + Y = K$, the narrator is also deeply interested in Spiritualism, and his reflections on this blend with his thoughts on aesthetics. More to the point, he is deeply interested in the Goligher story. The two lovers' favourite Belfast haunt, the place they first meet, is the 'XL Café' in Fountain Street. (In $X + Y = K$, Kilpatrick's parents are bombed and killed in the 'XL Café' in Fountain Street.) Meanwhile, the Golighers' séances, we are told, were held in 40 Fountain Street. On top of this, the narrator's lover works for 'MO2': a resurrected version of the English 'Mass Observation' project from the 1930s, transplanted to Northern Ireland, where it operates covertly and is 'supposed to report both to Home Affairs and the Northern Ireland Office'.[7] As such, *The pen friend* also becomes a meditation on the Northern Irish situation and intelligence, in every sense of that word.

It should be stressed that both novels are independent works, and each contain a multitude of themes and riches. Yet their combined concern with aesthetics, Spiritualism and surveillance does seem central, and this gives us a deeper understanding of Carson's poetics as a whole. Indeed, in many ways, all of Carson's works form a piece. We might imagine they are forged in what *The star factory* calls 'The Zone'. Those who enter 'The Zone', we are told, enter the story of themselves, a story endlessly proliferating and multitudinous: 'Of necessity, the

---

6 With their brilliant fusion of fact and fiction, *Fishing for amber*, *The star factory* and *Last night's fun: about music, food and time* have sometimes been hailed under the generic term 'faction' – apparently with a straight face.   7 *The pen friend*, 44.

story they had entered comprised many stories, yet their diverse personal time-scales evinced glimpses of an underlying structure, like a traffic flow-chart with its arteries and veins and capillaries' (*Tsf*, 62). 'The Zone' is 'an interactive blueprint; not virtual, but narrative reality' (*Tsf*, 63).

In *Fishing for amber*, however, Carson translated a passage from Séan Ó Ríordáin that seemed to disown narrative in favour of lyric poetry:

> Imagine two people in a room, a child and its father, and a horse going past in the street outside. The father looks out and says: 'There's Mary's horse going by'. That is a narration. From all appearances the father loses the horse because he remains outside it. Say a horse is a disease. The father doesn't catch that disease. The horse does not enrich the father's life. But as for the child – he perceives the sound of the horse. He savours the sound of the horse for the sake of the sound itself. And he listens to the noise grow dim – diminishing – finally becoming mute. And silence and noise are wonderful to him. And he gets the horse by its hind legs and ponders their antique authority. And the world blooms with horsiness and the magic of reins. It's like – like having another countenance. And that, I think, is poetry. The child dwells in his apparition of the horse. (*Fa*, 201–2)

While this is persuasive, the difference is ultimately artificial. All poetry involves narrative: the disease must pass by in order to infect; while the difference between prose and literary prose is surely the latter's ability to make us dwell in its apparitions.

In many ways, all of Carson's writing seeks to conflate these two poles of the aesthetic continuum. His narratives are predicated on a kind of intuited symbolic network more often associated with lyric poetry. And this is very much to the fore in *X* + *Y* = *K* and *The pen friend*. Towards the beginning of the former, we read:

> I ... began to delve into the history of Spiritualism, which I thought might be a parable for Ireland. The visible world, says AE, is like a tapestry blown and stirred by winds behind it; if it would but raise for an instant we would see Paradise. What is luxury and what necessity, says Yeats, when a fragment of gold braid or a flower in the wallpaper may be an originating impulse to revolution or to philosophy?[8]

8 *X* + *Y* = *K*, 16.

For W.B. Yeats, of course, Spiritualism and Symbolism seemed almost interchangeable, at least in terms of his doctrines of 1901: '(1) That the borders of our
mind are ever shifting, and that many minds can flow into one another, as it were,
and create or reveal a single mind, a single energy'; '(2) That the borders of our
memories are as shifting, and that our memories are a part of one great memory,
the memory of Nature herself'; and '(3) That this great mind and great memory
can be evoked by symbols'.⁹ A year earlier Yeats had stated: 'All sounds, all colours,
all forms, either because of their preordained energies or because of long
association, evoke indefinable and yet precise emotions, or, as I prefer to think,
call down among us certain disembodied powers ...'¹⁰

Carson's poetry has long been rooted in aspects of *symbolisme*, but of a kind
more unhinged than Yeats's, more influenced by Rimbaud. His translation of 'La
bateau ivre' fuelled the 'Babel-babble' of *First language*, while the opening and
closing sequences of *Opera et cetera* constitute one of the great explorations in
English of Rimbaud's 'Voyelles'.¹¹ Nevertheless, *The Alexandrine plan* fore-
grounded a more orderly form of *symbolisme*, translating Baudelaire and Mallarmé
alongside Rimbaud. And generally, much of Carson's work is suffused with a
symbolist aestheticism. Yeats wrote: 'The poet of essences and pure ideas must
seek in the half-lights that glimmer from symbol to symbol as if to the ends of the
earth, all that the epic and dramatic poet finds of mystery and shadow in the
accidental circumstances of life'.¹² A poet of essences, Carson's writing veers from
one theme or context to another in perpetual motion: forever seeking, amid
mystery and shadow, the half-light of insight.

The Alexandrine plan included Carson's second published version of
Baudelaire's 'Correspondances', frequently taken as an ur-text of *symbolisme*.¹³ A
straight translation of 'Correspondances' reveals an aesthetic that pre-empts
Yeats's:

9 W.B. Yeats, *Essays and introductions* (London, 1961), 28. **10** Ibid., 156. **11** Ciaran Carson, 'Drunk
boat', *First language*, 34–8. This poem refers to its language as 'Babel-babble' (34). Meanwhile, the
opening and closing sequences of Carson's *Opera et cetera* are called 'Letters from the alphabet' and
'Opera', 11–36, 67–92. Their emphasis on individual letters link them to Rimbaud's sonnet 'Voyelles',
the first line of which translates as: 'A black, E white, I red, U green, O blue: vowels'. Arthur
Rimbaud, *Collected poems*, trans. Martin Sorrell (Oxford, 2001), 134–5. **12** W.B. Yeats, *Essays and
introductions*, 87. **13** Carson's first version of this poem (transposing Baudelaire's sonnet into four
long couplets) appeared in *First language*, titled '*Correspondances*' (39). He later translated it into a
sonnet named 'Coexistences' in *The Alexandrine plan* (71).

> As the long echoes, shadowy, profound,
> Heard from afar, blend in a unity,
> Vast as the night, as sunlight's clarity,
> So perfumes, colours, sounds may correspond.[14]

Interestingly, however, both Carson's versions neglect Baudelaire's key idea of unity. One version opts, instead, for constellations and reflections:

> Like blue extended husky echoes from away
> Far off, which cloud together in the inner or
> The outer space of constellations in a mirror,
> Shimmery perfumes, colours, sounds, all shift and sway.
>
> ('Coexistences', *Ap*, 71)

It is probably no surprise that Carson's writing here side-steps the potential stasis of Baudelaire's unity, or Yeats's 'single mind', and yet his work is everywhere voltaged by the idea of correspondences, the sense that all things connect. In its most idealist guise, Carson's 'narrative reality' is held together by the promise of a final totality. *The pen friend* tells us 'any one thing in the universe implies the existence of every other thing'; and that 'Nothing is ever truly lost ... for every thing in the universe is in the place where it finds itself, and is observed by God, who sees everything'.[15]

On one level, this idealism is to be taken seriously. Even the quarry of Carson's most vigorous parodies are to be taken earnestly at some level: that nothing should be discounted is one his primary mantras. Yet such idealistic organicism is often nudged out of sync with a sly nod and a wink. Towards the beginning of *Shamrock tea*, for example, we get a wide-eyed agreement with Sherlock Holmes, in *A study in scarlet*, that 'from a drop of water ... a logician could infer the possibility of an Atlantic or a Niagara, without having seen or heard of one or the other; for all life is a great chain, the nature of which is known when we are shown a single link of it'.[16]

Such a poker-faced slip from plausibility to the incredulous is Carson's way of animating old ideas with a tantalizing *kitschiness*. Often he takes a sound principle and runs it to confabulation through a *faux-naïve* but infectious excitability, both

---

14 Charles Baudelaire, 'Correspondances', *The flowers of evil*, trans. James McGowan (Oxford, 1993), 18–19. **15** *The pen friend*, 50–1, 156. **16** Ibid., 12.

knowingly gullible and imaginatively genuine. In turn, this is an homage to the 'can-do' spirit of *Biggles*-era adventure stories, and to the scientific susceptibility of Jules Verne, H.G. Wells, and, indeed, Arthur Conan Doyle. This essentially comedic world's blend of rational aptitude and creative exuberance offers a quixotism that remains imaginatively vital to Carson: a prelapsarian archetype in fallen times.[17] And so, when perceived in its most positive guise, those who enter 'the Zone', with its glimpses of an underlying structure, assume the potential to 'see the world as it really is':

> [A] world in which everything connects; where the Many is One, and the One is Many. There will be no division, for everything in the real world refers to something else, which leads to something else again, in a never-ending hymn of praise. The world is an eternal story. (*St*, 236)

$X + Y = K$ links Spiritualism and Symbolism with the material universe through a form of pseudo-scientific apprehension: 'In reality', we are told, 'everything moves, because the universe consists of atoms perpetually swirling in a void, like dust-motes in a beam of light, colliding with each other, and, according to their nature, either rebounding from each other, or hooking together to form structures ...'[18] Such atomism becomes a means of keeping the ambit of Carson's Symbolism grounded in the real. It stops his 'matrix' from being a purely ethereal realm of essences hidden behind the veil.

$X + Y = K$ perpetually explores the processes behind sight and sound: the infinitesimally intricate chains of physical and mental agency through which our sensoria produce visual and sonic images. Stretching the normal parameters of such phenomena, Carson links them to his atomism to create a material universe in which all things constantly leave traces of themselves. All people, in every moment of their being, leave an indelible imprint of themselves upon the world around them:

> [I]n the world around us radiant forces were passing from all objects to all objects in their vicinity, and during every moment of the day and night were daguerreotyping the appearances of each upon the other; the

---

17 Carson's indebtedness to adventure stories is writ large in *The star factory*, but is implicit in most of his writing. In turn, this is another imaginative link with his contemporary Paul Muldoon, who recently cited Robert Louis Stevenson's *Treasure Island* as one of his key influences. See 'Invisible threads', the *Guardian* ('Review'), Saturday, 24 March 2007. **18** $X + Y = K$, 258–9.

images thus made, not merely resting upon the surface, but sinking into the interior of them; there to be held with astonishing tenacity, and only waiting for a suitable application to reveal themselves to the inquiring gaze. You cannot, then … enter a room by night or by day, but you leave on your going out your portrait behind you. You cannot lift your hand, or wink your eye, or the wind stir a hair of your head, but each moment is indelibly registered for coming ages. The pane of glass in the window, the brick in the wall, the paving-stone in the street, catch the pictures of all passers-by, and faithfully preserve them. Not a leaf waves, not an insect crawls, not a ripple moves, but each motion is recorded by a thousand infallible scribes; and this is just as true of all past time, from the first dawn of light upon this infant globe.[19]

Every sound that is made, each patterned phonic vibration, is likewise recorded in the atomic substructure of the world.

Again, then, Carson takes a plausible idea and skips with it to the marvelous. Again, the science predominantly comes from the age of Verne and Wells, which is also, of course, the golden age of *symbolisme*.[20] As such, $X + Y = K$ springs with a beguiling tonal ambivalence. While playfully knowing, the extent to which such elements in the novel are parodic depends upon the relativity of changing world-views over time. We are tickled, but, at the same time, we are dislodged from self-satisfied surety, any sense of metaphysical security, as the writing more deeply asks how certain we can be of our certainties.

And so, in the universe of $X + Y = K$, the conventional domain of Symbolism is not transcendental, but contrives to be literal. Material reality writhes with memory. The physical world becomes a great palimpsest that palpitates with the past, rendered as a potentially limitless layering of present-tense moments. History is part of the atomic infrastructure of the present:

> Walking in London, I was conscious that I walked on many palimpsests of London. Under me lay millions of overlapping footprints. I thought of Dr Johnson striking his walking-stick against doorposts and bollards, performing complex dance-step patterns so as to avoid the cracks in the

---

19 Ibid., 101. **20** In many ways, $X = Y = K$ reads like a fictive precursor to Marina Warner's more recent cultural history that explores 'ideas of spirit and soul' since the Enlightenment, but which spends much of its time on the Victorian era and the 'long' *fin de siècle*. Marina Warner, *Phantasmagoria: spirit visions, metaphors, and media into the twenty-first century* (Oxford, 2006).

pavement; of Virginia Woolf, gone out to buy a pencil, remarking how beautiful a London street is in winter, with its islands of light, and its long groves of darkness; of John Evelyn, during the Great Fire, watching the stones of St Paul's flying like grenades, and the molten lead from its roof running down the streets in a stream; of De Quincey's opium-driven excursions through a city full of enigmatical entries, and alleys without soundings, and sphinx's riddles of streets, so intricate and unexplored that it was doubtful if they had yet been laid down in the modem charts of London. The human brain, says De Quincey, is a natural and mighty palimpsest. Such a palimpsest is my brain; such a palimpsest, O reader! is yours. Everlasting layers of ideas, images, feelings, have fallen on your brain softly as light. Each succession has seemed to bury all that went before. And yet in reality not one has been extinguished.[21]

All knowledge is constructed out of experience in this palimpsestic universe, and all knowledge stems from story-telling, so that we do, indeed, live in 'narrative reality':

> [W]hen an organism interacts with an object, be it within body boundaries (for example, pain) or outside of them (for example, a landscape), it creates a narrative. This is true whether the object be perceived in the present moment, or recalled, for the past continues to influence our behaviour. The hippocampus is a vital structure in the mapping of multiple, concurrent stimuli .... In plain speech, it is the instrument by which we assemble ourselves. A human being is a story-telling machine, and the self is a centre of narrative gravity.[22]

And yet, given the unaccountably multitudinous nature of the world's palimpsest, each narrative could hardly tell the full story. Each narrative is also an interpretation, by nature blocking out other possibilities, even though all possibilities are potentially valid. The known knowns may change because known unknowns, or even unknown unknowns, might come to light at any given moment. Carson's world is similar in nature to Roland Barthes' ideal writerly text, in which 'the networks are many and interact, without any one of them being able to surpass the rest; this text is a galaxy of signifiers, not a structure of signifieds; it has no beginning; it is reversible; we gain access to it by several

21 $X + Y = K$, 103–4.   **22** Ibid., 299.

entrances, none of which can be authoritatively declared to be the main one'.[23] Yet Carson's vision complicates that of Barthes, and is far from utopian, as the lack of finality and authority is as troubling as it is enabling.

Both the apprehension of unity and of relativity are equally central to Carson's aesthetic. And this, in turn, indicates the antinomical rhythm at the heart of his work. Each positive is undercut by a negative, but neither can be discarded. Rather than dispensing with its propositions, Carson's antinomical rhythm seeks to convolute and confound its own foundations through a proclivity towards multiple worlds within worlds, startling juxtapositions, playful paradigm shifts, serendipity and paradox. Indeed, expanding on its core idea of atomism, the novel supplies us with a virtual manifesto for its own aesthetic, in the guise of the philosophy of one Edmund Edward Fournier d'Albe:

> As early as 1907 he had proposed a hierarchical clustering model for the structure of the universe which anticipated modern fractal theory. Fournier's fractal was a snowflake pattern consisting of five parts; each of those parts was a miniature copy of that snowflake; those miniature copies were composed of still smaller snowflakes, and so on, in a dizzying blizzard of self-replication. Worlds lay within worlds in nested frequencies. Atoms and stars, electrons and planets, cells and galaxies all moved to the same measure. Clouds, coastlines, earthquakes, the fluctuations of the stock market, all corresponded. A flag snaps back and forth in the wind, and a column of cigar smoke breaks into an anxious swirl. A pirouette of litter on a street corner heralds a tornado. A pin drops in an auditorium, a bomb goes off. Like patterns were apparent everywhere. The All was immutable, but the detail was ever new. The event, the incident, the individuality was unique, unprecedented, irrecoverable; but the equilibrium was eternal, and death could have no dominion over the infinity of worlds.[24]

In the midst of this Babel of forms, Carson's writing insists upon empirical accuracy and fastidious attention to detail: a dynamic that creates the scrupulous vivacity of his style. His assiduity is an aesthetic principle which seems to be an extension of broader ethical or existential codes. Early in $X + Y = Z$ we are

---

23 Roland Barthes, *S/Z*, trans. Richard Miller (London, 1975), 5.   **24** Ibid., 210.

introduced to 'A practical system for developing self-confidence, memory, mental concentration and character', penned, we are told, by a certain Victor Rocine:

> Pay attention to the quality of objects, says Rocine, figure their connections and their structural combinations. Notice buildings. Look at machines and determine how they are made, and how they function. Inspect houses. Build sentences and connect them according to grammatical rules. Look closely at alphabetic characters, and at footprints. Fix your eyes on things in such a way that your mind takes a mental photograph of their parts. Memorize time for the purpose of remembering time. Remember how old people are, and how they age. Read history, and memorize when wars took place. Ask yourself what time of day it is; answer the question first, then look at your watch. In all things, pay attention to the hour, the day, the week, the month, the year. Know the era, as it unfolds.[25]

This doubles as a guide on how to write and how to live, and such meticulous faithfulness towards 'seeing what's before your eyes' is another running obsession throughout Carson's *oeuvre*.[26] And yet, he is constantly teasing out empiricism's limits. 'Painting', we are told in *Shamrock tea*, 'is the art making things real, because you have looked at how things are', and yet, at the same time, 'painting requires you to discover things not seen, and present them to the eye as if they actually exist' (*St*, 50). In *Fishing for amber*, meanwhile, an absorption in detail can lead to potential social breakdown. After an outbreak of St Antony's Fire:

> People would sit for hours, engrossed in the folds of their garments, which seemed as undulating meadows shimmering with colour. Complex narratives could be discerned in the weave, as each thread proclaimed its origin and destiny, Shopkeepers were paralyzed by the magnificence of

25 *X + Y = K*, 13–14. This passage is cited, the novel informs us, from '*Dr Rocine's mind-training* – "A Practical system for developing self-confidence, memory, mental concentration and character, by Victor G. Rocine" – published in 1905 by the Human Science School at 130 Dearborn Street, Chicago, Illinois' (Ibid., 12). **26** Reviewing Seamus Heaney's *North* in 1975, Carson condemned it for mythologizing, and thus naturalizing, violence. Rounding on the claim of 'Exposure' to have 'Escaped from the massacre', Carson countered: 'No one really escapes from the massacre, of course – the only way you can do that is by falsifying issues, by applying wrong notions of history, instead of seeing what's before your eyes'. See Seamus Heaney, 'Exposure', *Opened ground: poems, 1966–1996* (London, 1998), 144; and Ciaran Carson, 'Escaped from the Massacre?', *Honest Ulsterman*, 50 (Winter, 1975), 86.

their stock. Angels appeared to many, in trees especially, which responded to the nearest zephyr with celestial whispers. Publicans and money-lenders were seen sprawled face-down in the common fields, examining the vast dimensions of the insect universe therein. (*Fa*, 57)

Thus, fidelity to what's there can lead to entropy, yet empiricism remains crucial and can never be disdained. Playful rather than parodic, Carson's often pernickety style is key to the verve of his incongruity.

Victor Rocine's guide sets up one of the central themes of $X = Y = K$, pitting William Jackson Crawford's scientific empiricism against the Golighers' spiritualism. And this dramatizes Carson's impish vision, as the scientist gets down on hands and knees to pedantically record levitations, strange banging noises and psychic rods at the limits of his credulity, since what's before his eyes exceeds rational understanding.

Spiritualism, of course, dovetails with $X + Y = K$'s vision of atomism:

In order to furnish some explanation ... spiritualists considered new theories ... some of which drew their inspiration from antiquity, notably the *De rerum natura* of Lucretius, who wrote that all matter was the unfolding of the primordial germs of things, which he called atoms, and that the universe was an ongoing, endless binding and unbinding of these elementary particles. Nowhere was this more evident than in the swirling restlessness of the earth's atmosphere, great ragged-edged clouds sweeping across the sky like windswept ocean billows, piled high on top of one another like mountain ranges, or collapsing into one another like the comb and wrack of tumbled surf.[27]

In turn, as this passage suggests, Spiritualism also dovetails with Carson's aestheticism. Spiritualism enables him to paint a canvas that is at once more physical and metaphysical, more mundanely normal and startlingly phantas-magoric, than would otherwise be possible within the rarified realm of *symbolisme* proper. Yet the consanguinity between Spiritualism and Symbolism remains unmistakable, and this correspondence links Carson's work with that of W.B. Yeats.

The choicest trope of Carson's Symbolism re-imagines Yeats's poetic in the context of Carson's own time; which is to say, it conflates Symbolism and

27 Ibid., 95.

Spiritualism with an atmosphere of political paranoia and a culture of seemingly omniscient surveillance. Carson's infatuation with the links between objects, senses, memory and reality makes his writing fizz with the immanence of Yeats's 'disembodied powers'. Like Yeats's 'Celtic Twilight', Carson's art is 'like a Twilight Zone' infused with 'Special Powers'. This conflates imaginative potential and historical coercion in a delicious pun, as such 'powers' in Carson's work are always potentially ambivalent: revelations of the deeply interwoven symbolic order, and intimations of covert British 'Special Forces' in Northern Ireland.[28]

It is this doublethink on Symbolism and surveillance that is writ large in $X + Y = K$ and *The pen friend*. As one would expect, in both novels, Carson's riffs on spiritualism and his riffs on art blend into a broad concern with consciousness, knowledge and identity. Broadly speaking, his atomistic, palimpsestic, fractal vision constitutes a *gestalt* in which the outer social world and inner consciousness are shared aspects of a semiotic universe, an ecosphere of information. All art, all cognition, all activity within the semiotic universe is simultaneously an act of symbolism and surveillance. The 'matrix' of information within which we live is a realm of interconnectedness, a realm in which all things coexist and interact: past and present, material and immaterial, real and unreal. But this same 'matrix' is also a realm of otherness and inequality; it is the realm of Power. Any given story might block out other possible stories; but more than this, it might also infect and oppress the lives of others as it takes shape in culture's narrative reality, which is never virtual. Moreover, the realm of traces which people and things incessantly leave of themselves and their actions is precisely the matrix that the surveillance units of 'Farset' penetrate, where 'any and all information about any person, place or thing might be obtained'.[29]

Carson's obsession with surveillance has been writ large in his work since *Belfast confetti*.[30] But $X + Y = K$ takes this infatuation to a new level:

> Belfast was the most surveillance-conscious environment in the Western world. Rooftops bristled with antennae. There were security cameras on every street corner, in every shop doorway. They swivelled on the tops of tall poles at sectarian interfaces. The city was a military grid of numbered

---

28 The poem 'Two to tango' from *First language* doubles as a kind of 'creative writing' manual and a guide to living under surveillance. The poem involves a shady 'They' – 'They can put you anywhere. Where's a mystery'; 'They make the place secure for you. It's like a Twilight Zone where they exert their Special Powers' (18–19). **29** $X + Y = K$, 175. **30** See, for example, 'Intelligence' in *Belfast confetti*, 78–82.

zones, patrolled by helicopters armed with thermal imaging devices and laser observation sets. Electronic bugs–parasitic transmitters, Trojan Horse transistors, 'synaptic grafts' or 'buds' – were planted everywhere, in phones and door-handles and light fitments, spiked like hat-pins into the backs of hotel room curtains, masquerading as martini olives in hotel bars, lurking in the ceramic chain-pulls of hotel toilets, or the matching ceramic insert H or C of the washstand taps. In smoke-filled back rooms the glint of an exposed floorboard nail was enough to invite suspicion. Cameras were concealed in smoke detectors, behind bar mirrors, and in bar optics, or were made to look like personal accoutrements: badges, buckles, brooches, bracelets, powder compacts, cigarette lighters.[31]

As the devil is in the detail, so these martini olives are quintessential Carson.

However, just as Carson is wary of symbolic totality, so his sense of Belfast's surveillance culture undercuts the idea of social control with a more deftly complex vision:

Taking into account that any conversation might be overheard, any covert action photographed, the players conducted conversations and actions accordingly, talking of this when they meant that, doing that instead of this. Silences were meaningful. A cough, a hiccup, some repeated verbal tic, a change of mood communicated by a hesitation or a lapse in grammar might define the grammar of the situation, since the totality of facts determined the case, and also all that was not the case. Everything was liable to mean its opposite, or anything in between: the pattern analysts referred to 'sliding definitions' and 'fluid dictionaries' … [32]

As such, culture is 'far from being regulated … by a panoptic administration'.[33] Rather, the city has become an impossible maze of agencies and counter-agencies that have swamped one another into stasis. There is a totality to this system, but no control or fixity.

On one level, then, Carson's vision of history is one of interminable and intractable entropy. $X + Y = K$ opens with a startling passage on The Church of the Holy Sepulchre: a symbol of labyrinthine conflict solidified to a Gordian knot. Here, the measure of Carson's meticulous detail intensifies into an almost vertiginous simulacrum of reality's excess of sense: his felicitous precision and

31 $X + Y = K$, 161–2.   **32** Ibid., 162.   **33** Ibid., 286.

controlled convolution of fact creating an impression of history that is as good as phantasmagoric. In Belfast, meanwhile, there are so many 'listening devices', they ultimately create nothing but 'a meaningless acoustic wash', a 'level of white noise', so that semiosis becomes a matter of 'Chinese whispers. Semantic creep'.[34] Similarly, in *The pen friend* we are told of MO2: 'we don't draw any conclusions, we just exist. The information is what we are'.[35] In this way, Carson's political and aesthetic visions begin to converge: they are aspects of one reality, one symbolic order.

Carson's vision of Belfast thus clearly surpasses any simplistic scenario pitting one force against another. In the logic of his work, any given semiotic act will partake of a power struggle, yet it may be impossible to know how, or to what end. Moreover, in this context, it becomes clear there can be no such thing as innocence. The narrator of *The pen friend* – working in an art gallery and circulating ideas of art – is shocked to learn he may inadvertently be in cahoots with MO2: complicit with indirectly oppressive forces without his consent. Yet his culture does not allow any position of inculpability.

To partake of the symbolic order – to think, to speak, to live – is to become an instrument of power, affecting the atomic structure of 'the matrix', no matter how obliquely or gently: the merest butterfly wing-beat could set off a proverbial hurricane. And yet, there is a freedom of sorts, since everything in this universe of semiosis and surveillance is fluid and ambivalent. However, because this world has ground itself into desistance, since it amounts to a virtual decomposition of self-cancellations, such freedom is ultimately circumscribed by entropy. It is framed within a broader curtailment of agency, as there can never be any definitive liberty or authority. In historical terms, there is no foreseeable way out of the political standstill, represented by the seething vortex of the Troubles.

In this manner, Carson dramatizes the historical situatedness of art. If anything, the pressures of such a historical reality create an ideal aesthetic environment, since all meaningful expression must be marked by cunning, subterfuge, invention and play. At the same time, however, there is a loss of revelation, as art becomes a potentially endless process of sliding interpretations and definitions. Disenfranchised from the finality of truth, art risks the asphyxiation of ineffectuality, threatening to become a hollow and self-perpetuating spectre of meaninglessness, a realm of the undead. And yet, paradoxically, such a scenario in fact keeps art living, for if semiosis was to be

---

34 Ibid., 286–7.   **35** *The pen friend*, 140.

somehow fixed and pinned-down to an ultimate meaning, this would amount to terminal petrifaction, a death of art.

What is crucial to the potency and scope of Carson's art is that his vision of art and history is in no way limited to Northern Ireland or the Troubles. Rather, Belfast becomes a symbol, in his writing, for the historical condition in general. And pivotally, his work also insists this historical condition isn't all bad. To be sure, he rails against the appallingness of history – against oppression, violence and murder – with vivid force. But his writing also realizes this same historical condition is our one and only site of the good. As such, he doesn't necessarily accept history, yet neither does he attempt to transcend it. Instead, while registering its disenchantments, his writing equally opens the doors to its splendours with creative authenticity. Carson is a materialist fabulist, a genuinely skeptical believer.

Given his predilection for Chinese boxes, his work might be understood as a simultaneity of concentric frameworks or horizons. Although his work's richness deserves a more nuanced approach, we might focus on two: an historical horizon, in the broadest possible sense; and a secondary horizon of experience, best registered in terms of style. In turn, each horizon is characterized by antinomies: each is manifested through oppositional figurative modes. In its positive aspect, the historical horizon is troped in terms of symbolic harmony: 'a world in which everything connects; where the Many is One, and the One is Many.' At the same time, as we have seen, another strain of his work sees this horizon in terms of conflict and entropy. Similarly, in its 'negative' aspect, the horizon of experience or style is entirely ironic: a web of narrative spin, pitched towards kitsch and parody. But, more frequently, the style is richly metaphorical. Metaphor is the trope through which things become simultaneously 'known and unknown', because it 'asserts that a similarity exists between two objects in the face of manifest differences between them'.[36] Thus, Carson's writing perpetually surprises with the shock of the new.

This is the heart of Carson's multifariousness. In the negative aspect of the historical horizon, the gap between self and otherness produces paranoia. In its positive mode, the same gap becomes the very locus of interest, empathy and imaginative invention. To say Carson's art creates a simultaneity of such apprehensions is to say that, in his work, these horizons and antinomies come into perpetual contradiction with one another: unremittingly colliding and combusting

---

[36] Hayden White, *Metahistory: the historical imagination in nineteenth century Europe* (London, 1973), 34.

in his writing. His work is antinomical rather than dialectic, because he doesn't attempt to fuse his oppositions into progressive advancement. Rather, differing modes and perspectives play upon and interrogate one another in an incessant orchestration of metamorphosis. In turn, this might suggest that entropy and irony have the upper hand in his aesthetic. Yet, crucially, his work remains vigilantly aware that one person's heaven may be another's hell. Positive and negative are relative terms: these modes are more precisely oppositional polarities of a continuum, complicating but also potentially redeeming one another.

Like his intuited symbolic unity, Carson's entropy and irony are never final. *The pen friend* tells us of surveillance: 'so-called intelligence is one thing; knowing what it means is another, and the same information can be used to draw very different conclusions by different parties, with different vested interests'.[37] This may seem to indicate a kind of hopeless relativity; but, crucially, such open-endedness is far from meaningless. History undercuts the finality of truth, but it remains brittle and violently real. The difference between one interpretation or narrative and another may well be a difference between life and death, and so the nuances of 'intelligence' are vital. Once again, it is central to Carson's aesthetic that reality is apprehended in its subversive, ultimately nihilistic horizon, while the opposite is equally true. Experience and history are fundamentally and simply ongoing.

Carson's 'negative' historical horizon doubles as a more generalized intimation of death. In many ways, his most crucial antinomy is between life and death, figured in his work as an aesthetic opposition. And this explains the centrality of flair and finesse to his poetic: there is a stark choice between style or enervation; existential nullity. In this respect, style and probity are one, and there is no hubris to the claim that, paragraph for paragraph, Carson is one of the greatest living prose writers 'on these islands' in terms of fulfilling the basic aesthetic criterion of making us see the world anew. Thus, in his work, we visualize an explosion: 'car, truck and tea-chests disintegrating with a boom and whoosh, an atomic cloud of tea like starlings boiling upwards, sifting, settling on the twisted shrapnel already scattered like bits of art'.[38] Against entropy, the honed detail and particularity of such writing forces our sensorium to continually adjust to, and question, the world. The more scintillating the sentence's fusion of momentum and precision, the more the antinomies between freedom and constraint, play and imprisonment, are registered with experiential verity.

The pen friend begins with a startling dream vision:

37 *The pen friend*, 140.   38 *X + Y = K*, 186.

I began to think of myself as an angler fishing a stretch of canal in the shadow of a dark semi-derelict factory leaking steam from a rusted exoskeleton of piping, who, after hours of inaction, feels his line bite, and, his excitement mounting, begins to reel in as his rod is bent by the gravity of what must be an enormous catch – a pike perhaps, glutted by its meal of barbel, perch, or one of the plump rats that scuttle through the soot-encrusted weeds of the canal banks – when to his consternation he finds he has snagged a smoothing-iron, which he discovers to be only the precursor of a series resembling an enormous charm bracelet dripping green-black beards and tendrils of slime, as the iron is followed by an iron kettle, pots and pans, a bicycle, a kitchen sink complete with taps, a pram, a harrow, a plough, forks and rakes, a gamut of broken looms, winding machines and spinning jennies, a string of dead horses, rotting straps and rusted buckles, tumbrils, wagons, engine tenders, locomotives, tanks, flat-bed trucks and howitzers, a crocodile of sunken barges, lighters, tugs, launches, cutters, gun-ships, battleships, amphibians and submarines sucked from the reluctant mud, the whole gargantuan juggernaut flying in midair for a second, as the angler's rod whips back, before collapsing all about him with an almighty thunderclap; and I would wake sweating and exhausted from my nocturnal Herculean labour.[39]

Such a passage indicates how Carson's style yields exhilaration through exactitude, as the sheer abundance of the world uncoils in supple paragraphs, translated into linguistic texture through lexical precision, imagistic dexterity and snaked syntax. Moreover, if imaginative invention is the crucial defence against oppression and negation, such a passage further exemplifies how this agon is inscribed at the very core of the literary enterprise, to the extent that the sentence itself implies an extraordinarily intensive duality of rigour and contingency, control and receptivity. Style incorporates constraint: this is key to Carson's comedic averment that the historical condition isn't *all* bad.

If the horizon of experience is chiefly registered through style, Carson's metaphoric fusions of particularity with fortuity may seem at odds with the other elements in his work of knowing kitsch, parody and ironic spin. Indeed, when artificially segregated, these elements do seem to be indicators of cultural and imaginative atrophy. Yet, for the critic Fredric Jameson, the simultaneity of

39 *The pen friend*, 3.

differing modes or horizons in a literary work simply relate to the contradictory state of the world: the uneven state of historical development whereby 'archaic' and 'progressive' elements co-exist in culture at the same time.[40] Simply put, then, the conflation of the clever-clever, the literary gamesmanship, with the imaginatively charged is a primary means of being – in the true sense – realistic. Without the archness, the 'poetic' would be self-aggrandizing at best, and, at worst, polluted with false innocence.

The kind of aesthetic that rails against historical curtailment and otherness, fuelled by a desire for a higher realm of freedom, has, of course, dominated Irish literary history. Carson's re-conceptualization of this desire has been as thorough as it has been invigorating. As argued, he inveighs against political and existential confinement vivaciously; yet, at a broader horizon, he is equally aware that this is akin to railing against language for stemming from a finite alphabet. And, in this regard, his secularization of Symbolism has been central to his historical realism. The atomistic, materialistic bent of his universe enables him to avoid conventional Symbolism's reification of an intuited realm of pure ideas and forces, while maintaining its basic Neoplatonic structure of the imagination. In Carson's work, the sense of an objective, essentialized, numinous order is replaced with a more diffuse and profuse ambit of subjective memory. Since the molecular infrastructure of the word seethes with memories – the atom itself is the core of physical reality, but doubles as a nucleus of memory – his Symbolism becomes republican and democratic. The desire for sensuous mental engagement with that which lies beyond the interpreted universe is freed from the shackles of monolithic purity and hierarchical exclusivity.

In a brilliant trope that runs throughout *Fishing for amber*, colour itself is seen to be part of the material world of natural resources and cultural practice, of labour and craft, as art is constantly traced back to the earth through attention to the pigments used in paint: how they are made, and what they are made from. Thus, the most numinous realms are intricately related to physical reality: to work, skill, and complex tradition. In a related manner, Carson's symbolism of the surface comes to the fore in *The pen friend*, which celebrates, among other things, Andy Warhol:

> Warhol's obsessive repetitions are a refusal to let go of the image, an
> insistence that we look again and again, that we do not forget. It doesn't

---

40 Jameson reads literature in terms of differing 'interpretive horizons' or 'concentric frameworks' in *The political unconscious: narrative as a socially symbolic act* ([1981] (Oxford, 2002).

matter whether the image is of a soup can, or a Coca-Cola bottle, or a shoe, or a Chanel No. 5 bottle. Warhol also made repeated images of electric chairs, car crashes, race riots, the atomic bomb, he did portraits of murderers and movie stars, and they are all about death and memory, they glorify the image of the thing or the person. The memorable icon that outlasts its subject, or that represents eternal subjects.[41]

Historically, we might say that the loathing of *symbolisme* for the utilitarian partially disenfranchised it from the real world, just as the commodification of the real world was increasingly aestheticizing the utilitarian. For Carson, the world of commodities is the symbolic realm *par excellence* – a domain of images with complex relations to reality and desire. Commodities beseech us to live in style.

Carson's embrace of this materialist symbolism of the everyday yields an imaginative pleasure that Yeats could never obtain from his far-off, most secret and inviolate Rose:

> Yesterday I bought a nice 1950s jacket in the Friday Market, lightweight grey Donegal salt-and-pepper tweed with heathery flecks, little hints of purple, blue and mauve that flicker in the sunlight. I'm wearing it with a pale blue soft-collared cotton shirt and white duck trousers, so when you appear through the door in a navy check box jacket over a high-necked cream *broderie anglaise* blouse and a flax-coloured maxi-skirt, like Bonnie of Bonnie & Clyde, I find myself indulging in a little scenario where we go well together, such a nice-looking couple, people would say.[42]

And yet, at the same time, commodities are, of course, merely the ciphers of a capitalist system that seeks to manipulate and profit from us. As mentioned, the most prominent commodities in *The pen friend* are fountain pens and perfume. The novel's obsession with pens as instruments of writing, art objects, and commodities, becomes another vehicle through which Carson dramatizes the historical situatedness of writing. And in this manner, we can begin to see how Carson's vision of Belfast mirrors his vision of the so-called 'normal' world: the historical condition in general. Both are states of symbolic intensity which entail a loss of agency due to their impossibly intricate and vast complexity of interconnections.[43]

---

41 *The pen friend*, 28–9.   **42** Ibid., 5.   **43** In 'Postmodernism, or The cultural logic of late capitalism', Fredric Jameson writes: 'The technology of contemporary society is therefore

The pen friend juxtaposes its interest in commodified style with a return to the Goligher story, while its love story is riven with paranoia about surveillance. Love and control, artefacts and spirits: the novel implicitly asks: what's the difference? To search for a single source behind commodification would be as daft as searching for who is behind either Farset or MO2. It would be as daft as William Jackson Crawford's search for the reality behind the Golighers' séances. It would be as quixotic as trying to pin down the reality behind love. The truth of any of these things is never pinned down in Carson's work. But his art is driven by the desire for such truth.

The perfumes of *The pen friend* are olfactory poems: simultaneities of precisely quantified elements, mixed with skill and care for pleasure. The smell of the perfumes creates a sensual influx of memory and artfully fused otherness: free-floating essences that make differing impressions, according to nuances of time, place and character. Simultaneously satiating, creating and driving desire through invisible but implicit technique, through intricate and on-going traditions of arcane knowledge, craft and labour, the perfumes are pure style. The memories they invoke might evoke counter-memories, which might provoke fictive memories, in a confabulation where truths are lies and lies are truths: a white noise, an acoustic wash that might be meaningless, or that might somehow contain the totality of every meaningful thing. At the heart of Carson's poetic is acoustic perfume.

mesmerizing and fascinating not so much in its own right but because it seems to offer some privileged representational shorthand for grasping a network of power and control even more difficult for our minds and imaginations to grasp: the whole new decentered global network of the third stage of capital itself. This is a figural process presently best observed in a whole mode of contemporary entertainment literature … in which the circuits and networks of some putative global computer hookup are narratively mobilized by labyrinthine conspiracies of autonomous but deadly interlocking and competing information agencies in a complexity often beyond the capacity of the normal reading mind. Yet conspiracy theory … must be seen as a degraded attempt – through the figuration of advanced technology – to think the impossible totality of the contemporary world system'. *The Jameson reader*, ed. Michael Hardt and Kathi Weeks (Oxford, 2000), 218.

Contributors

PETER DENMAN is Professor of English and Dean of the Faculty of Arts at the National University of Ireland, Maynooth. His publications include *Samuel Ferguson: the literary achievement* (as author), *Poetry Ireland Review* 34–7 (as editor) and *Sean Ó Tuama: Death in the land of youth: collected poems* (as translator).

ALAN GILLIS lectures in English at the University of Edinburgh. He is the author of *Irish Poetry of the 1930s* (2005). His debut poetry collection, *Somebody, somewhere* won the Rupert and Eithne Strong Award in 2004, and was shortlisted for the *Irish Times* 'Poetry Now Award'. His second collection *Hawks and doves* was a Poetry Book Society Recommendation in summer 2007 and was shortlisted for the T.S. Eliot Prize.

JOHN GOODBY is Senior Lecturer in English at the University of Swansea. He has written extensively on modern Irish poetry, and is the author of *Irish poetry since 1950: from stillness into history* (2000) and co-editor with Chris Wigginton of *Dylan Thomas: a new casebook* (2001), and editor of *Irish studies: the essential glossary* (2004). He has published two boks of his own poetry, and translations of Heine, the Algerian poet Adel Guemar (with Tom Cheesman), and Pier Paolo Pasolini. His latest work, with the Hispanic-Irish poet Carlota Caulfield, is *No soy su musa / I'm not your muse* (2008), an anthology of Spanish translations of contemporary Irish women's poetry.

TIM HANCOCK lectures in English at the University of Ulster, Coleraine. He specializes in twentieth-century poetry, and has published on contemporary poets from Northern Ireland (Heaney, Muldoon, Carson), the poetry of Mina Loy, and the poetry of Robert Lowell. He has also published on the traditions and academic reception of love poetry.

PATRICIA HORTON is Managing Director of Blackstaff Press, Belfast.

EAMONN HUGHES lectures in the School of English at Queen's University Belfast, where he is also Assistant Director of the Institute of Irish Studies. He specializes in Irish literary and cultural studies on which he has published widely. He has edited *Northern Ireland: culture and politics, 1960–1990* (1991), and co-edited with Fran Brearton, *Last before America: Irish and American writing* (2001) and with Edna Longley and Des O'Rawe, *Ireland (Ulster) Scotland: concepts, contexts, comparisons* (2003). He has particular interests in Irish autobiography and ideas of place in contemporary Northern Irish poetry.

JERZY JARNIEWICZ is a Polish poet, translator and literary critic who lectures in English at the universities of Lodz and Warsaw. He has published *The uses of the commonplace in contemporary British poetry* (1994) and *The bottomless centre: the uses of history in the poetry of Seamus Heaney* (2002), and has written extensively for various journals, including *Poetry Review, Irish Review, Krino, Arete, Agni* and the *Cambridge Review*. He is editor of the literary monthly *Literatura na Swiecie* (Warsaw), and has translated the work of many contemporary poets and novelists, including Seamus Heaney, Craig Raine, Christopher Reid, Philip Roth, Nadine Gordimer, Edmund White and Raymond Carver.

ELMER KENNEDY-ANDREWS is Professor of English at the University of Ulster, Coleraine. His books include *The poetry of Seamus Heaney: all the realms of whisper* (1988), *Seamus Heaney: a collection of critical essays* (1992), *Contemporary Irish poetry: a collection of critical essays* (1992), *The art of Brian Friel* (1995), *The poetry of Seamus Heaney: a reader's guide to essential criticism* (2000), *The poetry of Derek Mahon: a collection of critical essays* (2002), *Fiction and the Northern Ireland troubles: (de-) constructing the north* (2003), *Irish fiction since the 1960s: a collection of critical essays* (2006) and *Paul Muldoon poetry, prose, drama: a collection of critical essays* (2006). His most recent book is *Writing home: poetry and place in Northern Ireland* (2008).

MICHAEL McATEER teaches Irish writing in the School of English, Queen's University Belfast. He has authored *Standish O'Grady, AE, Yeats* (2002) and numerous essays on Irish poetry, drama and fiction. He is currently preparing a monograph on European influences in the drama of W.B. Yeats.

CIARAN O'NEILL is a research student at the Seamus Heaney Centre for Poetry at Queen's University Belfast. His current areas of research include the work of Walter Benjamin, Ciaran Carson and Frank O'Hara, on which he has a number of articles forthcoming in 2008.

FRANK SEWELL is a lecturer in English at the University of Ulster, Coleraine. He is the author of *Modern Irish poetry: a new Alhambra* (2000), and has co-edited with James Doan *'On the side of light': the poetry of Cathal Ó Searcaigh* (2002). Former Irish language editor of the *Honest Ulsterman*, he has translated poems and short stories by contemporary Irish language writers, including by Gearóid MacLochlainn, Nuala Ní Dhomhnaill and Micheal Ó Conghaile. He has also translated (from Russian) poems by Anna Akhmatova, Bulat Okudzhava and Regina Bondarenko. He co-translated with Mitsuko Ohno *Beyond the hedge: new and selected poems by Mutsuo Takahashi* (2006). Currently, he is working on a collection of his own poems and an anthology of twentieth-century poetry in Irish.

STAN SMITH holds the research Chair in Literary Studies at Nottingham Trent University. In addition to many essays and articles on modernism, twentieth-century British and Irish poetry, and the 1930s, he has published two books on W.H. Auden (1985; 1997) and edited *The Cambridge companion to Auden* (2004). He is the author of *History and twentieth-century poetry* (1981), *Edward Thomas* (1986), *W.B. Yeats* (1990), and *The origins of modernism* (1994). Recent work includes an edition of Storm Jameson's *In the second year* (2004), *Irish poetry and the construction of modern identity* (2005), *Globalization and its discontents* (2006), and *Poetry and displacement* (2007). His edited collection on Patrick Kavanagh, and a collection of poems, *Family fortunes / journeys to war*, appeared in 2008.

DAVID WHEATLEY lectures in English at the University of Hull, and is the author of three collections of poetry with the Gallery Press: *Thirst, Misery hill* and *Mocker.* He has been a recipient of the Rooney Prize for Irish Literature and the Vincent Buckley Poetry Prize. He has edited the work of James Clarence Mangan for the Gallery Press, and an edition of Beckett's *Selected poems* for Faber.

Index